The New Albanian Migration

The New Albanian Migration

Edited by
RUSSELL KING, NICOLA MAI
AND STEPHANIE
SCHWANDNER-SIEVERS

SUSSEX
ACADEMIC
PRESS
Brighton • Chicago • Toronto

2 4 6 8 10 9 7 5 3

First published in hardcover 2005, reprinted in paperback 2013, in Great Britain by
SUSSEX ACADEMIC PRESS
PO Box 139
Eastbourne BN24 9BP

Distributed in North America by
SUSSEX ACADEMIC PRESS
Independent Publishers Group
814 N Franklin St, Chicago, IL 60610, USA

British Library Cataloguing in Publication Data
A CIP catalogue record for this book is available from the British Library.

Library of Congress Cataloging-in-Publication Data
The new Albanian migration / edited by Russell King,
Nicola Mai, and Stephanie Schwandner-Sievers.
p. cm.
Includes bibliographical references and index.
ISBN 978-1-903900-78-9 (hardcover : alk. paper)
ISBN 978-1-84519-220-4 (pbk. : alk. paper)
1. Albania—Emigration and immigration. 2. Albania—Economic conditions—1992- 3. Albanians—Foreign countries. I. King, Russell, 1945– II. Mai, Nicola. III. Schwandner-Sievers, Stephanie. IV. Title.
JV8296.N48 2005
304.8′094965—dc22

2004020669

Typeset and designed by Sussex Academic Press, Brighton & Eastbourne.
Printed and bound by CPI Group (UK) Ltd, Croydon, CR0 4YY
This book is printed on acid-free paper.

Contents

Preface and Acknowledgmements

This book collects together several of the papers first presented at an international conference on Albanian migration held at the University of Sussex on 6-7 September 2002. It is the second major published output from that conference, following an earlier set of papers published as a special issue of the *Journal of Ethnic and Migration Studies* under the title 'Albanian migration and new transnationalisms' – see *JEMS*, 29(6), 2003, pp. 939-1096. The two collections should therefore be seen as complementary; together they offer a wide-ranging survey of one of Europe's most remarkable and still-evolving migration episodes of recent years. Interest in Albanian migration grows apace. As this book goes to press, a follow-up to the Sussex conference is about to take place in Korçë, southern Albania, in September 2004, this time focusing much more on the impact of migration on Albanian development.

Our first debt of gratitude, as organisers of the 2002 conference, is to the various organisations which sponsored the meeting: the Sussex Centre for Migration Research (SCMR) at the University of Sussex; the Nash Albanian Studies Programme at the School of Slavonic and East European Studies, University College London; the British Academy's International Conference Grant scheme; the Foreign and Commonwealth Office; and the British Association for Central and Eastern Europe. Without their financial support, it would not have been possible to organise such a successful conference, with over 40 participants and some 25 papers – far more than we ever expected when the idea for such a meeting was first mooted.

Several other votes of thanks must also be made: to Jenny Money at SCMR for her organisational skills in setting up the conference and maintaining contact with participants and paper authors; to Mark Thomson (also SCMR) for helping to materialise the final versions of the chapters of this book; and to Tony Grahame at Sussex Academic Press for his enthusiastic interest in the book right from the beginning. We also thank the chapter authors for their forbearance. All the chapters that were originally prepared as conference papers (a couple of chapters were later additions to the volume) have been revised and updated since 2002 and we are grateful for the contributors' willingness to take on board the editors' suggestions in this process.

THE EDITORS

1

Introducing and theorising Albanian migration

KOSTA BARJABA AND RUSSELL KING

In this ground-setting chapter for the book, we introduce Albanian migration and pay special attention to its phenomenological significance. We set the post-1990 Albanian migration in its historical and geographical settings and we explore its unique and defining characteristics as a 'new' type of international migration – but one which also has historical resonances. We build our analysis around some of our recent publications (Barjaba 2000, 2002, 2003, 2004a, 2004b; King 2003; King and Mai 2002; King and Vullnetari 2004), but we also introduce fresh perspectives and refer to newly-available data. In common with the other chapters in this book, we deal only with migration from the Republic of Albania, although some acknowledgement of Albanian migration from the wider territory settled by ethnic Albanians is made in historical references and in the notes to each chapter.

The chapter proceeds as follows. In the first part we highlight the nature and significance of the 'explosive' migratory events of the early 1990s. We then step back in time to examine the earlier history of Albanian emigration; our objective here is to demonstrate elements of continuity of Albanian migration across the pre- to post-communist periods, despite the undeniably 'new' nature and scale of the post-1990 exodus. In the third and longest part of the chapter we survey the pattern and chronology of Albanian migration since 1990. The role of spatial proximity and migration access routes, political and economic events in Albania, and host-society reactions, particularly in Italy and Greece, the two main destinations for Albanian migration, will be the main foci of attention in this section. We also show that Albanian migration is highly dynamic and continually evolving in response to new opportunities and constraints, both at home and abroad. Part four, the concluding section, is an attempt to theorise Albanian migration as a rather specific 'type' which, nevertheless, has similarities and parallels with other migrations.

Albania 1991: a 'migration explosion'

The meta-language of migration is full of pitfalls and stereotypes. Hence the use of such terms as 'crisis' or 'flood' to connote a large-scale migration event carries with it certain risks and potential prejudices (Scarpa 2002). In the same way, the use of photographs of migrants carries the same risk of constructing single images which subvert the complexity and diversity of migration processes.

These cautionary remarks ring very true in the case of Albanian migration, so often described by terms such as 'crisis' or 'emergency' and represented by the famously-iconic pictures of impossibly overcrowded ships full of Albanian migrants docking at the ports of southern Italy in 1991. Undoubtedly these photographs and news-film clips projected an image of crisis, drama, invasion; Europe's very own boat-people threatening the shores of 'fortress Europe'. Whilst to some extent true, this stereotypes Albanian migration: only a minority of Albanian migrants, even in Italy, arrived in those tottering, rusty ships.

But to speak of the events of 1991 in Albania as a migration explosion is not an exaggeration. Denied their fundamental human right to travel abroad during the previous 45 years, and with their country dissolving into economic anarchy around them, many Albanians were desperate to leave, pouring over their hitherto impregnable borders into neighbouring states which – at least initially – welcomed them with a mixture of curiosity and compassion.

The speed and intensity of the Albanian exodus yields another interpretative twist, in the sense of Albania being 'the exception to the exception to the rule'. Let us explain. Ever since Ravenstein's nineteenth-century laws of migration, conceived against a backdrop of transatlantic migration, it has been the case that most migrations are economically driven (Grigg 1977). By and large, this remains as true today as it did in the past, even if the routes and patterns have changed. Arguing along the same lines, many expected the fall of the Iron Curtain to lead to large-scale East–West migration driven by economic contrasts. But the East–West mass migration failed to materialise (King 1998).[1] This was an exception to the 'economic rule' that migrants move to places where wages and economic conditions are better. The exception to the exception was, of course, Albania – the one clear example of explosive mass movement across the previously uncrossable frontier.

Set within the contemporary European and global matrix of international migration flows, the recent Albanian migration, which started with a few thousand Albanians moving onto the 'foreign soil' of Western embassies in Tirana in July 1990, followed by some 26,000 'boat-migrants' to Italy in March 1991, another 20,000 in August 1991, and even larger numbers crossing the mountains to Greece in the early 1990s, was exceptional in many respects:

- its overall magnitude in relation to the size of the Albanian population – by 2000 an estimated 800,000 Albanians were abroad, compared to some 2.5 million living within Albania;
- its fundamental role in guaranteeing economic survival to so many Albanian households by providing an escape-route from dire poverty and starvation;
- the major impact it had on migration debates and politics in Italy and Greece, the two main destinations for migration;
- the contrast between the high level of stigmatisation the Albanians were subject to in Italy and Greece and their pragmatic and (by and large) successful integration in those countries in economic and social terms;
- its dynamic and rapidly-evolving character, involving practically all sections of the Albanian population in fluid mobility strategies which respond to the opportunities and constraints offered by various foreign destinations;
- the high rates of family, female and child migration.

It is worth recounting some of the events of 1990–1 for their poignancy and symbolism in setting the scene for the subsequent development of the Albanian migratory phenomenon.

Albania before 1990 was a closed society with a totalitarian political system and a centrally planned economy. Ruled for 40 years by Enver Hoxha, until his death in 1985, Albanian society was subject to unique levels of ideological and authoritarian control, coupled with increasing isolationism from the rest of the world, including other communist countries, criticised by Hoxha for their revisionism. Hoxha's successor as leader of the Albanian Party of Labour, Ramiz Alia, was a cautious reformer, and the pace of reform quickened in the run-up to Albania's first democratic elections in 1991. A multiparty system was created and private enterprise replaced the state-run economy. However, democratisation and economic transition were anything but smooth. Political and economic chaos surrounded the elections of March 1991, won by the Communists (later to become the Socialist Party), and March 1992, in which the Democratic Party under Sali Berisha was victorious. Albanian politics has continued to be dominated by cliques, corruption and financial scandals, although the general standard of political life has improved since the late 1990s, with a very respectable 5–7 per cent rate of annual economic growth during 2002–3.

Winding back to 1990 and winter of 1990–1, several symbolic events occurred which could be considered as prologues to the major migrations of 1991. These events were spontaneous challenges against what was seen by many Albanians, especially young people, as the state's long-term denial of one of the most fundamental of their personal freedoms – the right to travel abroad and hold passports.

The first event occurred in February 1990 when a family of six persons scaled the wall of the Italian embassy compound in Tirana and lived there in a shed in the garden for several weeks: a first symbolic 'migration' onto 'foreign territory'. By the summer several other Western embassies were occupied by around 4500 Albanians, most of whom were subsequently given asylum in Italy.[2]

At the same time (summer 1990) thousands of Albanians from all over the country trekked towards Tirana and the port of Durrës (see figure 1.1) where they commandeered a ship with the intention of sailing it to Italy. They were prevented from doing so by the security forces, who fought pitched battles with the would-be refugees on the beaches of Durrës (Vickers and Pettifer 1997: 27).

The next few months – across the winter of 1990–1 – were characterised by the almost complete collapse of the economy and a gradual slide towards civic anarchy. Food was in desperately short supply in many parts of the country, giving people a powerful motive to leave. Partly out of desperation, and partly because of the collapse of the moral order of collectivism which had been sustained by the coercive power of the one-party state, people 'interpreted demonstration as the right to appropriate common property regardless of its origins or purpose', including wholesale theft of livestock, crops and agricultural implements from state farms which promptly dissolved (Vickers and Pettifer 1997: 31). Meanwhile, in Tirana, students were openly demanding political pluralism, and in February 1991 the gold-leaf statue of Enver Hoxha in Skanderbeg Square was toppled by a huge crowd.

Two further proto-migration episodes occurred during those winter months. On 6 January 1991 more than 70 Albanians, using inflatable inner tubes and makeshift rafts, crossed the Buna river (which forms the border of northern Albania) to reach the town of Ulcinj (Ulqini) in southern Montenegro. Even more momentous were the events happening in the snow and ice of the mountainous southern frontier. In the words of Vickers and Pettifer (1997: 40):

> Small groups of refugees had begun to assemble . . . and they walked across the frozen limestone passes and waded across icy rivers into Greek territory . . . More and more refugees followed . . . Within days, thousands of people had arrived in northern Greece, penniless, hungry and desperate . . .

These examples established the means for future Albanian economic migration in the years to come. The mass migrations into Greece escalated during the early 1990s, on a larger scale but less publicised than the sea-

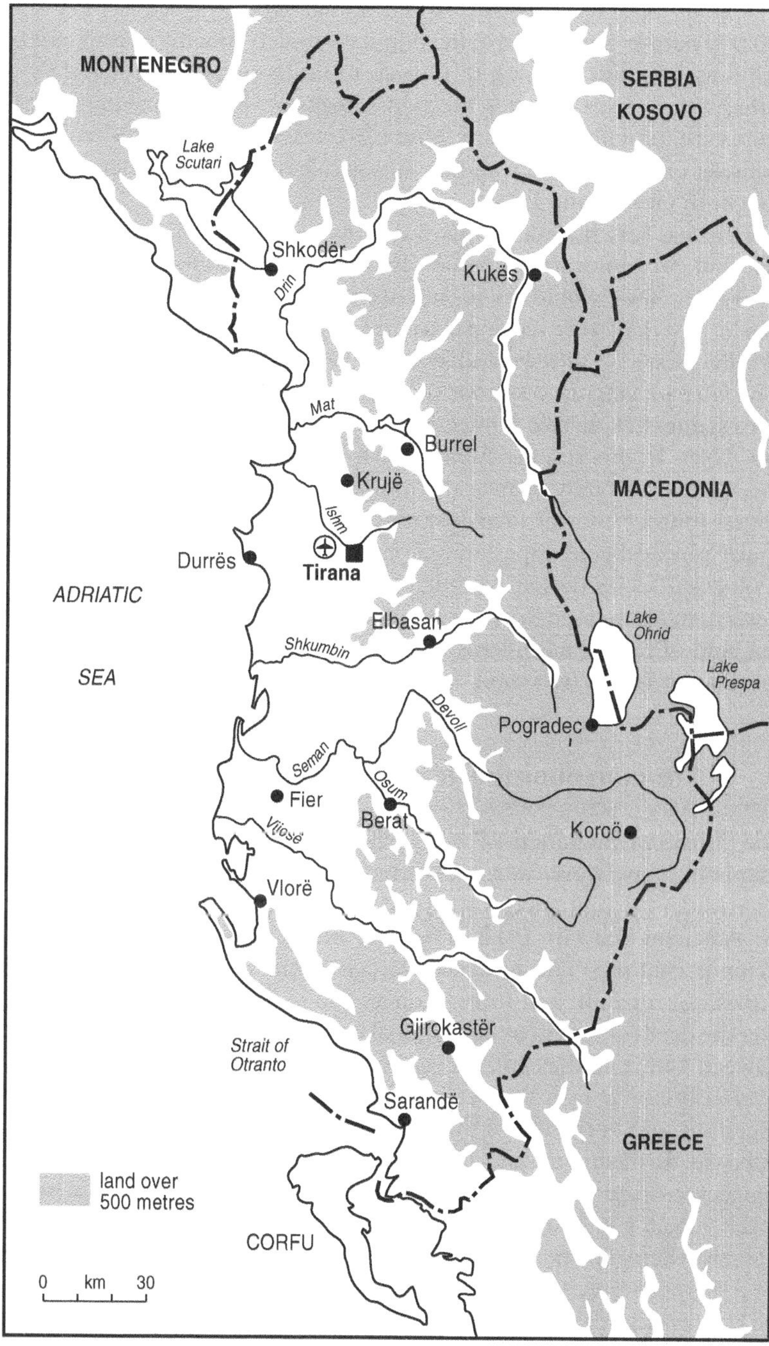

Figure 1.1 Albania: reference map

borne exodus to Italy. The overall figures are somewhat vague. Derek Hall, meticulous chronicler of Albanian life and geography, suggests that some 300,000 people – one in ten of the population – left Albania during 1990–3, including 150,000 crossing to Greece to find work (Hall 1994: 188–9). Perhaps this over-estimates the non-Greek movement. In any case the figures are difficult to judge in those early years because of the to-and-fro character of the movement and the large-scale repatriations after mid-1991 from both Greece and Italy.

What was less debatable was the wide-eyed reaction of Albanians on their first encounter with 'abroad'. Eye-witness accounts tell of how, once in Greece, 'they would stand and stare, often for minutes at a time in silence, as if they were seeking assurance that a prosperous modern society actually existed' (Vickers and Pettifer 1997: 40–1). One man reflected how, after looking at the shops in Greece, he was overcome by an enormous sadness: 'I realised how poor I had been all my life' (King *et al.* 1998: 160, 168). In this respect Albanians, migrating a few tens of kilometres across the sea to Italy or over the mountains to Greece, were making the longest journey: out of their history. Their short migration paths linked similar physical landscapes and climates, but bridged the chasm from an ideologised, collectivised past that was collapsing all around them to a utopian, mythologised West which for them, at least at that stage, was seen as a land of leisure and plenty, glimpsed mainly through the clandestine watching of Italian television.[3]

Pre-communist migrations: Arbëresh and kurbet

The Albanian migration of the early 1990s, although remarkable and unique in many ways, was not without precedent. Early migrations took place under the influence of the Ottoman Empire, before the founding of the Albanian state in 1912. The first major exodus took place in the fifteenth century. The refugees were Albanian Christians resisting the Turkish occupation and forced conversion to Islam. The exodus swelled after the death of the Albanian national hero Skanderbeg, reaching a climax between 1480 and the early sixteenth century, but with subsequent departures continuing into the seventeenth century. Although some of this migration was oriented north and south along the eastern Adriatic seaboard, to Dalmatia and Greece respectively, the greater part of the refugees crossed the sea to Southern Italy, where they settled in several dozen small yet scattered communities in Calabria, Sicily and other regions, where they became known as Arbëresh. By the eighteenth century the Arbëresh were estimated to number 100,000. In the Italian censuses of the late nineteenth and early twentieth centuries their numbers had grown to around 200,000, a figure that has remained fairly stable ever since (Hall 1994: 50; Vickers 1999: 9).

According to Logoreci (1977: 30), this emigration of the late middle ages removed a substantial part of the Albanian political and intellectual elite, resulting in serious economic and cultural impoverishment in the homeland. The other side of this coin has been the remarkable ability of the Arbëresh to preserve their language and customs to the present day; they played an important role in the Albanian national re-awakening in the latter part of the nineteenth century.[4] Many Arbëresh subsequently emigrated to the United States as part of the large-scale transatlantic emigration from Southern Italy during the years 1880–1914. Once in the US they joined the larger Albanian diaspora there, estimated to number around 60,000 in the early twentieth century. We return to the transatlantic branch of the Albanian diaspora a little later.

Meanwhile, many other types of migration took place during the five centuries of Ottoman rule over Albania. Source material on these migrations is scarce so our account, largely drawn from King and Vullnetari (2004), is somewhat sketchy. Many Albanian young men migrated within the military context of the Ottoman Empire, recruited, often coercively, into the infantry and cavalry and sent to fight and defend in regions of war and tension. Albanians were also recruited into the elite guard, the Janisseries, whose main residence was the High Porte in Constantinople. Some Albanians rose to occupy key positions in the Empire's military and administrative ranks. The Albanian Grand Viziers ruled in different parts of the Empire, some as far away as Syria. Mehmet Ali Pasha, founder of modern Egypt, was governor of Egypt for almost half of the nineteenth century; his dynasty came to an end with King Farouk, reportedly of Albanian blood.

Other Ottoman-era migrants were exiles, following the example of the Arbëresh. Those who were seen as a threat were often sent to live in other Ottoman-occupied territories. Others, from well-to-do families, went to study in France or Romania. Yet other Albanians were forced to emigrate by the repressive military campaigns of the Ottoman Turks; such was the case with the Albanian Christians and the Vlachs from south-eastern Albania, who fled to Greece and Romania after their towns had been destroyed.

Further population displacement and emigration ensued when the Ottoman Empire disintegrated during the late nineteenth and early twentieth centuries. Contested areas along the present-day Albanian borders saw large-scale uprooting of Albanians due to fighting; during the Balkan wars Serbs ousted Albanians in what is now Kosovo. This period also witnessed considerable emigration of destitute peasants to a variety of destinations – Turkey, Romania, Egypt, Greece, Bulgaria, Russia; later France, the United States and Australia. Significant Albanian communities formed in Istanbul (an estimated 60,000 in the early twentieth century) as well as in other key destination cities such as Boston and New York (Pollo and Puto 1981: 108).

Albanian emigration to the US started in the late nineteenth century, as noted above. Most migrants came from Korçë and other parts of rural southern Albania (figure 1.1). They were predominantly Orthodox young men who intended to return home after they had made some money (Lucas 2002: 164; Nagi 1988: 32–33). They were joined by Arbëresh migrants from Southern Italy. Boston and New York were the main reference points; it was in Boston that the first Albanian Orthodox Church (as distinct from Greek and other orthodoxes) was founded in 1908. Like the Arbëresh in Italy, the US Albanians voiced a strong nationalist sentiment; associations and weekly publications appeared in Boston and New York (Hall 1994: 50, 52). Soon, the pattern of migration shifted to become more family-based. After independence in 1912 some emigrants returned to Albania, only to re-emigrate subsequently for the purposes of more permanent settlement in the US. Whole families, and in some cases practically whole villages, departed. The origins were still firmly rooted in southern Albania; only very few emigrants left from the north (Lucas 2002). Further details on the more recent patterns of Albanian migration to the US are in Orgocka's chapter in this volume.

There are some similarities to the US case in the patterning and evolution of Albanian emigration to Australia, although this movement started later and the scale of the migration has been much smaller. The key period of migration was the 1920s, when around 1,000 Albanians arrived in Australia, nearly all of them men. One mechanism, noted by Price (1963: 96), was the migration to Australia during 1925–6 of Albanians who had returned from the United States but who could not go back to the US because of that country's quota laws set in place in 1922–4. Like the US, the first migrants to Australia were single men who wanted to work, earn money and then return home to improve their family properties in Albania. In the later 1920s and early 1930s, friends and relatives were brought over, changing somewhat the character of the migration. Nevertheless the sex ratio remained highly imbalanced: only 10 per cent of Albanians in Australia in 1947 were women, rising to 16 per cent in 1954 (Price 1963: 96). Chain migration was a fundamental driving force behind this migration; once again the Korçë area was the dominant district of origin. Korçë migrants settled above all in Shepperton (Victoria) and Moora (Western Australia), specialising in various farming and agriculture-related jobs. By contrast, migrants from Gjirokastër (figure 1.1) tended to settle in urban Australia (Sydney, Melbourne, Perth) where they opened small catering establishments (Hall 1994: 51, summarising Price 1963: 110–11, 150–1, 175–6). Since 1990 these chains linking southern Albania with specific destinations in Australia have become active again.

After 1944 Albania's borders were sealed by the communist regime, so that only a very small number of its citizens was able to cross to the 'other side' for the next 45 years. The trickle comprised a few defectors, mainly political opponents of the regime, who generally headed for Europe, sometimes moving on to the USA. Anti-communist parties were set up by these exile communities based in Paris and New York (Ragaru 2002).

This brief historical review of Albanian emigration reveals that the post-1990 exodus of Albanians is not an isolated episode. Rather, the recent emigration contains elements of continuity with this earlier history. Hence, the period 1944–90 can be seen as an artificial interlude within the longer-term historical framework of the migration of the Albanian people (Barjaba 2003; King and Vullnetari 2004).

Another element of historical continuity between pre- and post-communist articulations of migration, especially when seen from an emic perspective, concerns the nomenclature and cultural construction of emigration as a particular kind of 'absence'. There is a famous Albanian proverb which states that 'A man becomes a man out in the world, a woman becomes a woman over the cradle'. Quite apart from what this reveals about entrenched gender roles within traditional Albanian society, the Albanian word which we have translated as 'out in the world' is *kurbet.* Originating from the Turkish *gurbet*, this refers to a journey and stay in a foreign land, usually for work and family support. The act of going away and being distant is much referenced in Albanian folklore and originates in the travel and sojourn of Albanians within the borderless Ottoman Empire (Barjaba 2003; Barjaba *et al.* 1992; Tirta 1999). According to Robert Pichler (2002), these established practices of temporary labour migration were consistent with Albania's agro-pastoral economic and social history. Leaving the country and engaging in *kurbet* was, however, not merely a matter of labour migration; *kurbet* acquired over the centuries a strong moral connotation. The *kurbetlli* (the emigrant) was perceived as a proud and fearless man who had the courage to leave, while others stayed at home (Barjaba 2003). In de Rapper's analysis of migration patterns in Lunxhëri (Chapter 8 in this book) the era of *kurbet* is remembered as a time of prosperity and development – a 'golden age'. Today, particularly in rural Albania, the recollection of pre-communist mobility is still clear, and this reference to *kurbet* in memory, folksongs and narratives gives cultural meaning to themes of movement, loss and sacrifice, which have acquired a new intensity in the years since 1990 (Mai and Schwandner-Sievers 2003: 944–5).

The historic framing of Albanian migration through the culture of *kurbet* has important implications for the way that the phenomenology of post-communist emigration is experienced and interpreted – above all by the migrants themselves (Papailias 2003: 1064). First, there is the question of terminology. Albanians use many words to refer to migration. The strict term, *mërgim*, appears to be the least used. Far more common are *emigrant* and *refugjat* – terms that reflect the twentieth-century European discourse on international migration, sovereignty, territoriality and citizenship. Our preferred term for describing the Albanian migrants of the 1990s – 'economic refugees' – obviously captures elements of both these latter two terms. This approach underlines the inextricability of Albanian migration from the economic plight of the country in the early 1990s, which was, in turn, a result of the chaotic political situation. In other words, Albanian migrants, at least in the early 1990s, and again in 1997 when a serious financial crisis destabilised the country, tended to view themselves as refugees or as displaced people rather than as 'free' emigrants taking a cost-benefit decision to migrate to a more rewarding labour market (Papailias 2003: 1064). On the other hand, as opposed to the problematic subjectivities inherent in the terms *emigrant* and *refugjat*, both loan-words from the 'West', *kurbet* evokes a more neutral state of being distant. The common link is the separation from home and family and the sense of suffering that migratory absence entails.

Post-communist migrations: patterns and chronology

There are no systematic data to document the year-on-year development of Albanian migration post-1990. There are some data on individual migration episodes such as the 4,500 'embassy migrants' who were granted refuge in mid-1990, or the 26,000 'boat-migrants' who were enumerated as they landed in Italy in March 1991, but annual flow data do not exist. This data deficiency is more marked in the case of Greece where migrants have crossed the border in larger numbers but in a percolatory movement involving much to-an-fro transiting. In fact, a better idea of the scale of the early Albanian migration to Greece can be gained from the figures on the periodic mass deportations operated by the Greek authorities. Already in December 1991 100,000 Albanians were forcibly repatriated by the Greek government in the first of their major *skoupa* or 'sweeping-up' operations of irregular migrants. Three reasons were given for removing the Albanians: they were exacerbating the unemployment situation in Greece; they had a bad record for criminal behaviour; and they brought an Islamic presence into the heart of the Greek Orthodox state (cited in Hall 1994: 190). On all accounts, these reasons were largely spurious, as we shall see later. As Konidaris shows in his chapter in this book, the timing and motivations of these regularisations had much more to do with the fluctuating political tensions between the Greek and Albanian governments – and often these tensions had nothing to do with immigration *per se*.

The overall numbers of Albanian migrants living abroad at the end of the 1990s were estimated by the Albanian Ministry of Labour and Social Affairs at 800,000 (Barjaba 2000: 59): 500,000 in Greece, 200,000 in Italy, and the remainder scattered amongst a range of other European countries (Germany, France, Belgium, the UK, the Netherlands, Austria, Switzerland and Turkey) and the United States, Canada and Australia. These figures referred to the post-1990 exodus and did not include pre-1944 migrants; for instance, the Ministry estimate for the US of 12,000 was around one tenth of the number – 113,661 – recorded by the US Census of 2000 as 'being of Albanian ancestry'.

A second perspective on the scale of emigration was opened up by the 2001 Albanian census. Using the census residual method (calculating net emigration as the residual of inter-censal population change minus the net difference between births and deaths), INSTAT (2002: 19) nominated the figure of 600,000 as the number of Albanians who had emigrated and remained abroad during the period 1989–2001. However, the census calculation excluded persons abroad for less than one year; so the two estimates, 600,000 and 800,000, are not necessarily incompatible.

Further elaborations of the 2001 Albanian census (INSTAT 2002; 2004) reveal insights into the regional incidence of emigration, although it is not possible, thus far, to satisfactorily disentangle the relative roles of emigration and internal migration in regional population change. However, some general patterns are clear (King and Vullnetari 2004). Three regional migration systems can be recognised. The heaviest emigration abroad (mainly to Greece) has been from the southern districts close to the Greek border. However, within these districts there are often sharp contrasts from one village and ethno-cultural group to another, as de Rapper and Kretsi demonstrate in their chapters in this volume. Complex religious, linguistic and historical identities differentiate these southern Albanian populations, including their propensities to engage in different types of migration – internal, cross-border, overseas etc. Out-migration has also been heavy from northern Albania, especially from marginal mountainous districts. Here, however, there is much more internal migration (mainly to Tirana and Durrës) than from the south, and the emigration is more diversified – to Greece, Italy and, most recently, to the UK. Many families are engaged simultaneously in emigration and internal relocation, with different family members performing different migratory roles. Even more complex migration dynamics characterise the third region – central Albania. This is the main destination for internal migrants, but also a springboard for a diversified emigration, including both labour migrants, some of whom have left as irregular migrants, and higher-status migrants from the main urban areas: Tirana, Durrës and Elbasan (figure 1.1). These 'elite' migrants are less likely to have migrated to Greece, and more likely to have migrated, as students and professionals etc., to other European countries and North America.

We now examine the statistical records of Albanian migration for each of the two principal destination countries, Greece and Italy. This is followed by a profile of Albanian migrants in the same two countries, with particular reference to employment, social integration and the host-country reaction. Stress is laid on the dynamic character of the Albanian migratory process.

Figures: Greece

Estimates of the number of Albanians in Greece in the mid-1990s ranged between 200,000 and 400,000 (Fakiolas and King 1996). Meanwhile since 1992 an annual average of 200,000 Albanians have been deported by the Greek police (Fakiolas 2003). Care should be taken when evaluating these figures. Many migrants taken to the borders by the police simply re-crossed into Greece soon after, so that the *skoupa* figures include multiple counting of the same individuals. Even discounting the *skoupa* returns, the Albanian migratory relationship to Greece represents a complex amalgam of stock and flow patterns, with a great deal of seasonal, short-term and even daily cross-border shuttle migration, but also an increasingly large number of long-term residents establishing what will probably become permanent roots in Greece.

Greater statistical purchase on the Albanian presence in Greece was achieved by the first Greek regularisation of migrants in 1998. Out of a total of 371,641 applications for regularisation, 241,561, 65.0 per cent, were Albanians.[5] This share represents the approximate fraction that Albanians made up of the non-EU, 'non-ethnic Greek' foreign population in Greece; i.e. excluded from the calculation are EU nationals, Greek Cypriots, ethnic-Greek immigrants from the former Soviet Union (the so-called Pontian Greeks) and, probably, ethnic-Greek Albanians (who were given a special status and who therefore did not feel the need to apply for legalisation).[6] It was clear, however, that many immigrants, including Albanians, did not apply for the regularisation. Fakiolas (2003: 540) estimated that around 300,000 irregular immigrants did not apply. If we assume that 65 per cent of these were Albanians (and this is a rather big assumption), the total number of Albanians estimated to be in Greece in 1998 becomes 436,000 – plus an unknown number of ethnic-Greek Albanians.[7]

A second regularisation was initiated in 2001 and elicited a further 367,860 applications, 351,110 of which eventually resulted in a six-month permit. However, no national breakdown of these figures has yet been published; nor, of course, of the estimated 200,000 irregular migrants who did not apply (Fakiolas 2003: 540, 547). The same author estimated that, in 2003, there were 580,000 legalised migrants in Greece; plus, presumably, around 200,000 'irregulars'. Assuming that Albanians continue to make up around 65 per cent of the non-EU, non-ethnic Greek migrant total, this yields estimates of 377,000 legally-resident and 130,000 irregular Albanians in Greece – about half a million in all. When it is remembered that the total Greek population is less than 11 million, the scale of the Albanian migration into Greece can be appreciated.

Once again, these figures should be viewed with caution. The problem of to-and-fro mobility across the Albanian-Greek border has been mentioned earlier; although it is fair to say that an increasingly large core of Albanians in Greece are achieving stable settlement and are clearly building their family-based futures there. It also needs to be stressed that the boundary between 'regular' and 'irregular' migration status is as easily crossed as the geographical migration frontier. The short-termism of most permits, the bureaucratic obstacles and the discretionality and corruption involved in acquiring documents all mean that migrants' 'regular' status is a somewhat blurred concept (Psimmenos and Kassimati 2003).

Another perspective on the quantification of Albanians in Greece is offered by the 2001 Greek census, which enumerated 443,550 Albanians, again approximately 65 per cent of the non-EU, non-ethnic Greek population.[8] Further indications of the Albanian migrants' increasing stability were that half of them had been resident in Greece for at least five years, 46,000 were children enrolled in schools in Greece (plus another 7,000 ethnic-Greek Albanian pupils), and the female percentage of the Albanian presence was 41.[9] One aspect of the negative reaction of the host society towards the increasing presence of Albanian children in Greek schools is treated in Kapllani and Mai's chapter later in this book.

Other sources from the Greek government[10] confirm that the number of Albanian legal immigrants in Greece – based on those who pay social insurance – approaches 400,000, which leads to the conclusion that the total number of Albanians in Greece could be around 600,000. However, to repeat, the definitive total is hard to pin down because there is a constant movement, both legal and illegal, across the border.

Figures: Italy

Turing now to Italy, the second most important destination for Albanian migrants, we can note both similarities and differences from the Greek case. The most obvious difference is one of scale. In Greece, as we have seen, Albanians are approximately two-thirds of all non-EU immigrants, and they number more than 500,000 in a country of less than 11 million people. In Italy, in 2001, Albanians numbered less than half their total in Greece, accounted for only one tenth of all migrants in Italy, and their overall demographic impact, in a population of 58 million, is obviously much less. On the other hand, there are similarities too: rapid build-up of Albanian migrant numbers during the 1990s; the role of periodic regularisations in drawing erstwhile 'irregular' migrants into legality; and a progressive tendency to 'settle down', reflected in the increasing numbers of women and children in the migrant population structure. Further similarities, in terms of employment types, discrimination and stereotyping, and progressive socio-economic integration, will be analysed later in this chapter.

Two statistical sources exist to monitor the annual evolution of Albanian migration to Italy: the Ministry of the Interior's database on 'permits to stay' (*permessi di soggiorno*); and the municipal registers of population which report to the Italian National Statistics Agency, ISTAT. Both have faults: the municipal registers are often badly managed at the local level and hence may be out-of-date, in particular due to a failure to de-register migrants leaving the municipality; whilst the stay permits exclude most children (who are covered by their parents' permits) and, again, are not efficiently updated when permits expire. Regularisations (in 1995, 1998 and 2002) help to 'mop up' the pool of irregular Albanian (and other) immigrants.

Table 1.1 Albanians in Italy according to various statistical sources, 1991–2002: absolute numbers and share of total immigrant population

Year	Permits to stay		Population register		Regularisations	
	no. ('000)	%	no. ('000)	%	no. ('000)	%
1991	26.4	3.1				
1992	28.8	3.1				
1993	30.8	3.1				
1994	31.9	3.5	24.7	3.9		
1995	34.7	3.5	28.9	4.2	29.7	12.2
1996	64.0	5.8	33.2	4.5		
1997	83.8	6.8	55.6	6.3	39.0	18.0
1998	91.5	7.3	71.9	7.2		
1999	115.8	9.2	93.6	8.4		
2000	142.1	10.2	127.1	10.0		
2001	144.1	10.6	163.9	11.2		
2002	169.0	11.2			55.0	7.8

Sources: Bonifazi and Sabatino (2003: 970); King (2003: 290); Pittau and Forti (2004: 166).

Table 1.1 sets out the permit, register and regularisation data for Albanians in Italy since 1991. The first two sets of figures – annual data – display a modest degree of correlation. Generally the register totals are lower than the permit figures, except for 2001 when the census 'forced' the updating of municipal records. The broad similarity of the two sets of data, especially in recent years, might be construed as *prima facie* evidence for their broad accuracy; however, it could also be that they are missing the same (or different) groups of migrants. The main picture revealed, however, is undoubtedly true – the rapid growth of the Albanian presence in Italy throughout the 1990s so that by the end of the period in question (2002) Albanians seemed poised to overtake the long-term majority group, the Moroccans, with 168,963 and 172,834 respectively. In fact, no other immigrant group in Italy grew as fast as the Albanians during the period marked out by table 1.1: an approximate sixfold increase in aggregate number, from 3 to 11 per cent of the total immigrant population, and from seventh to second-ranked group. The effect of the regularisations is clearly seen in the jumps in numbers of permit-holders in the years during or immediately after the regularisation; the impact is more delayed with the register data because of the slowness of the municipalities' procedures. Pittau and Forti (2004: 166) aggregate the permit data for 31 December 2002 (168,963) with the regularisation figure (55,038) to yield a total for the Albanian community of 224,001, as of early 2003.[11]

As with the Albanian migration and settlement in Greece, in Italy too there are signs of a progressively successful integration and stabilisation, despite obstacles and discriminatory practices on the part of the host society. Demography gives strong clues about the consolidation of Albanian settlement in Italy. In the early 1990s females accounted for only 14 per cent of Albanians in Italy; ten years later the rate is 40 per cent. Albanian women are now more numerous, in absolute terms, than any other foreign nationality (since Moroccans are more male-dominated). The specific experiences of a small sample of Albanian women living in Bologna are described in the next chapter by Kelly. It is also the case that there are more Albanian pupils enrolled in Italian schools (32,270 in 2001–02) than any other nationality (cf. Moroccans 28,000) – another index of family-based settlement (Caritas 2003: 171).[12]

Host-country reactions: stigmatisation versus acceptance

The trajectory of reactions from the two main migrant-receiving countries has been both variable through time but also generally consistent between Italy and Greece. The gamut of reactions has run from an initial welcome followed by a more mixed, ambiguous and ultimately repressive reception, finally succeeded, in recent years, with a more moderate reaction, in which the negative stereotypes of Albanians as 'dangerous', 'criminals' etc. are still present but in a less overt form. As we saw earlier, within a few months in 1991 the Italian government executed a remarkable about-face in which it initially welcomed and settled the March wave of immigrants, considering them 'heroes of anticommunism' (Perrone 1998), but then, in August, after some episodes of indecision which resulted in inhuman treatment of the migrants, who were first kept on the quaysides and then herded into a football stadium in very hot weather, repatriated them (Zinn 1996). Further details on the Italian authorities' treatment of Albanian refugees and migrants in 1991 are given by Kelly in the next chapter. The Greek authorities have behaved in an equally contradictory fashion: allowing hundreds of thousands of Albanians to come into the country, but then ordering sudden and sometimes brutal mass repatriations in response to political tensions with Albania.

A shared feature of the Greek and Italian host societies has been the obsessive way Albanian migrants have been treated by the media. Cotesta's diagnosis of the situation in Italy is equally true for Greece:

> The role of the media, especially TV, has been absolutely decisive in the organisation of a negative perception of the phenomenon of Albanian immi-

> gration. To broadcast spectacles of desperation, poverty and violence in the world of the Albanian exiles – even when done with a Christian compassion – has generated fear and anxiety. The fear of being affected by this 'other world' has prevailed over other sentiments. Thus feelings of support for pro-immigrant groups have become weaker; and wider scope, if not encouragement, has been given to attitudes of indifference, and of rejection and expulsion of immigrants from Italy. (Cotesta 1995: 45)

Likewise in Greece, as Kapllani and Mai show in their chapter in this collection, the representation of Albanian immigrants by the media, combined with insensitive and sometimes violent army and police activities and the inflammatory remarks of a few politicians, have created a 'dangerous Albanian' stereotype which contributes further to their exclusion from Greek society (Droukas 1998: 361). Both in Greece and Italy this and allied stereotypes about Albanians' alleged tendencies to engage in violence, crime, smuggling and prostitution, become self-fulfilling prophecies, for they only enhance and reproduce their poverty, marginalisation and alienation. Especially for young Albanians, growing up in such a hostile, deprived and discriminatory environment, the danger is a rejection of the rules and a non-conformity to the law.

To some extent, however, the tide is turning. Particularly since 9/11, Albanians in Italy and Greece are no longer singled out for such heavy stigmatisation, despite the fact that most Albanians are Moslems.[13] Although stigmatisation has undoubtedly functioned as a mechanism of Albanians' social exclusion in the two main host societies,[14] and has been used as a mechanism for their exploitation within the labour market and in other ways, as time goes by and the process of migration and settlement matures, Albanians are becoming more socially integrated, above all through their improving status on the labour market and their decreasing tendency to exist solely as irregular migrants.

Employment and social integration

Evidence of Albanians' labour market progression must be set against the fundamental structural role that is assigned to them by the host-country economies: that of a workforce which is willing to do low-grade manual work and to labour under conditions of low pay and insecurity that are increasingly rejected by these countries' indigenous workers. This is true, once again, particularly for Greece and Italy, the two main destinations for post-1990 Albanian migration. The Greek case is the most exemplary, and hence is taken as the main reference point for the ensuing discussion. Here, Albanians' role as a 'replacement' labour force, picking up jobs which Greeks no longer want to do themselves, has a self-perpetuating mechanism built into it whereby jobs done by Albanians (and other poor immigrants) have become stigmatised for Greeks and are therefore even more decisively rejected by them. A dual labour market is thereby created (cf. Piore 1979), marked by different wage levels and working conditions, and reinforced by the irregular status of Albanians, at least in the first stage of their presence in the Greek labour market. On the one side exists a 'primary' labour market of secure, 'legal' jobs which are reasonably well paid; and on the other a 'secondary' or 'peripheral' labour sector of casual, flexible and poorly paid work done by Albanians and some other immigrants, many of whom are in an 'illegal' situation. This duality is further facilitated and reinforced by the size and dynamism of the informal or black economy in Greece, typically estimated to account for between 28 and 35 per cent of national product, the highest of any EU country (Baldwin-Edwards 1999).

It is important to recognise that a significant proportion of Albanians undergo occupational deskilling when they migrate: former engineers, teachers or artists may be employed as gardeners, cleaners or painters and decorators. Despite this demoralising downgrading and loss of their 'human capital', Albanian migrants earn much more doing low-status jobs in Greece or Italy than they could pursuing their careers in Albania. They are denied access to higher-status jobs in Greece and other European host countries because these posts are part of the primary labour market and are reserved for nationals or other EU citizens. Migrants' irregular status and the issue of non-recognition of their qualifications also play a role in blocking access to the higher-level jobs.[15]

Nevertheless, some occupational upward mobility over time has been observed, and sometimes this involves crossing the somewhat blurred divide between the informal and formal labour market. A survey of Albanians in the Thessaloniki area carried out in 2000 (Labrianidis and Lyberaki 2001) revealed that the migrants tended to move out of unskilled and poorly-paid farm labour, taking up jobs in construction, small firms and services. Of the sample surveyed (n=500), 82 per cent held steady employment and 57 per cent paid regular social insurance. For males in this survey, 30 per cent worked in construction and 24 per cent in small industrial companies; for women, 27 per cent were domestic cleaners and 28 per cent worked as housewives and mothers (the latter figure indicating a rapid process of family settlement). Subsequent, more qualitative research by Hatziprokopiou (2003) in the same city confirmed these trends with individual case-histories.

Moving away from Greece, Albanians' occupational improvement is certainly confirmed by Italian research too (Melchionda 2003). As in Greece, improved language skills, better understanding of employment opportunities, and increased legalisation rates were found to be some of the key factors governing this process. King and Mai (2004), studying Albanian immigrants in Modena (Northern Italy) and Lecce (in the South), found additionally that the emergence and consolidation of family-based networks helped newcomers to find job opportunities. The same authors noted substantial differences, however, in immigration integration trajectories between the two locations they studied. In the North of Italy, Albanian documented immigrants were given contracts and granted secure jobs and higher wages much more easily and rapidly than in the South, where 'good' jobs are at a premium. Undocumented migrants, on the other hand, although worse off than regularised migrants in both places, seemed to enjoy better working and living conditions in the South, where their condition of irregularity and precariousness is more shared with the rest of the Italian and migrant populations and where the magnitude of the informal economy is much greater. Housing is also cheaper in the South than in the North of Italy, where the shortage of affordable housing affects all sectors of the working population but especially immigrants whose entitlement to legal status and family reunification are dependent on their being able to meet stringent housing criteria.

A dynamic evolution

Almost everything about Albanian migration illustrates its dynamic character. Its phenomenology has evolved and changed constantly over a short arc of time, and it has become increasingly diversified as regards destinations, forms of movement, and categories of people migrating.

One way of appreciating this dynamic evolution over recent years is to make a simple comparison between the situations in 1997 and 2001 (Barjaba 2003). The former date closes the period of large-scale mass emigration triggered by recurrent political and economic crises in Albania, and is just before the first large-scale immigrant regularisation in Greece; the latter year represents a stage where the Albanian migration has matured and become more 'normalised', and when reasonably accurate and triangulated estimates of the scale of the emigration become evident.

Key features of the Albanian migration situation in 1997 were:

- Around 15 per cent of Albanians were abroad, having migrated since 1990; this rate of emigration was four to five times greater than those of other East European countries.
- Albanians were treated worse than any other immigrant nationality in Greece and Italy, the two main destinations.
- The ratio between 'illegal' and 'legal' migrants (as defined by the host countries) was abnormally high, higher than other immigrant groups in the receiving countries. Hence in Italy the illegal:legal ratio exceeded 1:1 and may have been around 2:1. In pre-regularisation Greece only 10,000 out of an estimated 400,000 Albanians were 'legal' – a ratio of 40:1.
- The ratio of Albanians to the native population was much higher, in terms of relative impact, in Greece compared to Italy – at least 15 times higher in fact.
- Despite this difference in impact, the general picture of Albanians in

the two countries – as regards their role in the labour market (casual, low-status jobs), limited access to services, partial integration, general lifestyles etc. – was approximately the same.

- Factors favouring a more successful integration were beginning to emerge, including general cultural and geographical proximity to both Greece and Italy, the relatively low cost of living for immigrants in these countries, the existence of help from NGOs, and the consolidation of Albanian family and social networks.
- Nevertheless, negative factors predominated, including: the concentration of Albanians in marginal jobs and housing, negative stereotyping by the mass media, and general economic pressures on Greece and Italy to have their economies meet EU criteria (some of these pressures being negatively transmitted to immigrants). In addition, compared to other immigrant nationalities, associative life amongst Albanians in Italy and Greece remained weak: this was linked firstly to Albanians' marginal economic and legal status, and secondly it reflected their antipathy to communal organisations in the wake of their experiences under communism.
- Finally there was, at this time, no 'successful' return. Some preliminary returns were negated by the pyramid crisis of 1997. Return migration was, if anything, linked to an ideology of failure, both personal and of the migratory project. At the same time, the continuing backwardness and instability of the Albanian economy discouraged return. Migration was continuing, geared above all towards economic survival.

Much of the above can be contrasted with the situation in 2001; however there are also similarities. The key features of 2001 are:

- Albania continues to have high rates of emigration, in both absolute and relative terms. Greece and Italy remain the key destinations, but other countries also come into the picture, such as the UK, the USA and Canada.
- There is evidence of the Albanian migration maturing and normalising, especially with family formation/reunion and a radical shift in the balance between 'illegal' and 'legal' migrants. By 2001 the illegal:legal ratio in Italy was around 1:2; in Greece it was about 1:1.
- Albanians in both countries have started to move away from their 'inferior' and marginalised positions in society towards a more 'recognised' status. New quotas have been established for Albanian migration to Italy, based on employment prospects and sponsorship mechanisms.
- Channels of integration have increased in both destination countries; nevertheless the barriers to full inclusion remain substantial.
- The Albanian government has begun to think about stimulating return migration and the productive investment of remittances and savings

earned abroad; but there is as yet no widespread cross-ministerial political support for an Albanian migration policy.[16]

- Over the long term, emigration has been a major contributor to the survival of Albania during the last decade and a half. Remittances constitute a major element of the national balance of payments, and this financial dependence will continue for some time.

For the future of Albanian economic and social development, much will depend on the last two of the above points, relating to return migration and remittances. These topics are respectively the focus of attention of two chapters in this book – by Labrianidis and Hatziprokopiou on return and by Piperno on remittances.

How can Albanian migration be theorised?

The foregoing analysis has given several clues as to the special, and complex, character of Albanian migration. In this concluding section we attempt a more generalised theoretical framing of the phenomenon. At the start of the chapter we set out the key features of the post-1990 migration: its scale, speed and intensity; its fundamental role in economic survival and poverty alleviation in the chaotic post-communist transformation; its spontaneous and 'irregular' character; its strong impact on migration policy questions in Greece and Italy; its diversity; and its dynamic and evolving character, leading to mostly successful adaptation and integration in host societies, despite ongoing reactions of stigmatisation and partial exclusion. The middle sections of this chapter have fleshed out some of the details of these defining characteristics, making it clear that we are dealing with a multifaceted and increasingly complex phenomenon.

How, then, can we explain Albanian migration with reference to theories of migration? Many standard theoretical tools apply. Push and pull factors, deriving from neoclassical economic principles and spatial proximity, are clear to see, especially the push factors operating from the country of origin. The strong family basis to much migration behaviour in Albania reinforces the importance of kinship, social networks and the 'new economics of migration' approach which stresses 'rational choices' from a family/household rather than an individual perspective. Family networks and obligations combined with geographical factors (transport routes, spatial proximity) also give rise to a strong transnational character in recent Albanian migration (Mai and Schwandner-Sievers 2003). Large-scale migrant flows have generated equally intense cross-border flows of remittances and capital/consumer goods, and Albanian migrants exhibit fluid transnational identities, as we have seen, and as other chapters will demonstrate in greater detail.

The economic push factors for Albanian migration are so obvious that they hardly need spelling out. They have been confirmed in survey after survey. To cite just one instance, in a survey reported in the Albanian Human Development Report for 2000 (UNDP 2000), 91 per cent of the Albanian migrants interviewed indicated economic and living conditions as the main reasons behind their decision to migrate. But perhaps the key element for an economic framing of Albanian emigration is that, not only were standard static economic variables such as wages and real incomes very low (and unemployment high) by comparison to neighbouring EU countries, but also that the economic (and social and political) situation was rapidly worsening over the years during which the country exited from communism. Unemployment increased from 9 per cent in 1991 to 29 per cent in 1993; GDP declined by 10 per cent in 1990, 27 per cent in 1991 and 7 per cent in 1992 (Korovilas 1998: 2). Moreover these negative economic trends, clear for all to see during the chaotic years of the early 1990s, continued a much less-documented, longer-term economic implosion which had been building up during the 1980s (Sandström and Sjöberg 1991). According to these authors, 'the Albanian economy, run . . . according to the principle of self-reliance, [was] far too weak to be able to employ productively at the margin an annual addition to the labour force of about 40–50,000 people . . . under the policy of full employment at any price' (1991: 935–6).

However, the equilibrium concept by which emigration helps to rebalance the equation between population and resources, and to counter unstable dynamic trends, only applies partially in the Albanian case. Certainly, the size of the Albanian migration has been on such a scale as to reflect the gravity of the economic, social and political push factors; but the mass nature of migration has played back into the Albanian context to introduce new types of economic and social fragmentation and dependency. In his essay on Albanian migration as a series of conflicts and crises, Pastore (1998) shows how mass emigration ended up by making a significant contribution to the worsening of the Albanian economic and political crisis. Emigrant remittances were the main fuel driving the expansion of informal pyramid saving schemes, in which unsustainable rates of yield were falsely guaranteed on the basis of further investments. As we saw earlier, the pyramid system collapsed in early 1997 wiping out the savings of hundreds of thousands of Albanians, provoking a complete collapse of law and order over much of the country which led, in turn, to the flight migration of 1997. Emigration had two further destabilising effects, according to Pastore: the establishment of emigration rackets by organised and semi-organised gangs who became increasingly bold in their confrontations with the authorities; and the unbalancing of the Albanian population by the wholesale removal of so many young persons.

The overriding importance of economic survival factors in the Albanian migration is all the more crucial because of the collapse of social support mechanisms in the free-for-all liberalism of the post-communist years. Collective services, such as kindergartens, canteens, homes for older people who had no family support, rural medical centres etc., which provided a platform of basic social welfare for the population at large, and especially for women, children and older people, were closed down (UNICEF 1998: 67).

To some extent these social changes reflected a wider ontological conflict between two competing cultural formations which framed the multiple relationships between political ideologies, models of lifestyle and behaviour, and migratory dynamics across the post-communist transformation. These complex interrelationships between politics, culture and society provide another layer of understanding in our attempt to explain the particular nature of Albanian migration.

This line of theoretical analysis starts with Artan Fuga's (1998: 28) identification of two cognitive worlds which have consistently confronted each other during this period of extraordinary change in Albania:

- a *homogenous* world, producing an ontologically secure social and moral order based on denial of difference and legitimation of authoritarian power; and
- a *heterogeneous* world, which constructs a mixed social environment by accepting difference and acknowledging it as a constitutive and non-threatening part of everyday life, expressed in democracy and freedom of thought and action.

Before the demise of the communist state, the former was represented by the authoritarian rule of Enver Hoxha and, after his death, by the legacy of his regime; whereas before 1990 the latter was either excluded or infiltrated clandestinely via foreign influences, above all Italian television.

Post-1990 Albania sees the continuation and re-working of these cognitive models, including within the setting of migration. Against the recently-introduced neo-liberal and democratic model one finds revitalised elements of tradition, patriarchy and customary law in which violence (for instance between families, or against political rivals or women) is legitimised by reference to earlier codes of behaviour, including those resuscitated from the pre-communist era (Schwandner-Sievers 2001).

In his account of the trafficking and exploitation of young Albanian girls in Italy, Mai (2001b) has shown how such processes can only be understood within an analysis of the social and cultural dynamics which are currently transforming and dividing Albanian society, and which have to be historically interpreted. This historical perspective sees the return, in mutated forms, of traditional gender relations of 'honour', power and violence, re-worked by new social actors who are no longer the patriarchal family and clan heads but marginalised young men who can otherwise find no place or role for themselves in modern Albania.

These conflicting and contradictory cognitive and moral systems create confusion and unrest throughout Albanian society, including amongst migrants and potential migrants, and give rise to a complex differentiation of migration types. In the first years of post-communist emigration, those seduced by the capitalist utopia portrayed by glitzy Italian television wanted to emigrate not just to escape poverty and taste the hitherto forbidden fruits of the tantalisingly 'near-West', but as a gesture of political protest against the old regime which had denied them so much in terms of material goods, freedom of movement and political rights. They were, in a sense, both political and economic refugees (Barjaba and Perrone 1996: 133). But different cultural formations also divide the present-day population of Albania. On the one hand the educated elites from the main urban centres, with their skills in languages and their cosmopolitan outlook, have been able to adapt to the needs and opportunities offered by the neoliberal economy; and when migrating they have generally been able to construct a more successful and efficient migratory project. However, this gives rise to worries over a brain drain, as Albania's brightest students, academics, scientists and intellectuals take every opportunity – and understandably so – to go abroad (Gedeshi *et al.* 1999). On the other hand, emigrants from rural areas, with poor education and intercultural skills, have often found it difficult to escape the circuit of irregular migration and exploitation when abroad.

Meanwhile, new forms of internal social and economic marginalisation have emerged within Albania. These have generated widespread and intense pressures for internal migration and urbanisation, whereby rural values and outdated codes of honour are transplanted to new peri-urban squatter settlements where people of diverse backgrounds are thrown together. According to Fuga (2000: 275), the uneven modernisation of Albania has created a 'periphery of the periphery' whereby the urban world pushes to the extreme margins the categories of people who cannot benefit from the economic liberalisation of the country.

All this means that Albania offers itself as a superb laboratory for the study of a range of contemporary migration forms and their links to social integration abroad and development at home. This academic objectification of Albanian migration is not, of course, to ignore its more tragic effects – for instance on the exploitation of trafficked young women, or on the abandonment of elderly people left behind by the departure of their family members and support networks. The chapters which follow tackle only a selection of the themes and interrelationships which suggest themselves for analysis. As Albanian migration continues to unfold, new scholarly challenges for migration experts will emerge, which will also have an undoubted policy relevance as the country struggles to harness the beneficial effects of the phenomenon, turning 'migration of survival' into a 'migration for development'.

Notes

1 Just as the enlargement of the EU to the East in May 2004 failed to produce the predicted large-scale westward flows of would-be migrants. For geographical overviews of the likelihood of mass East–West migration post-Iron Curtain see Fassmann and Münz (1994), Kupiszewski (1996), White and Sporton (1995).

2 As Vickers and Pettifer point out (1997: 26–7), no one has ever researched the 'embassy migrants' and hence there is no clear judgement as to whether this was a spontaneous movement of demonstrators, or, as alleged by Alia, planned with the help of foreign powers. Vickers and Pettifer favour the view that it was a purely indigenous response to a local situation – poverty, impending chaos and denial of the right to go abroad. We incline to the view that the embassy occupations were a first step in the rapid transformation of a considerable migratory pressure and potential into a tangible flow, promoted by political and many other factors.

3 The role of Italian television in framing Albanian perceptions of the West and in conditioning migratory ambitions is considered in Mai (2001a).

4 For details, see Hall (1994: 50), according to whom the nationalist movement amongst the Arbëresh was encouraged by Italy's wish to further its own influence in the Mediterranean and by the fact that Italy's prime minister in the 1870s, the Sicilian Francesco Crispi, was himself of Arbëresh origin.

5 After Albanians, the next most important groups to apply for regularisation were mostly from former Warsaw Pact countries: Bulgaria (25,168; 6.8 per cent), Romania (16,954; 4.6 per cent), Pakistan (10,933; 2.9 per cent), Ukraine (9,821; 2.6 per cent), Poland (8,631; 2.3 per cent) and Georgia (7,548; 2.0 per cent).

6 There has been – and continues to be – enormous controversy over the issue of Albania's ethnic-Greeks, who live in southern Albania. Their numbers are hotly disputed and their treatment by the Albanian authorities, during and after communism, has been fiercely criticised by the Greek government, often for propaganda purposes. Some of the complications of this debate are brought out in three chapters of this book – by Konidaris on the 'Greek side', and by de Rapper and Kretsi on the 'Albanian side'.

7 The Ministry of Public Order refuses to give such information on the grounds of 'national security'. Fakiolas (2003: 540) estimates their number in Greece at 40,000–60,000.

8 It is not clear how many Albanian ethnic-Greeks are included in this figure. Baldwin-Edwards (2004) suggests many were probably counted as Greeks by the census enumerators, so the true Albanian total may be somewhat higher. We should also make the general point that censuses have a marked tendency to under-estimate migrants because of language difficulties, migrants' unstable residential patterns, and, sometimes, their wish to avoid enumeration for fear of being expelled. As with the 1998 regularisation, Albanians were ten times more numerous than the next largest groups in the census – Bulgarians 37,230, Georgians 23,159, Romanians 23,066 etc.

9 In the 1998 regularisation only 18 per cent of the Albanians were females. It is unlikely, however, that the sex ratio has changed so much in three years; probably females are under-represented in the applicants for regularisation.

10 Information from the Greek Ministry of Labour and Social Policy communicated to the Albanian Ministry of Labour and Social Affairs, Tirana, 2003.

11 This puts the Albanians in third position after the Moroccans (227,055) and, surprisingly, Romanians (239,781), the latter group leaping into first place because of their massive participation in the 2002 regularisation (143,947 applications, added to the 95,834 existing permit-holders). For the full set of data, and commentary, see Pittau and Forti (2004: 164–7).

12 Unfortunately there is also a much darker side to the story of Albanian children in Italy. A study by Campani *et al.* (2002: 81–151) on unaccompanied child migrants in Rome shows that Albanians are by far the largest group, accounting for 40 per cent of such children in the city.

13 But Albanians profess a rather secular Islam, partly because of the suppression of all religion during the communist era (Hoxha declared Albania the world's first atheist state in 1967), and partly because of a longer history of religious sycretism and switching under the Ottoman Empire. Most authorities nominate the following percentages for Albanians' religious allegiance: 70 per cent Moslem, 20 per cent Orthodox (mainly in southern Albania) and 10 per cent Catholic (mainly in the north): see the useful discussion in Hall (1994: 42–9). For obvious reasons (geographical and religious), the Orthodox southern Albanians have migrated mainly to Greece. However, even in migration, Albanians continue their tradition of religious fluidity. Many Moslems in Greece have converted to, or claimed, Orthodoxy and taken or given their children 'Greek' names; some Albanians in Italy have likewise baptised their children in the Catholic Church. These actions can be seen, at least partly, as instrumental strategies of assimilation, especially for the second generation.

14 Much less is known about Albanians' experiences in other countries, where their numbers, and hence their 'profile', are very much lower. Indeed, the literature on Albanian migration to other European countries, outside of studies of Kosovan labour migrants and refugees, is practically non-existent. One exception is a study of Albanians in the UK (King *et al.* 2003) where the migration is very recent (mostly post-1999) and mainly from rural northern Albania. These migrants have an uncertain legal status and work mainly in the informal economy, especially in construction. Partly as a result of recent media reports of Albanians' involvement in human smuggling and the sex business, elements of stigmatisation are beginning to be evident. By contrast, Orgocka's chapter (this volume) portrays a broad picture of success for highly-educated Albanian women in the US.

15 Thus, to take some specific examples, non-recognition of Albanian doctors', teachers' and architects' qualifications prevents them taking these jobs in destination countries; what often happens, however, is that they are allowed to practise their professions at a lower level – e.g. as a hospital technician, nursery assistant or draughtsman. Albanian students moving to foreign universities may suffer similar problems of 'underqualification' and have to repeat some of their exams in the destination country.

16 The Inter-Ministerial Committee and Working Group on Migration, established in 2004 and supported by the EU Delegation in Tirana, seems to be having little effect in stimulating governmental progress on addressing migration issues.

References

Baldwin-Edwards, M. (1999) Where free markets reign: aliens in the twilight zone, in Baldwin-Edwards, M. and Arango, J. (eds) *Immigrants and the Informal Economy in Southern Europe*. London: Frank Cass, 1–15.

—— (2004) Albanian emigration and the Greek labour market: economic symbiosis and social ambiguity, *South-East Europe Review*, 7(1): 51–66.

Barjaba, K. (2000) Contemporary patterns in Albanian migration, *South-East Europe Review*, 3(2): 57–64.

—— (2002) *Ondate senza Ritorno: Scritti e Saggi sull'Emigrazione Albanese*. Rome: Organizzazione Internazionale per le Migrazioni.

—— (2003) *Shqiptaret, Keta Ikes te Medhenj*. Tirana: Korbi.

—— (2004a) Ethnicity and migration in Albania: synergies and interdependencies, *Brown Journal of World Affairs*, 11(1): 231–9.

—— (2004b) Albania: looking beyond borders, *Migration Information Source*, online journal of the Migration Policy Institute, Washington, DC, 1 August 2004.

Barjaba, K. and Perrone, L. (1996) Forme e grado di addatamento dei migranti di cultura albanese in Europea (Italia, Grecia, Germania), 1992–1995, in Perrone, L. (ed.) *Naufragi Albanesi. Studi, Ricerche e Riflessioni sull'Albania.* Rome: Sensbili alle Foglie, 123–62.

Barjaba, K., Dervishi, Z. and Perrone, L. (1992) L'emigrazione albanese: spazi, tempi e cause, *Studi Emigrazione*, 107: 513–38.

Bonifazi, C. and Sabatino, D. (2003) Albanian migration to Italy: what official data and survey results can reveal, *Journal of Ethnic and Migration Studies*, 29(6): 967–95.

Campani, G., Lapov, Z. and Carchedi, F. (eds) (2002) *Le Esperienze Ignorate: Giovani migranti tra accoglienza, indifferenza, ostilità*. Milan: Franco Angeli.

Caritas (2003) *Immigrazione Dossier Statistico 2003*. Rome: Anterem.

Cotesta, V. (1995) *Noi e Loro. Immigrazione e Nuovi Conflitti Metropolitani.* Rubettino: Soveria Manelli.

Droukas, E. (1998) Albanians in the Greek informal economy, *Journal of Ethnic and Migration Studies*, 24(2): 347–65.

Fakiolas, R. (2003) Regularising the undocumented migrants in Greece: procedures and effects, *Journal of Ethnic and Migration Studies*, 29(3): 535–61.

Fakiolas, R. and King, R. (1996) Emigration, return, immigration: a review and evaluation of Greece's postwar experience of international migration, *International Journal of Population Geography*, 2(2): 171–90.

Fassmann, H. and Münz, R. (1994) Patterns and trends of international migration in Western Europe, in Fassmann, H. and Münz, R. (eds) *European Migration in the Late Twentieth Century*. Cheltenham: Edward Elgar, 3–33.

Fuga, A. (1998) *L'Albanie entre la Pensée Totalitaire et la Raison Fragmentaire*. Paris: L'Harmattan.

—— (2000) *Identités Périphériques en Albanie*. Paris: L'Harmattan.

Gedeshi, I., Mara, H., Dhimitri, R. and Krisafi, K. (1999) *Emigrimi i elitës intelektuale nga Shqipëria gjatë periudhës së tranzicionit*. Tirana: Shtëpia Botuese 'Luarasi'.

Grigg, D. (1977) E.G. Ravenstein and the laws of migration, *Journal of Historical Geography*, 3(1): 41–54.

Hall, D. (1994) *Albania and the Albanians*. London: Pinter Reference.

Hatziprokopiou, P. (2003) Albanian immigrants in Thessaloniki (Greece): processes of economic and social incorporation, *Journal of Ethnic and Migration Studies*, 29(6): 1033–57.

INSTAT (2002) *The Population of Albania in 2001. Main Results of the Population and Housing Census*. Tirana: INSTAT.

—— (2004) *Migration in Albania*. Tirana: INSTAT.

King, R. (1998) Post-oil crisis, post-communism: new geographies of international migration, in Pinder, D. (ed.) *The New Europe: Economy, Society and Environment*. Chichester: Wiley, 281–304.

—— (2003) Across the sea and over the mountains: documenting Albanian migration, *Scottish Geographical Journal*, 119(3): 283–309.

King, R. and Mai, N. (2002) Of myths and mirrors: interpretations of Albanian migration to Italy, *Studi Emigrazione*, 145: 161–99.

—— (2004) Italians in Lecce and Modena: narratives of rejection, survival and integration, *Population, Society and Place*, 10(6): in press.

King, R. and Vullnetari, J. (2004) *Migration and Development in Albania*. Brighton: University of Sussex, Development Research Centre on Migration, Globalisation and Poverty, Country Background Paper.

King, R., Iosifides, T. and Myrivili, L. (1998) A migrant's story: from Albania to Athens, *Journal of Ethnic and Migration Studies*, 24(1): 159–75.

King, R., Mai, N. and Dalipaj, M. (2003) *Exploding the Migration Myths. Analysis and Recommendations for the European Union, the UK and Albania*. London: The Fabian Society and Oxfam.

Korovilas, J. (1998) *The Albanian Economy in Transition: The Role of Remittances and Pyramid Investment Schemes*. Bristol: University of the West of England, Working Papers in Economics 28.

Kupiszewski, M. (1996) Extra-Union migration: the East–West perspective, in Rees, P., Stilwell, P., Convey, A. and Kupiszewski, M. (eds) *Population Migration in the European Union*. Chichester: Wiley, 13–37.

Labrianidis, L. and Lyberaki, A. (2001) *Albanian Immigrants in Thessaloniki*. Thessaloniki: Paratiritis (in Greek).

Logoreci, A. (1977) *The Albanians: Europe's Forgotten Survivors*. London: Victor Gollancz.

Lucas, P. (2002) *Rumpalla, Rummaging through Albania*. Tirana: Dritan editions.

Mai, N. (2001a) 'Italy is beautiful': the role of Italian television in Albanian migration to Italy, in King, R. and Wood, N. (eds) *Media and Migration: Constructions of Mobility and Difference*. London: Routledge, 95–109.

—— (2001b) Transforming traditions: a critical analysis of the trafficking and exploitation of young Albanian girls in Italy, in King, R. (ed.) *The Mediterranean Passage: Migration and New Cultural Encounters in Southern Europe*. Liverpool: Liverpool University Press, 258–78.

Mai, N. and Schwandner-Sievers, S. (2003) Albanian migration and new transnationalisms, *Journal of Ethnic and Migration Studies*, 29(6): 939–48.

Melchionda, U. (ed.) (2003) *Gli Albanesi in Italia. Inserimento Lavorativo e Sociale*. Milan: Franco Angeli.

Nagi, D. L. (1988) *The Albanian-American Odyssey. A Pilot Study of the Albanian Community of Boston, Massachusetts*. New York: AMS Press.

Papailias, P. (2003) 'Money of *kurbet* is money of blood': the making of a 'hero' of migration at the Greek–Albanian border, *Journal of Ethnic and Migration Studies*, 29(6): 1059–78.

Pastore, F. (1998) *Conflicts and Migrations. A Case Study on Albania*. Rome: Centro Studi di Politica Internazionale, Occasional Paper.

Perrone, L. (1998) I flussi migratori albanesi tra stereotipi e pregiudizi, *Da Qui*, 4: 32–48.

Pichler, R. (2002) Hirten, Söldner and Wanderarbeiter. Formen der mobilen ökonomie in der Dörfern des albanischen Hochlandes, in Kaser, K., Pichler, R. and Schwandner-Sievers, S. (eds) *Die weite Welt und das Dorf: Albanischen Emigration am Ende des 20. Jahrhunderts*. Vienna: Boelhau, 129–61.

Piore, M. J. (1979) *Migrant Labor in Industrial Societies*. New York: Cambridge University Press.

Pittau, F. and Forti, O. (2004) Italia, paese di immigrazione: tra flussi regolari e irregolari, *Studi Emigrazione*, 153: 157–68.

Pollo, S. and Puto, A. (1981) *The History of Albania, from its Origins to the Present Day*. London: Routledge.

Price, C. A. (1963) *Southern Europeans in Australia*. Melbourne: Oxford University Press.

Psimmenos, I. and Kassimati, K. (2003) Immigration control pathways: organisational culture and work values of Greek welfare officers, *Journal of Ethnic and Migration Studies*, 29(2): 337–71.

Ragaru, N. (2002) The Albanian-American community in the United States: the story of a diaspora. Paper presented at the International Conference on 'Albanian Migration and New Transnationalisms', University of Sussex, 6–7 September 2002.

Sandström, P. and Sjöberg, O. (1991) Albanian economic performance: stagnation in the 1980s, *Soviet Studies*, 43(5): 931–47.

Scarpa, F. (2002) The language of migration studies in English and Italian, *Studi Emigrazione*, 148: 811–32.

Schwandner-Sievers, S. (2001) The enactment of 'tradition': Albanian constructions of identity, violence and power in times of crisis, in Schmidt, B. E. and Schröder, I. W. (eds) *Anthropology of Violence and Conflict*. London: Routledge, 97–120.

Tirta, M. (1999) *Migrime të Shqiptarëve*. Tirana: Shkenca (Ethnografia Shqiptare 18).

UNDP (2002) *Albania Human Development Report 2002*. Tirana: UNDP.

UNICEF (1998) *Situation Analysis 1998: Children's and Women's Rights in Albania*. Tirana: UNICEF.

Vickers, M. (1999) *The Albanians. A Modern History*. London: I. B. Tauris.

Vickers, M. and Pettifer, J. (1997) *Albania: From Anarchy to a Balkan Identity*. London: Hurst.

White, P. and Sporton, D. (1995) East–West movement: old barriers, new barriers? in Hall, R. and White, P. (eds) *Europe's Population: Towards the Next Century*. London: UCL Press, 142–60.

2

Lifestyles and integration of Albanian women in Bologna

Two steps forward, one step back?

ELLEN KELLY

This chapter concerns the lifestyles and integration of female Albanian migrants living in Bologna, Italy. It situates their experiences within the wider framework of Albanian migration to Italy and the Italian reaction to this migration, with a specific focus on the media portrayal of Albanian migration and the effect of this image upon public opinion. Above all, I aim to demonstrate the specificity of the female migratory experience and to investigate the reality of life in Bologna for Albanian women. The study is based on fieldwork carried out in 2002: I interviewed 17 Albanian women, who can be roughly divided into two groups: students and workers. It examines their individual experiences, and draws out common themes and salient issues, such as the construction of migration by the women as a progressive step and the extent to which this reflects reality. I also comment on the contrast between widespread public prejudice and individual reception, a theme which resonates in other studies on Albanian women in Italy (King and Mai 2002; Zinn and Rivera 1995).

The chapter is divided into five main sections. First, I examine the context of Albanian-Italian migration: the Albanian political, economic and social situation; the Italian political, media and public reaction to it; the consequent image of 'the Albanian' in Italy; and the negative stereotyping surrounding it. Secondly, I briefly review the gendering of migration studies, and explore some of the issues that arise out of studies of female migrants elsewhere in Italy and Western Europe. Then I introduce Bologna and my research methods. The fourth, and most important, section consists of the results and analysis of my fieldwork, based on in-depth interviews with a sample of Albanian women living and working in and around the city. This section is sub-divided into two parts: the first consists of a description of the lives of six of the women interviewed, with particular focus on parts of their stories which exemplify the experiences of the group; the second is a thematic analysis of certain issues which emerged from the interviews. Finally, I present some conclusions concerning the key features and themes of the lives of Albanian women in Bologna.

Albanian migration to Italy

The receiving context

The Albanian migration to Italy came to a country which had, itself, a long tradition of emigration. Indeed, perhaps no other European country has sent as many emigrants abroad as Italy – more than 26 million during its history (King 1992; King and Andall 1999). Since the early 1970s, triggered by the oil crisis and the subsequent economic restructuring, the rise in immigration to Italy has been very substantial. Estimates of the total number of immigrants living in Italy in 2000 put the figure at around 1.5 million – approximately 2.5 per cent of the total Italian population, but latest estimates, deriving from the 2002 regularisation, suggest 2.5 million and 4 per cent (Caritas 2003). Migrants arriving from Africa and Asia increased proportionally during the 1980s, stabilising in the 1990s, when the main driving force behind the continued growth in immigrant numbers became Eastern Europe. The countries of origin which have shown the biggest increase in numbers in recent years are Albania and Romania; these two countries, plus Morocco, are the leading nations in terms of absolute numbers. Long-term residence of migrants has also been increasing, likewise the share of so-called 'foreign births', up from 1.5 per cent of births in 1992 to more than 4 per cent in 2000, and the proportion of female migrants. These are all signs of an increasingly stable and settled migrant population.

The immigrants are drawn by opportunities in the Italian labour market, as was pointed out in Chapter 1. The increasingly prosperous Italian economy, especially its well-established informal sector, has provided ideal conditions for an increase in economic migration, filling the sectors in the job market which Italians are unwilling to occupy. There has been a progressive redistribution of immigrants towards the north of the country, which can be seen as evidence of their search for more stable and well-paid employment and for a better chance of regularisation and, if desired, family reunion (King and Andall 1999: 148). Bologna, in the region of Emilia-Romagna, can be considered as a typical city in the 'rich North' of Italy.

The Italian government has been fairly slow to respond to the issue of immigration, and has tended to use a series of ad hoc measures to deal with the latest situation or crisis. Moreover, the legislation that has developed seems generally to have done so in restrictive ways. The first law dealing with immigration, Law 943 of 1986, offered regularisation to immigrants already present in the country. Law 39 of 1990, the 'Martelli Law', also regularised many migrants, in this case 235,000 of them, including special provisions for the first arrivals from Albania. However, this law made visas compulsory for those coming from 'high emigration risk areas', including Albania. The New Nationality Law, 91 of 1992, introduced different conditions for people wishing to acquire Italian citizenship. EU citizens had the residence requirement reduced to four years, whilst the requirement for those from outside the EU was increased to ten years. The 'Turco-Napolitano' law, passed in 1998, established annual quotas for immigrants granted a *permesso di soggiorno* (permit to stay). It also made moves towards combating illegal immigration and set up procedures for expulsion of illegal immigrants.

Most recently, under the current Berlusconi administration, the 'Bossi-Fini' law has been enacted. Its main provisions are as follows:

- The *permesso di soggiorno* to be linked to work contracts. The migrant worker to leave Italy upon termination of the contract. The employer to guarantee adequate housing for all immigrant employees, and to pay the return journey to the country of origin when the contract ends.
- The *permesso di soggiorno* to be renewed every two years, instead of every four, the maximum allowed under previous legislation.
- Family reunification only to be allowed for spouses, minor children, and parents over 65 with no other children.
- All immigrants found not in possession of a *permesso di soggiorno* to be immediately expelled.
- All immigrants to be fingerprinted upon applying for a *permesso di soggiorno*.
- The more long-term residence permit, the *carta di soggiorno*, only to be issued after six years, instead of the previous five.
- A *sanatoria* (amnesty) to be held for all domestic workers (known as *colf*) and *badanti* (carers). Only one *colf* to be permitted per household.

As can be seen, this law follows the trend of those preceding it, being increasingly restrictive. Some of these measures are obviously of relevance to female migrant workers, particularly those concerning family reunification and the amnesty for domestic workers and carers, and will therefore have a direct impact on the lives of Albanian and other immigrant women.

The sending context and the link to Italy

The recent emigration from Albania has been dramatic, as Barjaba and King stress in the previous chapter. This mass exodus does not seem quite so surprising given its background. For more than forty years, Albania had been ruled with an iron rod by the dictator Enver Hoxha, whose ill-conceived plans designed to achieve complete autonomy meant that Albania never lost its title of poorest nation in Europe. There was a total ban on emigration. This all changed dramatically with the death of Hoxha in 1985 and the eventual collapse of the communist regime. In March 1991, before the first promised multi-party elections, strikes broke out on a wide scale, statues of Hoxha were toppled across the country, and thousands of would-be emigrants, mostly unemployed young men, commandeered ships in the ports of Vlore and Durrës and sailed to the Italian port of Brindisi (Vickers 1995: 220). The Italian authorities, unprepared, reacted to the situation with emergency measures. It was obvious that repatriation was impossible for humanitarian reasons, and that the new arrivals should be treated as refugees. Soon, they were dispersed in small groups all over Italy.

While this 'first wave' were still being settled, new arrivals complicated the situation during the summer. As a democratic government had been established in Albania in the interim period, the Italian government was reluctant to treat this new group as refugees and instead decided that they were 'illegal' economic migrants. The consequent policy was to refuse entry to Italy, and to support the Albanian government in its efforts to prevent people leaving. The situation reached crisis point in August 1991, when the Italian authorities were again caught unawares by the mass arrival of several overloaded ships with 20,000 people on board. This time, although the authorities were forced to allow them to dock, the arrivals were packed into Bari football stadium, where they were kept in appalling conditions until the eventual decision was taken to repatriate them all.

The dramatic change in attitude was due to a number of factors. Media and public opinion were crucially important. Whilst the first wave were greeted positively, seen as 'Adriatic brethren' escaping the evils of communism, a different current of opinion had built up by the time of the arrival of the second group (Zinn 1996). Largely led by media, a stereotype had quickly emerged – 'Albanians were incapable of organising themselves, work-shy, prone to thieving and violence' (King and Mai 2002: 166). Another factor in the Italian government's radical change in policy was the changing nature of the political relationship between the two countries. In order to show support for nascent Albanian democracy, Italy felt it could not accept the 'second wave' as refugees (Dell'Agnese 1996). I shall say more about the media stigmatisation of Albanians later in the chapter.

The general policy of discouraging Albanian immigrants from coming to Italian shores has continued, save for a brief period in 1997, when the spectacular collapse of private pyramid investment schemes in Albania prompted another mass exodus of around 11,000 'boat people'. Again, while the first of these arrivals were accepted as refugees, the reception then became more restrained. However, despite restrictive measures designed to halt the entry of Albanians into Italy, the evidence is that the movement has continued steadily, using clandestine means.

A less obvious, but perhaps even more important factor influencing the desire of Albanians to migrate specifically to Italy, is the impact of Italian television (Mai 2001a). Although the viewing of foreign television had been banned under the Hoxha regime, Italian television had become a passion, with people often tuning in for several hours a day. This equipped them with language skills, useful for migration, but also, more crucially, with an image of Italy as a land of consumer pleasures and wealth – a stark contrast with the bleak reality of Albanian poverty.

The Italian media portrayal of Albanians and public opinion

A recurrent theme throughout the academic literature on Albanians in Italy is that of the media reception and portrayal of the events which marked this migration, and of the people who make up the migratory flow. As has been shown by Giovanna Campani (2001), the Italian media and public passed through a series of different stages in their reactions to, portrayals of, and views on immigrants; and, as she again points out, these views are crucially dependent on the views and policies of the various Italian political parties and financial groups which have important stakes in Italy's major newspapers. In her analysis, the portrayal of migrants has swung from a picture of a poor refugee, victimised and in need of support and asylum, and has hardened into an image of a dangerous criminal and economic migrant, who can only bring harm to Italy, and who thus should be kept out at all costs The difficulties which migrants encounter once on Italian soil are then used to blame the migrants themselves; their very marginalisation and poverty are used against them. This anti-immigrant sentiment is echoed even in the highest political chambers; Irene Pivetti, former President of the Italian Parliament, was allowed to get away with saying that the Albanians should be thrown back into the sea (quoted in Campani 2001: 46). The immigrant population as a whole is thus stigmatised, marginalised, and constructed as a source of danger.

It seems that, within this general discursive picture, Albanians have been particularly harshly treated. It has been suggested that this specific reaction to the Albanian situation may be related to the very proximity of the country, its culture, and its people. In the words of Dorothy Zinn (1996: 244), 'The Albanian Crisis of 1991 forced Italy to confront its own Utopian myths and the precariousness of the *benessere* (wealth) it has achieved'. Especially for the southern Italians who first received the Albanian arrivals, their social and economic progress and development are relatively recent, and Albania seems in a way to embody that which they have left behind, rejected. In this way, therefore, the Italian population seems to an extent to be reacting against an 'Other' constructed as their own near past, and reflecting the negative aspects (criminality, illegal economic activity, threatening sexuality) of their own society.[1]

Migrant women, on the other hand, although occupying some of the space created by this general image of 'the immigrant', have generally been portrayed as maids or domestic workers; hence an unthreatening, vaguely reassuring image has emerged. Although this has been modified more recently by the increased attention paid to the presence of Islamic women and to migrant prostitutes, a unifying theme remains that of the female migrant as subordinate. This may be simple economic subordination to her employer, marital and cultural subordination, or sexual exploitation in the case of prostitutes. In the way that migrant women have been constructed by the Italian press, they are denied both agency and voice.

Gender and migration

Until recently, migration studies have been gender-blind, or perhaps more accurately, blindly gender-biased. 'The migrant' was always assumed to be male, and when women were mentioned it was either as dependants, or in conjunction with the dependent unit, the family. Now, in the light of several important studies (see for instance Anthias and Lazaridis 2000; Buijs 1992; Kofman *et al.* 2000), this stance is no longer excusable.

Migration not only impacts in differing ways upon men and women; it may also have an effect on the gender relations within a particular community. These dynamics of change brought about by migrancy itself are an important area for exploration.

A recurrent theme in the writings on gender and migration is the important role which women play within migrant communities as the agents of maintenance and recreation of cultural forms from the home society. Women coming from traditional, patriarchal societies, it is often hypothesised or observed, act as upholders of tradition, culture and propriety within the home setting. The move to a new society impacts radically upon this role, either serving to reify and perhaps 're-traditionalise' the idea of woman as cultural symbol and marker of boundaries, or to 'threaten' the traditional cultural role of women by supplying them with new and conflicting economic and social roles within the host society. The role of female migrants differs greatly between different immigrant communities. Some groups, such as Filipinos in Italy, are predominantly female, composed of women migrating specifically for economic reasons to a labour market with a growing niche for them, i.e. domestic service. Other women see their role more as one of offering support to their menfolk, who have led the migration process.

It is, however, crucial to avoid a straight-line continuum based on the association of 'Westernisation' with modernisation and emancipation. Migrant women may find themselves exploited in their new environment, especially when an extremely limited range of employment opportunities is available to them, and even more so when these jobs exist primarily in unregulated sectors, such as domestic work and the sex industry. The effect of altered economic and social roles within families also depends fundamentally upon the way this change is mediated within the household, and is dependent on the cultural context. In the case of Albanians, the situation perhaps differs from the norm, in that Albanian women under communism were used to being in work, only experiencing unemployment with the economic crisis which accompanied the fall of the regime. Thus Albanian women living as housewives in Italy are following a different trajectory, with consequent differing effects on household structures and relations (Zinn and Rivera 1995).

One group of factors highlighted as crucial in affecting adaptation are the constraints of the host society. The possibilities available for employment, and for contact with the local community, are vital criteria which influence the ability of immigrant communities to survive and adapt to their new environment. The little research done to date on Albanian women in Italy seems to suggest that the very presence of women – especially married women with children – facilitates contact with local people:

> the presence of the Albanian women allows for the inclusion of the couple in the neighborhood network, which is a significant element of local life . . . This effect is especially important for the inclusion of the Albanian man who, as a single, might simply be spied upon from a distance. (Zinn and Rivera 1995: 5)

The evidence from this preliminary research conducted by Zinn and Rivera in the southern Italian regions of Apulia and Basilicata suggests that, although Italian public opinion is undoubtedly predominantly negative,

> when the Other becomes the pole of a real, interpersonal relationship, element of a concrete relational experience, he/she ceases to be perceived in un-real and phantasmal terms. He or she is no longer the incarnation of the type which summarizes the essence attributed to the group of membership, but becomes individualized and therefore humanized. (Zinn and Rivera 1995: 6)

Their research, however, was on the experiences of immigrants in small southern towns, where neighbourhood networks, and the emphasis on domestic solidarity, may be more marked than in an affluent, medium-sized city such as Bologna.

Another contrast to these rather positive findings on the integration of Albanian women in (southern) Italy is provided by the link, both in reality and in its exaggerated perception, between Albanians and prostitution in Italy. Studies on the trade and position of prostitutes in Italy have found that Albanians tend to be among the youngest (on average between 14 and 18 years of age upon arrival), least autonomous, and most exploited group of sex workers (Campani 2000). Estimates put the number of migrant sex workers in Bologna alone at between 600 and 800, whilst in 1998 the Italian Home Office estimated the total number of Albanian sex workers in Italy to be 10,000–15,000, two-thirds of all foreign sex workers (Mai 2001b). The traffic in these women seems to be growing, and becoming increasingly connected to other criminal networks, such as those dealing in drugs and arms (Jamieson and Silj 1998). Mai links this to a fundamental adjustment in Albanian social values and relations, conceived in reaction to the enforced collectivisation of the communist period, and leading to 'a counter-process of anarchic and individualistic privatisation of life in all of its aspects', which, in its most extreme form, results in 'gangs of young men, unemployed and virtually illiterate, who are directly involved in new kinds of violence such as the trafficking of drugs, weapons and people into neighbouring countries' (Mai 2001b: 273, 275). However important this aspect of Albanian female migration may be, I choose deliberately not to include it in my study for two reasons. First, there is extreme difficulty in accessing these women, since they are highly controlled and monitored by their so-called 'protectors'. Secondly, and perhaps more fundamentally, I wish to avoid doing anything which might enhance the 'Albanian prostitute' stereotype.

The other economic sector which is of great importance in the field of female migration, particularly in Italy, is that of domestic service and, to a lesser extent, care or nursing work. As mentioned above, this is one of the most precarious of all economic sectors, and an area in which undocumented labour flourishes. Studies on migrant domestic workers in Italy have highlighted several issues connected to the undertaking of such work, primarily the way in which the 'modernisation' of the Italian economy and Italian women's increasing presence on the labour market, combined with the survival of traditional ideas about the role and importance of the family and home, have led to an increasing reliance on migrant domestic labour, particularly in the form of live-in maids. This situation has led to the argument that Italian women are asserting their freedom by abusing that of migrant maids from poor countries (Campani 2000: 151). Although this points to vital issues concerning the 'triple oppression' of migrant women (through race, gender and class), it also seems over-simplistic as a viewpoint, ignoring the ways in which migrant women can use their employment to combat other oppressions; and also, unforgivably, laying the blame (and thus the assumed responsibility for all domestic work) on Western women, ignoring male complicity. Having said that, the coping strategies used by women in these situations are vital in understanding their lifestyles, and often revolve around friendship and kinship groups, generally within their particular immigrant community.

Bologna: field site and methodology

The city of Bologna makes an interesting case study for two reasons: first, because of its well-established and renowned status as the heart of the Left in Italy, although for the first time since the end of World War II, a centre-right administration has been in power for the last few years. Despite these recent developments, the liberal socialist history of the city is evident in the proliferation of NGOs, the local feminist tradition, and the rhetoric produced by the administration, notably the *comune* (municipal council) internet site, which declares Bologna to be '*la città multietnica*' (the multi-ethnic city).[2] Secondly, as one of the richest towns in Italy, with a thriving economy, Bologna is a logical destination for migrant workers. For 2001, the council put the number of foreigners in Bologna at 14,489, making up 3.8 per cent of the population. Nearly half (47 per cent) of the immigrants are female. Albanians are the fourth largest immigrant group in Bologna.

However, the rhetoric of inclusion and multiculturalism in Bologna has been sharply contrasted with a reality of exclusion (Però 2001). Despite the city council's charter, which explicitly aims to 'facilitate the full social, cultural and economic integration of non-EU immigrants present in the area', actual policy fails to live up to this objective, particularly concerning issues of housing, work and contact with the Italian population. Però (2001: 181) concludes that

> people have been geographically ghettoised, patronised and infantilised. Apart from providing for their most basic needs, the council policy has achieved little in terms of a more thorough incorporation, especially in the spheres of housing and work.

Orsini-Jones and Gattullo (2000: 135) come to similar conclusions, stating that

> further initiatives are needed in order to create a more tolerant environment for migrant women in Bologna, improve basic services such as housing and welfare and set up opportunities for those migrant women who are still left out of participation and are still invisible.

However, they also point out that in relation to other Italian cities, such as Florence, 'the efforts of the local institutions in Bologna with regards to anti-racism, multiculturalism and acknowledgement of gender-related issues are still quite impressive' (Orsini-Jones and Gattullo 2000: 135). It seems that the progressive *Bolognese* tradition has indeed had a certain impact on the reception of migrant women, although mainly as regards those communities which are able to organise themselves effectively – which, as we shall see, the Albanians are not.

My research was conducted using a variety of methods, each chosen for its appropriateness and utility in a given situation, including time constraints. Preliminary investigations were carried out through means of a self-completion questionnaire distributed through an Albanian website specifically for Albanians living outside their country of origin. Whilst recognising the limitations and bias of such a highly specialised forum, it proved a useful way to obtain an indication of the issues which are important to Albanian women in Italy, and which could be topics for the interviews to follow. The interviews were semi-structured, focusing on themes thought to be of particular interest and importance, but flexible enough to allow a wide variety of responses and to follow the contours of a still inadequately documented subject.

Somewhat contrary to expectations, I found that the women I contacted to request interviews were extremely accommodating. I encountered only one refusal: from the husband of one woman who turned down my request before I was even able to speak to her. This general willingness to participate seemed to me to be partially due to three factors: first, the Albanian tradition of hospitality (I had a distinct feeling that many of the women I spoke to felt it would have been rude to refuse); secondly, a desire to 'prove' in some way that the Albanian community in Italy is not made up of the criminal networks and delinquents portrayed by the Italian media; and thirdly, a sense of their own worth (most respondents seemed interested in the very idea of studying Albanian women specifically, and indeed pleased by the fact that I was uninterested in speaking to men). On the other hand, many of the respondents were extremely diffident, particularly at the start of the interview. This was often demonstrated through a desire to stress that they were perfectly happy in Italy, and a reluctance to go into further detail about their lives. I found, however, that this attitude generally softened as the interview progressed, and often very different realities emerged.[3]

I made initial contact with the Albanian community through the centre for foreign workers run by the multi-sector trade union CGIL. Through this office I was able to make direct contact with some respondents, and also with two specific organisations for Albanian immigrants: 'Drita', which was initially set up to focus on the particular circumstances of Albanian women; and 'Skanderbeg', an organisation born out of an effort to assist the 59 Albanian minors sent to Bologna in 1991 as part of the dispersal programme for the first refugees. Using these organisations, I was thus able to meet a fairly wide range of women, from market traders to domestic care workers. I also made contact with a group of Albanian students studying at Bologna University through students I had met when previously living in Bologna.

The interviews were carried out in various locations according to the lifestyle and wishes of the respondent. Often I was invited to the house of the respondent, a situation in which they were obviously at ease, but where the potential presence of a male relative might influence the responses, particularly those concerning gender relations. Other interviews were carried out in bars, at places of work, and in my own accommodation. All the interviews were conducted in Italian, a language which is neither my mother tongue nor theirs. Only rarely did I feel that this impacted on the ability of the women to express themselves. In my translations of quotes from interviews, I have tried to be as faithful as possible to the original Italian, sometimes even to the detriment of entirely fluent English.

The respondents can be roughly divided into two groups, a division which I use to structure my analyses throughout. Seven of the women are students at Bologna University, present in Italy on student visas.[4] The other ten are all working full-time.[5] There are some areas of overlap, in that one of the workers previously had a student visa, and most of the students also have jobs.

I first present the stories of six of the women I interviewed, focusing on areas of specific interest or importance in their lives, and picking out ways in which their experiences illustrate the position of Albanian migrant women in Bologna. Following this, several more general themes are drawn out, both from their accounts and those of the other respondents.

Portraits of Albanian women

Six women have been chosen for the representativeness of their lives and situations; their stories, taken as a whole, paint a picture of the way in which these women live, and provide a framework for the subsequent in-depth analysis of certain issues. Their names are fictitious.

Zamira

Zamira is typical of many Albanian women living in Bologna, in that her husband had preceded her, and she entered the country through the process of family reunion, bringing her two children with her (one girl aged 9 and a boy of 14). When I went to meet her in her flat, she had recently had a car accident and broken her arm, which was preventing her from working. She lives with her family in a large flat, in a pleasant area just outside central Bologna. Her husband was present at the interview and sometimes acted as interpreter, as Zamira's Italian is still at a fairly basic level, despite having lived in Italy for two years. She is 40 years old and comes from a medium-sized town in Albania, where she worked in a factory. Since her arrival in Italy she has worked firstly as a care assistant in an old people's home, then as a cleaner in a hotel.

The main purpose behind Zamira's presence in Italy is obviously her family. In explaining her aims and desires, she constantly mentions her children:

> We are here for the children. I'd like to go back to my country when they've finished school, but not before. I want to give them a good future. It's not possible in my country.

Her desire to integrate her children into Italian society seems absolute. Her daughter, also present during the interview, seemed to have become thoroughly italianised, speaking fluent Italian and nodding her head vigorously when I asked if she liked it in Italy. This trend did not seem to be tempered by any great parental effort to maintain 'Albanianness' in the children.

> They can choose if they want to find out about Albanian culture and life in the future, when they're grown up. For now, it's just important that they fit in and have no problems.

Zamira seems relatively satisfied with her life in Italy, in the sense that it has enabled her to achieve her most immediate aims, which are to earn more money than in Albania and give a 'better life' to her children. Yet she still finds life in Bologna a struggle, economically and emotionally. While she earns approximately 750 euros a month, and her husband around the same amount for his work as a builder's labourer, the rent on the house alone is 750 euros, which they find extremely expensive. However, the current Italian legislation on family reunion specifies that a house of certain dimensions must be found and rented before a visa will be issued granting entry to the family members.[6] These restrictions meant that the family had to wait for two years before joining Zamira's husband, who unsurprisingly found it difficult to rent a house of this size on a single wage, adding to the difficulties already experienced by Albanians in finding any accommodation. Eventually, he was able to rent a house through the company he worked for, which acted as guarantor.

On an emotional level, Zamira feels isolated in Bologna, knowing few people besides her family and having little free time.

> I miss my country. I don't know very many people here and I miss the friendship and community that exists at home. In this apartment block the people are very nice, but they don't have much time.

Since her arrival in Bologna two years ago, she has not returned to Albania due to financial constraints. She worries about this, missing her parents and other family. Despite this feeling of isolation, she maintains that it has not been difficult to meet other people, both Albanian and Italian; and she found her job through some friends of her husband's.

Within the family, the gender roles seem fairly traditional. Although she insisted that all the family helped with the housework, it was still Zamira who prepared the refreshments with her one functioning arm. She also bears the responsibility of child-care, in common with most female migrants, and this has affected her position on the job market. She was in fact forced to leave her last job as she was unable to combine an altered shift with obligations of taking the children to school and back.

Juliana

Juliana is one of a group of respondents who all work at the main fruit and vegetable market in Bologna. Among the market traders, there is a sizeable group of Albanians working in family, or extended family, units. When I met Juliana, she was at work at the stall. She is 25 years old, and has been in Bologna for four years, having come with her husband.

> We got married and came straight over here. I came the same way as everyone else, in a motorboat. It was our 'honeymoon'! (Laughs).

So Juliana had entered Italy illegally, but by the time I met her, she had managed to get most of the documents she needed (permit to stay, work permit). This seems to be a standard pattern for the Albanian women resident in Bologna, that of arriving as a *clandestina* (illegal immigrant) and applying for the relevant documents once in the country. The majority of Juliana's family also live in Italy, having entered in the same way:

> We're all here. I'd say that 80 per cent of my family are in Italy. The other 20 per cent are still back in my country. They're the older ones. Everyone under 50 has come over here. The only one left in Albania is my little sister and now she wants to come over. She's 17 years old, she's just finished school and she already speaks some Italian. So she'll come soon.

The presence of family networks is an extremely important factor in facilitating the integration of newer arrivals, offering job and housing possibilities either through connections or directly. For example, Juliana has been able to accommodate a recently-arrived cousin in her house. Juliana currently works on her brother's stall, as do her brother, cousin and husband. The other women working at the market told a similar story. Out of four of them, Juliana was the only one not to work with her husband on the stall (he is a builder). Juliana seems happy with the work she's now doing, although she describes it as

> very tiring. I have to get up at 5.30 three or four times a week, and I work long hours. I work from 6.30 to 12, then have a break and start work again at 4 until 7. But I enjoy my work. I really like the contact with people. Maybe if I'd done more studies, I'd like to get a different job. But this one is OK for me.

Another positive aspect of their work which all the women working at the market emphasised was the autonomy it allowed them, and the consequent flexibility. The stalls are privately owned, in Juliana's case by her brother, and the other three women either own theirs independently or jointly with their husbands. This means that their wages depend directly on the income of the stall, a fact which all of them appreciated.

> The amount I earn depends on the period, but I never earn less than 1,000 euros a month. I'm happy with this wage. I have to work a lot, but the money is good.

Juliana's husband earns more than her, being paid 8 euros an hour for his work as a builder. With the money they earn, she is able to send money back to her parents in Albania, to 'help them out'. The rent for their house comes to 570 Euros a month, which she considers a fairly normal price for what she describes as 'quite a nice house, but not as nice as the one I had in Albania'. Finding the house, however, was:

> an absolute nightmare. It took us seven months to find a house, and the whole time was just a nightmare. I would hate to have to go through that again. I would go to see houses, and then as soon as they found out I was Albanian they would say 'Oh, the landlord doesn't want any foreigners' and that was that.

In the end, they managed to find their house through an Italian friend, a customer at the stall. She describes him as a

> very nice man. He didn't even ask for guarantees, like everyone else. He just trusted us.

This seems a fairly typical story concerning the housing difficulties for Albanian immigrants. Going through standard channels (agencies, etc.) proves largely fruitless and frustrating, so housing is often eventually found through friends and acquaintances. On this more personal, less structural level, Juliana seems well integrated in local society. She says she now feels almost more comfortable speaking Italian than Albanian, having already had a good level of Italian before arriving in the country due to her previous work with an Italian company in Albania. The majority of her friends are Italian, apart from the other Albanians she meets at the market, and her social activities are:

> the same as everybody's. We go out to eat, go for picnics, or to the cinema. Whatever comes up really. Sometimes we go bowling. Most of the time we go out with another (Italian) couple. I used to love going dancing, but I can't go any more.

The reason for this recent change is that Juliana is currently six months pregnant. While she is concerned that the pregnancy goes well, she is confident that she will be able to cope, using the public services available.

> the services for mums are really good. You can book a nursery five or six months in advance. Extra services are provided for immigrants. Things like free medical services.

She does, however, expect some financial difficulties, and plans on returning to work soon after the birth.

Juliana has no plans to return to Albania, and declares herself happy to be in Italy, where her whole life is now based. One reason she gives for her reluctance to return is that

> There is nobody left in my country. All my friends have gone abroad, to Italy, Germany, America. Out of thirty people in my class at school, only about two or three of them are still in Albania.

Among the younger respondents (below the age of around 30) this was a common theme. The very exodus from Albania seems to have contributed to its own sustainability.

Odeta

I met Odeta through her nephew, whom I had met at a conference on immigration. The meeting took place at his house, and he was present throughout, again partly to help with any language difficulties. She is 40 years old, and unmarried. When we met, she seemed exhausted: the reason for this became clear as the interview progressed.

Odeta arrived in Bologna three years ago, coming on a tourist visa to visit her 'sister' and 'nephew' (they are in fact a cousin and her son). Her 'sister' was only recently arrived at the time, having also arrived on a tourist visa and been persuaded by her son to remain. Odeta gives her reasons for leaving Albania as purely economic:

> I didn't earn very much money in my country. Here you can earn more. I didn't suffer in Albania, but I wanted to be able to have a better life.

Her 'nephew' is well established in the area, and his work as a nurse brings him into contact with many local people. It was through one of these connections that Odeta was able to find work. She has been working for almost three years now as a live-in care worker for an old woman suffering from Parkinson's disease, before which she was employed as a general assistant in a hospital.

As the demands of the job are so high, Odeta has very little time in her life for anything else.

> I work for 22 hours a day, seven days a week. I have two hours off every afternoon, and then I come and visit my sister. The rest of the time I am in the house with the woman.

At present, this is the only job available for Odeta as she remains undocumented, a fact which she blames on her employer.

> She hasn't done my documents for the three years that I've been with her, so I think she doesn't want to do them. She could have done them for me, she could have helped me, but she hasn't. I've asked her lots of times.

She was pinning her hopes on the possibility of an amnesty for undocumented *badanti*, which would enable her to receive the desired documentation.

On an economic level, Odeta is achieving her aims to a certain extent. She currently earns around 1,000 euros a month, and as she lives with, and cooks for, the old woman, has no expenses for food or lodging. Her lack of free time also means that she spends little money on activities. She is thus able to save money, and to send some back to her mother in Albania, although she only does this in specific instances when the money is needed. However, as she says

> I think the money I earn is OK, but if an Italian person did the same job, they would earn much, much more. It is very difficult for a foreigner to have the same situation as an Italian. For a foreigner, this is a good wage.

On an emotional level, however, Odeta finds her situation very difficult. The work is emotionally and physically draining, she sees almost no other people apart from her 'sister' and 'nephew' during her break, and the uncertainty caused by her illegal status worries her. She would like to be able to find a job more suited to her experience and training (she has a degree in Business Economics and in Albania worked as an accountant), but is impeded by several factors: her undocumented status, the insular nature of the Italian job market, and her lack of language skills (despite having been in the country for three years, her lack of contact and conversation with other Italians has meant that her Italian has remained at a fairly basic level). As things stand, Odeta feels stifled and oppressed. She has no time or space of her own, even sleeping in the same room as the old woman she looks after.

> I don't like living in Italy. My problem is the situation that I live in, the job that I have, the friends that I don't have. I can't express my own personality. Here, I don't have a life or a personality.

In the future, Odeta hopes to be able to get the appropriate documentation for working, at which point she would return to Albania to finish the law exams she had been studying for. She would like to have documents before she leaves in order to enable her to return to Italy in the future.

> I would like to live in my country, but if I go back and I can't find a job, what can I do? I will have to come back here. I had a job before, but many people didn't and it may be difficult for me to find another one. My plans are: documents, home, exams, future.

Mirela

Of all the women I met, Mirela seemed to me to have rejected her background the most and to have become the most italianised. She came to my apartment before going to work, and was extremely eager to tell her story and opinions. She is now 25 years old, and arrived in Italy eight years ago, making her the longest resident of all the women I spoke to. She had left Albania before finishing her schooling, and characterised her departure as an escape:

> I left Albania to make a better life for myself, a better future. I wanted to be free. In Albania, you're not free, you're controlled. You can't do what you want, other people always tell you what to do. I always wanted to leave, so I left.

Whenever Mirela mentioned Albanian culture and society, she did so with dislike and almost disgust, complaining of the family-based societal structure:

> In Albania, there are people around you the whole time. The family's always there. I don't like it. You can't be on your own, do what you want to do. Here you can make your own decisions. I like having my independence.

Whilst her desire to leave Albania and all things Albanian behind her was evident, she also seemed to be struggling somewhat with continued family obligations and worries. Her brother had recently migrated to Bologna, and Mirela had had the responsibility of paying for his travel, arranging his documents and finding accommodation and a job for him. Her brother had then 'behaved badly' in Bologna, returned to Albania and then came back again, at which point she again arranged everything:

> He expects me to do everything for him. I've found him a job and a house twice. He can't do anything for himself, he's just a typical Albanian man. Now, I've washed my hands of him. I don't see him anymore, and I don't want anything to do with him.

Although she had made this decision, it was causing problems with her parents, who expected her to help her brother in all possible ways.

> They don't understand how things are here. They think that because I'm his sister I'm obliged to look after him. I've argued with them about this.

She found the situation distressing, particularly as she had not been able to send money to her parents during the period when she was supporting her brother. The tension of her dual identity, caught between two radically different types of family structure, was obvious.

Although Mirela is now very well integrated into Italian society, she had difficulties getting to this position. She initially entered the country as a *clandestina*, was unable to get a work permit, lived for a few years on a student visa, and has only had work documents for the past three years. She currently works as a care worker in a nursing home:

> I like my work. It's much better than other jobs I've done in the past because it's specialised. I had to take a course to train for this job, and I like working with people, even though it's difficult sometimes.

Mirela earns approximately 800 euros a month, based on 40 hours per week, and is one of only two unionised respondents. The other people she works alongside are mostly Italian. Even though she enjoys her job, she feels unrewarded:

> I don't get much money for the work I do. I have to deal with people, with disease, with death. People like us [carers] don't get paid enough for what we do.

The money she is earning enables her to live as she has wanted to – independently. She has a small studio flat, for which she pays 230 euros a month. In common with almost all respondents, her search for accommodation was extremely difficult:

> I've lived in all kinds of different places. I've shared a flat with other girls, lived in a *collegio* (long-term hostel, normally run by nuns), and now I've finally found a place of my own. It's not perfect, but I've had to move around so much that I'm staying put now, even if there are problems.

Again, Mirela had found her flat through connections: some people she knew happened to be renting it. She blames her difficulties in finding appropriate accommodation on the competitive and expensive housing market in Bologna, rather than on her nationality.

On a social level, Mirela has found it easier to meet Italians than Albanians. She has had one bad experience of a hostile reaction when she tried to forge a friendship with an Albanian woman, and is now wary. But, 'it's really easy to meet Italians, especially men, if you're a girl.' Mirela is in fact involved in a relationship with an Italian man, and has been for the past three years, although she feels it is not going particularly well. She was one of only two unmarried respondents to have a boyfriend, and felt that Italian attitudes to relationships suited her much better than the equivalent Albanian view:

> In Albania, you have to be really serious about a relationship. When you are together with someone, everybody assumes you're going to get married. That's not for me at all.

In terms of societal norms, and more specifically gender roles, Mirela had once again rejected what she saw as traditional Albanian ideas, and for this reason felt no desire to return to her country of origin, imagining instead that if she were to move, it would be to the United States.[7] Whilst the majority of respondents cited the family-centred and communal values as positive features of Albanian society, which they felt to be missing in the Italian environment, Mirela insisted on the importance of independence and autonomy which the Italian setting offered her. However, when questioned about her main concerns, she immediately referred to her family:

> I worry that I can't do enough for my parents. They're both ill. I'd like to send them more money. They've had a hard life, they've always suffered. If I earned more money, I would be able to give more to them – maybe even bring them here for medical care, I could pay for their hospital treatment. It's not that their everyday life is bad; if they had a decent house and were healthy, they'd be OK.

Mirela's case seems to exemplify the tensions inherent in the integration process of Albanians in Italy. Although on a structural level she has encountered setbacks (documents, housing, employment), on a personal and social level, she has found the *Bolognese* setting to have offered more opportunities than obstacles, and it is largely through these personal contacts that she has successfully negotiated appropriate, if not perfect, solutions to the structural problems facing her.

Xhilda

Xhilda belongs to the student group of the sample and is studying foreign languages. She is also one of three respondents who are actively engaged in the issue of immigration, as she works as a volunteer for the 'Drita' association. Xhilda left Albania in 1997. She cites the period as one of the main reasons for her departure:

> There were lots of difficulties in my country at that time. My parents said to me 'Why don't you go to Italy, it will be better for you'. I was very enthusiastic, as I had always wanted to have different experiences, to go abroad. You know there is this image in Albania of the fascinating and exciting West. Italy was the obvious choice because it's near home.

The adventure of coming to Italy is a common theme throughout the student group, as well as the enticing image of the West. This reflects the construction of Italy amongst Albanian youth as a land of opportunity, and particularly consumerist pleasures, through the medium of television (Mai 2001a).

Xhilda had obtained her student visa through the Italian embassy in Tirana, and arrived in Bologna by plane, alone. Her only connection in Italy was a cousin in Rome, who had taken a course at a residential convent.

Through referral from this cousin, Xhilda was able to obtain accommodation in a linked *collegio* in Bologna, at a reduced rate. She has now lived there for almost five years, sharing a double room with an Italian girl, and paying 155 Euros a month.

> I'm lucky, because I found this room and it's quite cheap. I think it would have been very difficult to find a house otherwise, because I was a first-year student and also an Albanian. People don't want to rent rooms to Albanians because they worry that they might not be able to pay the rent. You have to show you can afford it.

Since her arrival in Italy, Xhilda has been financially supported by her parents: her father is a pharmacist, and her mother a state employee in a bank. This puts her in a privileged position amongst her compatriots in Italy. However, she feels herself to be a burden on her family, and has consequently worked at various temporary, part-time jobs throughout her studies. These she finds through a work co-operative, which some Italian friends introduced her to. She chose to work with this co-operative, which pays somewhat less than other jobs, for the flexibility it offers her. She uses her earnings to

> buy extra things for myself, like books, clothes, going out and things like that. I try to spend as little of my parent's money as possible. I only spend it on absolute essentials, like my room and food.

Xhilda has found adjustment to life in Italy fairly easy in the university context. She has made several Italian friends, and copes well with the language. Her life is almost entirely focused around her studies, allowing little time for social activities:

> I don't go out very much, only once in a while. In the first year, I didn't go out at all because I hadn't met the right people. Now I have friends, but it's difficult because of the curfew at the *collegio*. My friends know about it, so I can stay over at their houses, but I don't like doing it very often. I maybe go out once a week, or every ten days. You need it sometimes.

Xhilda's plans for the future are still unsure. Although she does not particularly want to return to Albania, she thinks it would be easier to find a job there than in Italy:

> It would be really difficult to find a good job in my field in Italy. I would like to work with languages, maybe to be a translator or something, but people here would rather give a job to an Italian than an immigrant. I don't see that many opportunities for a good job, other than cleaning and things like that. I think you would need Italian citizenship first.

Xhilda's uncertainties about her future also involve trepidation at the prospect of return:

> I think it would be difficult to go back to my country. I've been away for so long now. Most of my friends there have left the country, and the ones who are still there will have changed. If I found a good job here, then I would definitely stay. Having said all that, I wouldn't dislike to live in Albania though.

Xhilda definitely feels that her experience of living in Italy has changed her, and her attitude to life and gender relations:

> In Albania you still have to depend on the man. Your husband should take care of everything. I don't feel that way anymore. I think the experience of living abroad has changed this for me and my generation. Now I want to be able to take care of myself, support myself. The dream of every woman is to have a family, but now I realise that I have to do something for myself, and for society first.

Although she rejects traditional gender roles of support and dependence, she still maintains a critical attitude to Italian norms:

> I would like to be a woman between the two societies. Italy gives a woman the opportunity to fulfil her potential, but in some circumstances she is also forced to do things to survive. It should be a decision, not an obligation.

and particularly Italian men:

> Italian men are sweeter, more romantic, but you can't depend on them. They're all 'mummies boys'. Although Albanian men are 'harder', I still prefer them. They're not afraid of responsibility, because they've had to survive, to depend on themselves, so they're more mature.

Mirjana

Mirjana also belongs to the student group of respondents, but her lifestyle is extremely different from that of Xhilda. The most obvious difference is the fact that Mirjana is obliged to support herself whilst in Bologna, as her parents are unable to help. Her father is unemployed, having previously been a military official, whilst her mother works as a nurse, earning only 1,000 euros a year. Mirjana has been in Bologna for three years, and studies medicine. Before coming to Italy, she had been studying at the University of Tirana, but decided to leave for several reasons:

> I wanted to be able to study in a better school, with better resources. The university in Albania isn't as good, the teachers pay less attention to you. And even though university is free there, life can be quite expensive and I found it difficult to support myself. But I also came to give myself a better future. There is more opportunity here than in my country. Also, it had always been a dream of mine to study abroad, since I was a child. Not particularly in Italy, but just in another country.

Mirjana had been able to have her three years of study in Albania accredited, so that she started university in Bologna approximately half-way through the degree. She had decided to come to Bologna because her brother was already living nearby, in Rimini, which made it much easier for her:

> My brother had already been in Italy for two years. When he came home on holiday one time, I decided I would return with him. So we came back on the plane together.

Her brother's presence made it possible for her to survive the first year, when she found it very difficult to find work:

> I have found jobs mainly by word of mouth. It's very difficult at first, when you don't know people, or the work environment. When you first arrive, people treat you with suspicion, or want to try and take advantage of you. You have to be very careful. The first year I had to live off my brother.

As she has got to know people, Mirjana has found it easier to get jobs. She has worked in several different environments: in a bar, baby-sitting, cleaning houses, looking after old people, teaching English and French, and doing clerical work at the university. She has also worked two summer seasons in a hotel on the Adriatic coast:

> I have done all kinds of different jobs. The only jobs that I have liked a bit have been teaching and working in an office, because of the contact with people and the nature of the work, which is much more stimulating . . . I do other jobs because I need the money, but for a medical student to have to clean houses 'weighs' on me a bit.

Although there is a legal limit of 21 hours work a week for students in Italy, Mirjana had been able to do more by working *in nero* (literally 'in the black', or illegally). She generally earns between 6 and 8 Euros an hour, whether her work is declared or *in nero*. This year, however, Mirjana is entering what she hopes will be her last year of university, and is consequently keen to work less. She has applied for a scholarship, awarded on the basis of academic merit, and is waiting for a response.

Mirjana tells a similar story to many other respondents about the difficulty of finding housing:

> It was very, very difficult to find accommodation. Firstly, it's very expensive, and then there's the problem of being Albanian. People don't want to take risks, they think that Albanians destroy things, they 'throw all of us in the same sack'. It took five months from when I started looking for us to find a house. Now I live with my brother in a small studio. It's nice, just the right size for two of us.

They presently pay 425 euros a month between them, which she finds expensive, but is fairly average for Bologna.

Although Mirjana has found superficial social integration in the student community fairly easy, which she puts down to the fact of speaking good Italian when she arrived, she finds that the difficulties of living in Italy outweigh the advantages. Financially, she characterises her survival as a struggle, and she is particularly worried about her future prospects:

> Italy is not a country which offers foreigners the possibility to get ahead. A law has just been passed, without anyone paying much attention, which says that non-EU immigrants can't take the exams to enter medical specialisation courses unless they can prove that they can afford to pay the fees. This means I would have to have 90 million lire (around 45,000 euros) to become a practising doctor in Italy, even though I have done my degree here. There's no way I could afford that, so I don't know what to do.

Because of this, Mirjana has decided to take the US Medical Licence Exams, a series of three exams which, if she passes, would allow her to study to practice medicine in the US. She feels that structural difficulties and the lack of opportunity for advancement are pushing her away from Italy.

Another factor which troubles Mirjana is the level of latent prejudice in Italy against immigrants in general, and Albanians in particular. Even though, in common with all my respondents, she herself has not experienced specific severe problems, she finds it difficult to deal with.

> Italians are racist. When I'm talking to someone and then I tell them I'm Albanian, they're always shocked, and say 'Oh, but you don't seem like an Albanian' as if it's a compliment . . . And then people are so ignorant, I've met people who thought that Albanians were black. They have a negative impression that comes from the TV. You get used to it. It still hurts, but not as badly as when you first arrive.

Speaking of the media portrayal of Albanians in Italy, Mirjana gives a very succinct description of the effect it has:

> On TV, if an Italian kills someone, or commits a crime, they call them by their name. But if it's an Albanian, they just call them 'an Albanian', as if that were their name. And that annoys me, because that's my name too.

Thematic analysis

Several key issues emerge from the interviews, which impact in differing ways on the migratory experiences of all respondents. Here I select four themes which give an insight into both the differing ways these women have lived their migrations, and the experiences and challenges which are common to the majority of them.

Migration: the great leap forward?

Although migration usually arises from a complex combination of factors, a striking feature was the extent to which respondents described their migratory experiences as a positive advancement, a step towards 'a better future'. This was evident throughout the range of different situations and experiences, although it manifested itself in certain distinct forms.

The mothers, or expectant mothers, felt that, in migrating to Italy, they were offering the possibility of a better life to their children, indeed often subordinating their own feelings of displacement and anguish to the present and future well-being of their children. They echoed Zamira's sentiments:

> I'm here for my kids. (. . .) I wouldn't stay away from my country if I were on my own. But they need to grow up here, to finish school, and to fit in here. After that, we'll see. (Lira, aged 34)
>
> My daughter is very good at school. She's studying English and she speaks it well. (. . .) she's like an Italian girl now (laughs) she doesn't like being around other Albanians. That's just the way she is. (Alma, 35)

This desire for complete integration, even to the point of assimilation, is in marked contrast to certain other migrant communities, particularly those with strong religious identities, where the need to maintain cultural markers of difference is emphasised. Many of my respondents told me of families in which the parents had decided to baptise their children in the Catholic church, although the parents were themselves either Muslim or Orthodox Christian.

Among parents of children of university age, there was evidence of a similar pattern, in that parents experiencing difficulties supporting their children studying at Italian universities on an Albanian wage would consider migrating simply in order to earn the extra money required:

> I arrived in Italy on a tourist visa, for two weeks, nearly three years ago. I came to visit my son, and he said to me 'Don't leave, stay with me', so I stayed. In my country I earned enough money to live, but not enough to support my son here in Bologna. For his rent, university fees, books, life. Here I can earn more and help him. (Viola, 48)

In several families, the children's studies seem to take on the role of a common improvement project:

> I have a friend whose parents came with her when she came to Italy, so they could support her through university. Now she's nearly finished and they're all planning to go home together. (Mirjana, 22)

For the student group of respondents, there was also a clear sense of migration to Italy as a means to a better future, although this was almost always combined with a feeling of adventure, to a much greater extent than was true for the older women I spoke to. For example, Eda told me that:

> I wanted to leave to get away from home. As I live in Tirana, it was impossible to do this in Albania, so I came abroad. (Eda, 21)

Yet the sense of progression, of forfeiting present comfort for the sake of future reward, remained strong. Eda continues:

> I would like to stay in Italy after I finish my degree, to get some work experience in my particular field (she studies Business Economics). I know that I have made some sacrifices, working so hard and being away from home for four years. It would be a shame to go straight back. I want to be rewarded for the effort I have put in.

Eda has been able through personal contacts to create the possibility of appropriate work experience. A young couple for whom she has been baby-sitting throughout her time in Bologna, and with whom she has become close friends, own a small business in the area. As Eda is studying economics, they have offered her a position working for them, dealing with accounts and administration. She is thrilled at the prospect:

> I'm really, really happy about it. I have the possibility to get relevant work experience even before I've finished my degree. I think it will really help with my integration into Italian society and work.

As previously mentioned, the project of migrating and creating a better life abroad had in some ways become a self-fulfilling prophecy for many of these young women, who found it difficult to contemplate the prospect of return to an Albania in which their generation is severely depleted. However, many of them were also finding that Italy failed to offer as many opportunities as they had previously hoped, leaving them with an acute dilemma. Public *concorsi* (competition examinations for entry to certain jobs) in Italy are only open to Italian (and EU) citizens; passing one of these *concorsi* is a prerequisite for holding any job in the public sector, and is well regarded even when applying for a job in the private sector. As Italian citizenship can only be obtained after ten years of residence in Italy, even Albanian students leaving Italian universities with good degrees are not eligible.

> A new generation of young Albanian students are about to finish university in Italy, and I will be very interested to see what they do, whether it will be possible for them to get good jobs on the Italian job market, with this problem of citizenship. (Enkelejida, head of 'Drita' association, aged 39)

A similar problem faces the older, already qualified women who migrate to Italy. As we saw, Odeta, although a qualified accountant, was only able to find work as a domestic care worker. Enkelejida put the dilemma thus:

> People have to make the choice between staying in Albania and doing the job they want and are trained for, but for very low pay, or moving to Italy and getting a low status job that is paid more.

The project of moving to Italy for a better future is thus fraught with difficulties, and has proved much less straightforward than many of the women expected. The students especially, and particularly those nearing the end of their studies, are facing the realisation that they are not on an equal footing with their Italian peers; further sacrifices may be required if they stay in Italy, and high ambitions are likely to be thwarted.

Housing – the immigrant's nightmare

> You must say this – our biggest problem is finding a house. The biggest problem for any foreigner is this. We don't need help for other things, but this is very, very difficult. (Lira, market trader, 34)

One point which cannot be over-emphasised in the lives of Albanian women in Bologna is the difficulties which they have experienced in finding appropriate accommodation. Other researchers agree: as Zontini (2002: 162) puts it, 'housing is the principal problem immigrant women face in Bologna'. The pressure on the private housing market in Bologna is extremely high, due to several factors: the large student population, often able to pay relatively high rental prices; the high average wage in the city which further pushes rents up; and the pull of the city for immigrants, both internal and external. These factors mean that property owners have the pick of their tenants, a situation particularly unfavourable to immigrants. A combination of racism, concerns about documents, and a desire for a quiet life mean that landlords are frequently unwilling even to consider potential tenants from outside the EU.

Finding housing posed acute difficulties for almost all the women I spoke to. It was, as Juliana calls it, 'a nightmare'. Indeed, the only respondent who did not cite accommodation as her foremost difficulty was Eda, a student who, as soon as she arrived in Bologna, was able to move into a room which became vacant in the flat where her cousin was living. As mentioned previously, most of the women were eventually able to find housing through informal networks of employers, friends and acquaintances, bypassing the 'normal' routes of advertisements and agencies. When asked about assistance in finding a house, one respondent replied:

> We had no help at all. Finding a house is the last thing they (the *comune*) would help us with. They don't do any other, more basic things, so why would they help us with that? (Alma, market trader, 35)

When she first arrived, Alma had lived for four months in a cheap hotel with her daughter; her husband, already present in Italy for two years before her arrival, had never been able to find stable accommodation during that time. Other respondents had coped by making use of alternative living arrangements. Two students to whom I spoke had lived in a *collegio* (Xhilda was still living there), Odeta was living with her employer, and Mimoza was the only one to have benefited from the *casa di accoglienza* (reception house) provided by the *comune* for immigrants in specific difficulties.

Whilst none of the women, excluding Mimoza (who came on a medical visa, and therefore was entitled to special provisions), had contacted immigration services or local migrant service providers concerning housing, this was not through lack of need, but rather through a widespread and probably well-founded belief that nothing would be done to help them. As they would not have been considered as especially vulnerable cases by the authorities, the chances of assistance or of being allocated council housing are almost negligible. Here I would reiterate the words of Zontini, who says:

> housing is a problem . . . although not in the sense that the Council understands. Rita (her respondent, a Filipina domestic worker) in fact does not need an emergency shelter nor a room from an employer. What she needs is good quality accommodation at a price she can afford. (2002: 174)

Rent is, inevitably, the chief expense for all the women I spoke to. A job as a full-time cleaner earns about 750 euros a month, while a market trader can expect to make a bit more. The rent of a small apartment for a couple in Bologna is around 600 euros, and that of a family apartment approximately 750 euros. This means that the wages of one of the couple are almost completely consumed by rent alone, even more so when extra costs such as the ubiquitous *spese condominiali* (building service charges, often as much as 150 euros per month) are taken into account.

Italian friends, the Italian foe

The general level of prejudice against immigrants in Italy, particularly Albanians, is high. It is generally accepted that much of this anti-immigrant sentiment is fuelled by the media, a fact which many of my respondents made reference to when asked about experiences of discrimination.

> The TV sends the message that all Albanians are bad people, it blames all crimes on Albanians. (Mimoza, 28)

> Every murder, every crime in Italy is blamed on an Albanian by the television news. It's true that some Albanians have committed crimes, but not all of them. The government is using foreigners as a scapegoat. (Ariola, 21)

These feelings of disillusionment were most marked and prevalent within the student group. The students had arrived in Italy with higher expectations of integration and adventure, were expecting to be treated as any other foreign student, and had therefore been taken aback by the realisation that, for many Italians, they formed a distinct and somehow inferior group. Ariola described a situation which had taken place during her first year in Italy:

> I was in the lecture theatre with an (Albanian) friend and we were talking. A good-looking boy was sitting in the room and turned round to talk to us. He asked 'Do you speak Italian?', we said yes, then he said 'Are you English?', 'No', 'French?', 'No', 'Where are you from?', and when we said 'Albania' he just lost all interest. He turned back and stopped talking to us. It's only a small thing, but it really hurt me.

A striking aspect of the respondents' views on discrimination was the extent to which they would themselves blame fellow-Albanians. Many of the media-driven negative images of the Albanian community seemed to have been accepted, and to an extent internalised, by these women who then found their own scapegoats in 'other', unknown parts of the Albanian population in Italy.

> For me, there are two different Albanian communities. Firstly, there are the people I know, and then there are the Albanians you hear about. (Xhilda, student, 23)
>
> (the reason for the bad image of Albanians is that) some Albanians have done some bad things in Italy. When I see a certain type of Albanian in the street, I avoid speaking Albanian, I avoid coming into contact with them. (Eda, student, 21)
>
> The Albanian community is a bit divided, into let's say, the good part and the bad part. I don't know the bad part of the community. (Juliana, market trader, 25)

It seems that a widely-used strategy amongst these women to cope with the pressures of prejudice has been to create another 'Other' within the Albanian group, onto which they are able to project the negative images of Albanians which surround them, and which otherwise they would be forced to accept as racism against themselves. By using this 'get-out clause' they are able to exist peacefully in a society which attempts to alienate and reject them. This image of the other, 'bad' Albanian may go some way to explaining the lack of association and community networks within the Albanian immigrant group.

Whilst all respondents cited widespread popular prejudice, the majority also emphasised that on a personal, individual level the situation was markedly different. Perhaps linked to the weak community bonds amongst Albanian immigrants, informal social contact with Italians was common. Of the 17 interviewees, ten said that the majority of their friends were Italian, two that they were both Italian and Albanian, and of the five remaining, two said that they had no friends due to work commitments. The general picture seemed to be of relative ease of integration at a social level. Indeed, many informants told stories of the ways in which individual Italians had helped them to overcome difficulties.

> The only people who have helped us since we arrived here have been Italians, some of them are very good people. I have friends who have helped me find work and to sort out my documents. (Alma, market trader, 35)

I therefore concur with Zinn and Rivera's conclusion that:

> Despite the fact that in recent years a xenophobic attitude has been spreading in Italian public opinion, in the concrete experiences of the immigrants the elements of sympathy, aid and solidarity on the part of the Italians have prevailed. (1995: 4)

Albanians' insertion into Italian society and into job and housing markets therefore seemed much more dependent on informal personal contacts with the indigenous population than on any more formal arrangements. With reference to help supplied by the *comune* or the state, the general attitude was negative:

> The state in Italy doesn't try to help foreigners, it just puts obstacles in your way. In banks, and schools, and things like that, they just create problems and ask for more and more documents. I've had to do everything on my own. (Alma, market trader, 35)
>
> The immigration system is badly organised, it always takes longer than they say to renew your permit. And they could do more for integration, instead of just stopping at giving you documents. (Xhilda, student, 23)
>
> I haven't had much contact with the social services here, but from what I see around me I think that they're not good enough. People have problems when they arrive here, but they're not helped. And they need help, to find a house and a job. (Odeta, carer, 40)

The only public services which respondents felt had served them well were the medical services, which Juliana had used during her pregnancy and had found to be very efficient and affordable, and which Mimoza had had much experience of, having spent several months in hospital:

> The medical services here are good. They're not what I expected of course, I thought they'd be absolutely amazing, but they're good enough. I stayed in the hospital for a whole summer, and then had lots of treatment afterwards, and I never had to pay anything. (Mimoza, 28)

The experiences of these women point to a somewhat contradictory, but ultimately explicable situation, in that while levels of public prejudice are high against Albanians, the attitude of many Italians with whom they have had personal contact has been hospitable and helpful. Again this backs up the findings of Zinn and Rivera that:

> The presence of the Albanian women in these concrete relations with Italians has given some space, if limited, to a de-essentialized view of the Albanian refugees as a whole. (1995: 5)

The relations with local residents in Bologna, however, seem to be less warm than those observed by Zinn and Rivera in the context of the South of Italy. I would suggest that this is due to the more urbanised, individualistic lifestyle which prevails in Bologna in which, in my experience, close contact on a domestic, quotidian level between neighbours such as that described in the small towns of the Italian South is uncommon.

Where's the difference?

The lack of community feeling and association within the Albanian population in Italy has been noted elsewhere. A paper by de Bonis (2001), entitled 'The Albanian non-community in Rome', focuses on the fragmentary and rivalrous nature of Albanian organisations in Rome. It is suggested that this tendency towards non-association is due to a rejection of their communist/collectivist past, or suspicion of their compatriots. Whilst I found some evidence of this feeling, highlighted in the conceptual separation of 'good' and 'bad' Albanians, I would propose that the lack of impetus towards community groups and organisations is largely caused by a feeling of similarity to the Italian population, and a consequent lack of need to assert difference through association. This is reinforced by a tendency towards individual self-reliance.

> It seems like Albanians are the only community that don't stick together. There are lots of us, so there could be a strong organisation, but people prefer to be alone, independent. (Mirjana, student, 24)

Although several of the women had at least one Albanian female friend, there was no evidence of the type of community 'friendship groups' which have enabled migrant groups to cope elsewhere. Women had made friends just as readily with Italians as with Albanians:

> I haven't looked for Albanians here. I've met a few, by chance, but I haven't really got to know them. I don't know where they go, what they are like, or any of that. (Mimoza, shop assistant, 28)

For one respondent at least, the lack of a strong Albanian community feeling was liberating. She had come to Italy looking to escape from Albanian norms of 'control', and valued her independence highly.

> In Italy, women have much more independence. I can be completely independent, not like in Albania where people are watching you all the time. (Mirela, care worker, 25)

The feeling of similarity to Italians was especially strong amongst the younger respondents, who often responded to questions about Albanian culture by asserting that it was no different from Italy, particularly southern Italy. They therefore felt that there was no great cultural gulf between them and the Italians around them, especially as many Italian students in Bologna originate from the southern regions of the country.

In spite of this feeling of cultural similarity, there was a sense in which many of the women felt they had been changed by their experiences of living in Italy. Again, this feeling was more pronounced among the younger respondents.

> We try to maintain Albanian culture a bit. For example, we speak Albanian together, we play Albanian games, and cook Albanian food. We want to stay Albanian, but you can't help becoming a bit Italian. (Flutura, student, 22)

> My generation is changing, becoming more open. I think this is partially because of the experience of living abroad. Now I'm more keen to be independent, to look after myself instead of relying on a man. (Xhilda, student, 23)

The way this change manifested itself was often in terms of views on gender roles. All but two of my respondents agreed that Italian society was much better for women than Albanian society, and many related this to their own life and position.

> Italian society is wonderful (*bellissima*) for women. For everything. Jobs, behaviour, attitudes, rights. In Albania a woman's voice doesn't count. Here, if you make a woman angry, you better watch out! So, I feel like I have more power here. (Juliana, market trader, 25)

Another striking way in which some of the women had been changed by Italy, and were to a degree assimilating, was in being baptised into the Catholic Church. Four respondents had been baptised since their arrival, and another attended church on a regular basis, although all of them were from nominally Muslim families. When asked for further explanation, all of them explained that as religion had been prohibited in Albania, their attachment to a particular church was weak, and that for them belief in God was the same in all religions. This seems to exemplify the pattern of integration through flexibility. None of the women felt that they were losing their cultural identity, although they were for the most part willing to adapt their patterns of behaviour and attitude in order to cope with life in Italian society.

Some conclusions

Whilst Bologna's boast of being '*la città multietnica*' may be increasingly true at a numerical level, there is no real evidence – as perceived by the Albanian population – of the *comune* working to facilitate the full social, cultural and economic integration which is its stated aim. The picture which emerged from my fieldwork was of a national group isolated from the civic life of Bologna, having very little contact with municipal services or institutions of any kind. My findings reinforce the general conclusion that, although general levels of prejudice against Albanians are high in the Italian population, individual women and couples have encountered at best welcome and support from their Italian friends and acquaintances, and at worst indifference and minor incidences of cowardly hostility. It would seem that the presence of the more recently-arrived female element in the Albanian immigrant group has served to 'soften' the image of, and attitude to, Albanians among the people with whom they are in contact. The traditional masculinised stereotype of a criminal, destructive Albanian has been challenged and, to an extent, altered by the female presence. It must be stressed, however, that this shift is noticeable only through the evidence of the Albanian women's personal experiences, and does not seem to be reflected by a significant change in the media representation, nor in the general public and political discourse, which continue to conform to the aforementioned stereotype. This apparent lack of direct personal experience of aggressive prejudice means that life in Italy is relatively easy to adjust to on a social level. This is achieved to a certain extent by the construction of an internal Other, a 'bad Albanian' or group upon whom the blame can be placed for creating the negative Italian attitude.

However, at an economic and structural level, difficulties are much more evident. The interviews show that housing has remained the foremost problem, both in terms of availability and cost, and the anxiety which it causes. The women I spoke to have often been forced to use alternative, non-ideal housing solutions, such as living in a *collegio* or staying long-term in a hostel. This is partly due to the prohibitive cost of accommodation in Bologna, and partly caused by the unwillingness of property-owners to rent to an immigrant group considered untrustworthy and unreliable. On the job market the problem is similar, though less acute. Whilst there seems to be an occasional reluctance on the part of employers to take on Albanians, generally work is available. Indeed, it is this very ease of finding work which initially attracts immigrants to Bologna. The restrictiveness of the labour market, however, is sectoral. While domestic, cleaning and care work, and bar and baby-sitting work for students, are relatively easy to find, the same cannot be said of higher status, better paid jobs, demanding higher qualifications, which many Albanians have, or soon will have. The 'better life' which many respondents are seeking may be just about obtainable in terms of material wealth, but there remain substantial obstacles to advancement in the world of employment and social status.

The women for whom this posed the most acute dilemma were the student group, who considered themselves as substantively no different from the Italian students around them, particularly those from the South of Italy, whose 'culture' the Albanian girls identified as almost identical to their own. The realisation that their situation was in fact markedly different to their classmates was often a painful one, exacerbated by the difficulties in returning to their home country, now denuded of their friends and schoolmates. These women faced the difficult choice between attempting to continue their lives and careers in the country where they had pursued their university studies, but in which the labour market is loaded with restrictions against them; or returning home to a country and culture which now seem almost alien, and certainly restrictive; or of moving to another country to face more unknowns. The market traders among my small sample seemed in a way to have achieved the most successful negotiation of their position. They were able to define and control their own situation in the labour market to a far greater extent than women working elsewhere, and felt less exploited as they were self-employed.

Acknowledgements

I am deeply indebted to the women I spoke to, who gave willingly of their time and stories. I trust and hope that I have represented them faithfully. I would like to thank Giuseppe, of 'Skanderbeg', Roberto of CGIL, and Enkelejida of 'Drita' for making it possible for me to contact the women who are the focus of this study. I also thank Russell King at the University of Sussex for his advice and guidance in supervising the MA dissertation on which this chapter is based. Finally, thanks to Johanne Mygind and Julie Billaud for some lovely Danish dissertation days.

Notes

1 The theme of Italians identifying their own poor and half-forgotten past in the 'Albanian Other' is at the core of Gianni Ameglio's film *L'America*. For a sophisticated analysis of the mutual relationships between Italy and Albania see Mai (2003).

2 See www.comunebologna.it/immigrati

3 One particular woman, for example, started the interview trying to convince me that she was extremely happy to be in Italy and had no problems, only to say later 'If I'm honest, I'd go back to Albania tomorrow if I could'.

4 Albanian students are able to study at Italian universities under an accord system between the two governments, administered by the Italian embassy in Tirana. As well as proving academic merit, the families of these students are obliged to open a current account in Italy in the name of their child, into which they must deposit a sum of money. The students are then issued a student visa, which entitles them to a *permesso di soggiorno* which must be renewed every year. Whilst in Italy on a student visa, the maximum number of working hours allowed is 21 per week, although many students exceed this by working illegally.

5 Four work as market traders, selling fruit and vegetables. These women work on stalls owned either by themselves or a member of their immediate family, and as such are self-employed. Four other women work as domestic workers and carers, mainly for elderly people. One woman has a job in a pastry shop and the remaining respondent, through whom I was able to meet some of the others, works as a cultural mediator for 'Drita'.

6 A bedroom for one person must be 9 square metres, and for two people 15 square metres, whilst the house must also comprise a sitting room, kitchen and bathroom.

7 Several respondents talked about the possibility of moving to the US in the future, and always talked of it in classic terms of a 'land of opportunity'.

References

Anthias, F. and Lazaridis, G. (eds) (2000) *Gender and Migration in Southern Europe*. Oxford: Berg.

Buijs, G. (ed.) (1992) *Migrant Women: Crossing Boundaries and Changing Identities*. Oxford: Berg.

Campani, G. (2000) Immigrant women in southern Europe: social exclusion, domestic work and prostitution in Italy, in King, R., Lazaridis, G. and Tsardanidis, C. (eds) *Eldorado or Fortress? Migration in Southern Europe*. Basingstoke: Macmillan, 147–69.

—— (2001) Migrants and media: the Italian case, in King, R. and Wood, N. (eds) *Media and Migration: Constructions of Mobility and Difference*. London: Routledge, 38–52.

Caritas (2003) *Immigrazione Dossier Statistico 2003*. Rome: Anterem.

de Bonis, M. (2001) La non comunità albanese di Roma, *Limes: Rivista Italiana di Geopolitica*, 2: 273–6.

Dell'Agnese, E. (1996) Profughi politici e rifugiati economici: il doppio esodo albanese nel 1991, in Gentileschi, M. L. and King, R. (eds) *Questioni di Popolazione in Europa: Una Prospettiva Geografica*, Bologna: Pàtron, 69–81.

Jamieson, A. and Silj, A. (1998) *Albanian Immigration: A 'Criminal' Invasion?* Rome: Ethnobarometer Working Paper No. 1.

King, R. (1992) *Patterns of Italian Migrant Labour: The Historical and Geographical Context*. Bristol: University of Bristol, Centre for Mediterranean Studies, Occasional Paper 4.

King, R and Andall, J. (1999) The geography and economic sociology of recent immigration to Italy, *Modern Italy*, 4(2): 135–58.

King, R. and Mai, N. (2002) Of myths and mirrors: interpretations of Albanian migration to Italy, *Studi Emigrazione*, 145: 161–99.

Kofman, E., Phizacklea, A., Raghuram, P. and Sales, R. (2000) *Gender and*

International Migration in Europe: Employment, Welfare, Politics. London: Routledge.

Mai, N. (2001a) Italy is beautiful: the role of Italian television in Albanian migration to Italy, in King, R. and Wood, N. (eds) *Media and Migration: Constructions of Mobility and Difference*. London: Routledge, 95–109.

—— (2001b) Transforming traditions: a critical analysis of the trafficking and exploitation of young Albanian girls in Italy, in King, R. (ed.) *The Mediterranean Passage: Migration and New Cultural Encounters in Southern Europe*. Liverpool: Liverpool University Press, 258–78.

—— (2003) The cultural construction of Italy in Albania and vice versa: migration dynamics, strategies of resistance and politics of mutual self-determination across colonialism and post-colonialism, *Modern Italy*, 8(1): 77–94.

Orsini-Jones, M. and Gattullo, F. (2000) Migrant women in Italy: national trends and local perspectives, in Anthias, F. and Lazaridis, G. (eds) *Gender and Migration in Southern Europe*. Oxford: Berg, 125–44.

Però, D. (2001) Inclusionary rhetoric/exclusionary practice: an ethnographic critique of the Italian left in the context of migration, in King, R. (ed.) *The Mediterranean Passage: Migration and New Cultural Encounters in Southern Europe*. Liverpool: Liverpool University Press, 162–85.

Vickers, M. (1995) *The Albanians: A Modern History*. London: Tauris.

Zinn, D. L. (1996) Adriatic brethren or black Sheep? Migration in Italy and the Albanian crisis, *European Urban and Regional Studies*, 3(3): 241–9.

Zinn, D. L. and Rivera, A. (1995) Notes on a displaced womanhood: Albanian refugee women in southern Italy, *Anthropology of East Europe Review*, 13(1): 23–9.

Zontini, E. (2002) Female domestic labour migrants and local policies in Bologna: the story of a Filipino woman, in Grillo, R. and Pratt, J. (eds) *The Politics of Recognising Difference: Multiculturalism Italian-style*. Aldershot: Ashgate, 159–76.

3

Examining policy responses to immigration in the light of interstate relations and foreign policy objectives

Greece and Albania

GERASIMOS KONIDARIS

Greece has been an emigration country for most of its modern history. It became a country of positive net migration in 1975, through a combination of return migration of Greeks and immigration of foreigners (Fakiolas and King 1996). However, the overall size of the migratory inflow in the course of the subsequent 15 years was very moderate. Then, after the collapse of the East European communist regimes, the situation changed dramatically. During a very short period of time in the early 1990s, the country became host to a large number of immigrants from Eastern Europe. The overwhelming majority of these entered illegally, and by the mid-1990s the undocumented immigrant population was estimated to be half a million people (see, for example, Athens Centre for Workers and Employees 1995: 13; Fakiolas 1997: 1). Although nationals from many East European countries have been coming to Greece, the main source has been Albania. In the mid-1990s Albanian nationals constituted at least half of the undocumented immigrant population in Greece. The scale of their migration was such that the term 'Albanian' began to be used by Greeks as a synonym for 'immigrant'.

The unexpected mass influx from Albania and the other Eastern European countries not only surprised the Greek state, but also found it completely unprepared. Being a sending country for so long, Greece had for decades been more interested in putting forward emigration policies

(Fakiolas and King 1996: 184; Lazaridis 1996: 341). The adoption of a more contemporary immigration policy framework had not been seen as a priority; the one in use was based on Law 4310, enacted in 1929. Realising that the existing policy instruments were inadequate for addressing the new situation, the authorities acted swiftly. On 5 November 1991 the Greek Parliament replaced Law 4310 with Law 1975, which came into force on 4 June 1992.

For the most part, this new legislation was designed to deal with illegal migration. It introduced numerous strict stipulations aimed at controlling the entrance, stay and employment of clandestine immigrants. The measures included the penalisation of undocumented entry; immediate deportation of illegal immigrants without the application of formal procedures; creation of special police squads for patrolling Greece's land and sea borders; and prohibiting the illegal employment of immigrants. However, despite the introduction of these policies, the number of Albanian illegal immigrants living in the country remained high. Finally – after a lot of wavering – Greece's rigorous official stance changed in 1997 with the introduction of a programme for the regularisation of the illegal immigrant population.

Why did it take six years for Greece to put forward such a regularisation plan? Why did the Greek governments of the period show such a reluctance to legalise the existence of the (predominantly Albanian) irregular immigrants? Had this anything to do with the state of the relations between Greece and Albania, given the marked historic antagonism in their affairs and the tensions that existed in the 1990s? And was the delay because of the fact that Albanians – being by far the most numerous ethnic immigrant group – would have benefited the most from such a development?

This chapter will try to answer these questions by examining what role Greece's relations with Albania played in the country's policy response to the migratory flow from Albania. The analysis will be centred on the years 1990–97 because it was during this period that migration and international affairs were most entwined. The chapter will be divided into three main parts which follow a chronological order. In the first, I will make a brief and selective presentation of the main events that shaped relations between the two countries in the twentieth century, up to the end of the 1980s. The second will cover the period from 1990 up to the time before the regularisation process was officially initiated in 1996. The third will cover the events that took place from 1996 to 1997, when the final decision on the form and scope of this process was taken. A summary of the main findings of the analysis will be presented in the conclusion, as well as a concise account of developments post-1998.

The discussion and analysis will be based on secondary sources as well as on my own empirical research. This primary material is the product of in-depth semi-structured elite interviews I conducted in Greece in 1998 and 1999. Interviewees were people who have dealt with the migration issue in their own capacity; some have been involved in policy-making on migration at a state level. Thirty-nine such interviews were conducted with high-ranking ministerial officials, representatives from Greek political parties, non-governmental organisations, as well as with individual politicians and specialists.

I acknowledge that the nature of my research design privileges the Greek view of the issues discussed. My interviewees were all Greek and many of my secondary sources are also Greek. And of course my informants were aware that they were talking to a Greek researcher, which probably coloured the emphasis of their responses. They may have slanted their remarks in a different way if they were addressing a researcher of another nationality, such as an Albanian. Although I have done my best to present the contested nature of some of the issues my analysis deals with, for example in some detailed footnotes, I have to be honest with my readers about my positionality in this research. It would have been a challenging and revealing exercise to collect a parallel set of interviews with Albanian politicians and officials about the same issues – an avenue for further research.

The background of the uneasy Greek–Albanian relationship

In the years that followed the creation of the Albanian state by the Great European Powers in 1912, Albania and Greece have not had the good fortune of establishing good neighbourly relations with each other. Rivalry, tension and mistrust have characterised their dealings for most of this period. The core cause for friction has been their dispute over the territory of south Albania and its inhabitants. This area, called 'Northern Epirus' by many Greeks, is regarded as geographically, historically, ethnologically and culturally connected with the northern Greek territory of Epirus since antiquity. However, the geographical boundaries and ethnological composition of this area have constituted a heated debate between the two countries for nearly a century. The term 'Northern Epirus' (which Albania rejects as irredentist) started to be used by Greece around 1913. It should not be seen as corresponding to specific geomorphologic features but rather as a political and diplomatic term (Dodos 1994: 119–20; Kallivretakis 1995: 25, 29; Winnifrith 2002: 24). A characteristic element of the dispute is that, to a great extent, the historiography of both sides stresses the continuing presence of the two peoples in the area.[1]

An important parameter that would influence events in the modern era was the way in which people in the area were categorised during Ottoman rule. For the Ottomans, being Greek meant that the subject was also an Orthodox Christian. Thus, Orthodox Albanians, Vlachs and other smaller ethnic groups were also classified as Greeks (Kallivretakis 1995: 31–3;

Kondis 1994: 13). The view that those who were Orthodox also had a Greek ethnic identity would underline Greece's perception and attitude towards the population of south Albania for much of the twentieth century (Tsitselikis and Christopoulos 2003: 21, 23, 28).[2] In reality the ethno-cultural history of the area was much more complex and fluid; some of this complexity is brought out in de Rapper's chapter in the book.

In the early 1900s, the Greek army occupied this territory twice – during the Balkan War of 1912–13 and in October 1914, during World War I. Eventually the Great European Powers forced it to withdraw. On 18 February 1914, an attempt made by the ethnic Greeks to declare this area autonomous within the territory of the Albanian state met with success, but due to the outbreak of World War I this autonomy was never implemented. In March 1916 Greece officially declared its unification with south Albania, only to be forced again to revoke by the Great Powers. With the end of World War I, Greece again laid its claim for the annexation of south Albania in the Peace Conference at Versailles in January 1919; without, however, any success.[3]

In the period 1921–39 the tension between the two countries revolved mainly around educational issues affecting the Greek minority. From the 360 Greek-language schools that existed before the Balkan War, there were only 10 functioning in 1933. Greece appealed to the League of Nations (LoN), which ruled in 1935 that Albania should re-open the schools. With its accession to the LoN in 1921, Albania had committed itself to protecting the rights of minorities. Questions naturally arose as to the size of such minorities. In 1922 Albania recognised the Greek minority as 16,000, but a LoN special committee estimated 35,000–40,000 as the number who spoke Greek in their homes. In 1922 the British Consul in Durrës gave an estimate of 25,000–35,000. A later estimate (1934) gave 37,000 (Baltsiotis 2003: 65–6; Divani 1995: 271; Kondis 1994: 153–7; Tsitselikis 2003: 169–72).

Greece entered World War II after Italy's attack on 28 October 1940. Albania – which by 1939 had become Italy's colony – was used as the base for the Italian operations against Greece and also participated in the hostilities. During the subsequent occupation of Greece by the Axis powers, Albanian-speaking Muslims living in the Greek territory of Epirus (the Chams) collaborated with the invaders. They fought fiercely against the Greek partisans, who in 1944 were ordered by the Allied forces to push them out of Greece and into Albania. The violent clash that followed and the extensive reprisals exercised by the Greek guerrillas resulted in the migration to Albania of almost the entire Cham population, many of whom would not have been active collaborators of the axis. In 1945, a Greek Special Court on Collaborators condemned in absentia 1,930 of them (many to death), while their immovable property was confiscated by the Greek state. According to the 1951 census, only 487 Albanian-speaking Muslims remained in Greek territory.[4]

When World War II ended, Greece resurrected its territorial claim on south Albania, this time at the Ministerial Council of the four Great Powers (15 May 1946). In the Paris Peace Conference that started on 29 July 1946, the Albanian delegation, under its new leader Enver Hoxha, voiced strong anti-Greek views, also raising the Chams' issue. Greece managed to bring onto the agenda the issue of south Albania, but after procedural manoeuvres on the part of Yugoslavia (which along with other East European states was against Greece's plans), the Allies asked, and Greece agreed, to withdraw the issue from the agenda and reintroduce it to the Ministerial Council in November of the same year. When that happened, the Council referred the issue for settlement at a later date.

In the period up to the early 1970s, the relations between the two states remained highly hostile (see Antonopoulos 1999: 106–9; Vickers and Pettifer 1997: 188–90). To past antagonisms were added the rivalry of the Cold War and the alleged persecutions to which the Greek minority was subjected under the Hoxha regime. Although the existence of the minority was recognised by the regime, its presence was pinpointed to a 'minority zone' that included 99 Greek-speaking villages mainly in the districts of Gjirokastër and Sarandë, leaving out the three villages of Himarë, which had been recognised as minority areas in 1921, and people who lived in towns (Baltsiotis 2003: 61–2; Kondis, 1994: 174). On this basis, people outside the 'minority zones' were deprived of their rights to learn the Greek language, to have four years of Greek education and to speak the Greek language in public; possibilities available to the rest of them in the acknowledged minority areas. The regime also proceeded to transport Albanian settlers to the minority regions, and to the parallel transfer of ethnic Greeks to the north of the country, in what was seen by many ethnic Greeks as an attempt to alter the demographic composition of these areas.[5]

The unprecedented repression (even by the standards of a communist regime) of religion was a further attack on the identity of ethnic Greeks, many of whose traditions and customs related closely to Orthodox Christianity. The process started in 1949, with the confiscation and nationalisation of Church property and intensified in 1967, when the regime launched its atheistic campaign.

As would be expected, the alleged mistreatment of the minority bolstered anti-Albanian feelings in Greece during this period. Such was the hostility that, for example, the then Greek Prime Minister Karamanlis said to his British opposite number in 1961 that, 'Albania is not a state, it is a den of thieves' (*Kiriakatiki Eleftherotypia*, 13 June 1993). Furthermore, Greece's territorial claim on south Albania continued to be on the agendas of both the right and the centre political parties which dominated the country's politics until the coup d'état of 1967. As the moderate co-leader of the Centre Union party and subsequent Prime Minister George Papandreou said in the Greek Parliament in 1960, 'what all Greek governments ought to know is that the issue of Northern Epirus exists. And what will always be prohibited is to renounce this sacred demand. Our claim on Northern Epirus is sacred and inalienable' (Georgiou 1994: 392–3).

The first serious efforts for achieving better neighbourly contacts and releasing the accumulated tension were made in the 1980s, initiated by Greece (see Antonopoulos 1999: 111–13; Vickers and Pettifer 1997: 190–2). The main factor that allowed such initiatives to take place was the accession to power of Andreas Papandreou's Panhellenic Socialist Movement (PASOK) in 1981. PASOK introduced significant changes in many aspects of public life, in the way the country was governed and in the way it handled its foreign affairs. So in February 1984, Prime Minister Papandreou declared at a public speech in Epirus that the principle of inviolability of European borders, which had been included in the Helsinki Final Act of 1975 to which Greece was a signatory, applied also to the Greek–Albanian border. He also emphasised, though, Greece's particular concern for the 'miserable conditions in which the Greeks of Albania live' (Antonopoulos 1999: 111). The most significant development took place on 28 August 1987, when the Greek Cabinet lifted the state of war with Albania that had been declared in November 1940, cancelled during the occupation and re-declared in 1944. In that way it hoped to remove Albania's suspicion that the state of war was still in force, due to Greece's supposedly still-existing territorial claim. As Mr. Papoulias – the Minister of Foreign Affairs in 1987 – said to the author, with the decision of lifting the state of war the Greek government was aiming

> to progressively open the hedgehog (as Albania was called at that period); to surmount the absolute mistrust of its government in relation to Greece's intentions. Because for sure, many of the things which created that mistrust had to do exclusively with Greece's behaviour; Greece's territorial claims were always there.[6]

The government believed that by achieving that, the human rights of the minority could be progressively improved, in a country where the population in general had been seriously deprived of its liberties.

Having presented elements of the highly problematic past of Greek–Albanian relations, I now proceed to the main discussion on the relations between the two countries from 1990 to 1997, and how these have influenced Greece's policy response to the migratory wave from Albania during that period.

The period 1990–6

At the beginning of 1990, Albania was the only country in the East European block that was still resisting the flood of change that had swept the rest. Since 1985 – the year that its hard-line communist leader Enver Hoxha died – it was ruled by Ramiz Alia, a protégé and close associate of

Hoxha. Alia had introduced some reforms, but they were too modest to adequately appease the fast-growing popular dissatisfaction with the situation in the country (Pano 1997: 299–302). Among these changes were the liberalisation of the issuing of passports, travelling abroad and the right to emigrate, the latter being no longer a crime of high treason.[7] However, the number of people who were given the opportunity to leave the country continued to be very small, due to the fact that the infamous *Sigurimi* (the Secret Police) was still in control of the Ministry of the Interior issuing the passports. So in July 1990, around 6,000 Albanian citizens attempted for the first time to leave the country by entering the embassies of Western European countries in Tirana and seeking asylum. Despite condemnation by the regime, the overwhelming majority of them managed to acquired visas and leave Albania; 30 (mostly ethnic Greeks) were flown to Greece (Antonopoulos 1999: 116; Pano 1997: 303).

In the months following the embassies' 'invasion', popular unrest became progressively widespread and more violent, as was pointed out by Barjaba and King in Chapter 1. This prolonged internal turmoil weakened the regime which was finding it increasingly difficult to exercise tight control over the country and its people. The flight of Albanians to Greece remained, however, on a small scale. This was to change dramatically in late December, when thousands started crossing the Greek borders. In the single night of 30–31 of that month more than 800 Albanian citizens (many of Greek origin) were recorded as having entered Greece (Antonopoulos 1995: 84), and the pace of this inflow continued during the first days of 1991. These developments forced Mitsotakis, the Greek Prime Minister and President of the New Democracy party (ND), to visit Albania on 13 and 14 January 1991. In the talks he held with Alia it was agreed that it was for the Greek minority's best interest to remain in Albania, while the Albanian side guaranteed that minority members returning from Greece would face no consequences. The two leaders emphasised their commitment to respecting the principles of territorial integrity, inviolability of borders and non-interference in the internal affairs of other countries. This visit was not without problems, however, as the Albanian Premier raised the Chams' issue, which his opposite number refused to discuss. Mr. Mitsotakis also visited one of the minority areas, where he urged the ethnic Greeks not to leave their ancestral homes. At the end of the year (25 December), the Albanian Ministry of Foreign Affairs reacted strongly to deportations of illegal immigrants and accused Greece of exercising 'an anti-Albanian campaign and a pogrom against Albanian immigrants and of an unacceptable violation of human rights' (Antonopoulos 1995: 137). Greece rejected the accusations by saying that the deportations were a legitimate response to the increased criminal activity on the part of Albanian irregular immigrants.[8] On 28 December Albania took its complaints further, to the Council of Europe and the United Nations. Two days later, Mr. Alia said in an interview that the two states had close relations, but he also raised the Chams' issue. He stated that Albania had no territorial claim on Thesprotia, but was asking for the return to the Chams of the properties they had left in Greece at the end of World War II. Greece responded by saying that that issue was non-existent and bringing it up it would not contribute to the further development of Greek–Albanian relations.

In February 1992 the ethnic Greeks created the Human Rights Union party in order to take part in the March elections, since the Omonia Party with which they had participated in the 1991 polls had been disqualified by the Alia government. The debarring of Omonia was due to a new electoral law that banned political parties with a regional, ethnic or religious basis (Omonia continued to exist, but as a cultural not political organisation). The Greek government and the minority protested strongly against that decision, but Albania rejected their complaints as well as those of the European Union (EU) and the Council of Europe. In the elections of March 1992, Sali Berisha became the first non-communist President of Albania. The day after his victory he stated: 'Our views are clear . . . Because the Chams had been forced out of Greece when the latter had a non-democratic government, now the new democratic one has to grant them the right to return to their properties' (Antonopoulos 1995: 144). Greece once again replied that that issue was non-existent.

In an effort to prevent the creation of new tension, Prime Minister Mitsotakis again visited Albania on 11 April. In the talks he held with his opposite number, the latter insisted that Greece put no obstacles to immigration from Albania, and recognise all Albanian immigrants in the country as legal, while he raised again the Chams' issue. With respect to immigration, Mitsotakis said that Greece could agree only to the admission of some seasonal workers, the number of whom would be in accordance with the regulations of the EU. Regarding the Chams, he characterised them as war criminals who would not be allowed to go back to Greece. He proposed a trade-off in relation to their properties, by saying that some form of compensation could be agreed only in cases when it could be established that Chams had not been convicted for or participated in crimes against Greeks and their fleeing from the country in 1944 was only due to fear; and if Albania would agree to mutually compensate ethnic Greeks who had lost properties due to (alleged) persecution in the communist era. The visit by the Greek Premier clearly did not produce any results. That became evident during the following months when senior Albanian politicians including the President, the Prime Minister and the Minister of Foreign Affairs accused Greece of having territorial claims against Albania, and of denying the issues of the Chams and the supposed existence in the country of an Albanian minority. In December, the Albanian Ministry of Education prohibited the opening of new Greek schools in the country.

Greece repeated its intention to reach an agreement with Albania on the issue of illegal immigrants during the visit to Athens of Albanian Premier Mexi on 16 and 17 May 1993, one month before relations between the two states were to undergo the first of their two most serious crises in the post-communist period (Doudoumis 1994: 94–8). This was occasioned by the arrest and deportation by the Albanian authorities of Chrisostomos Maidonis, a Greek Archimandrite and representative of the Orthodox Archbishopric of Albania in the minority area of Gjirokastër, on charges of anti-Albanian activities: namely, that he was propagandising the unification of south Albania with Greece. Greece proceeded right away to deport Albanian illegal immigrants on such a scale that around 10,000 were sent back within three days. The Greek government insisted that the Maidonis incident had nothing to do with the ongoing deportations, which were just a way of dealing with the serious problem of illegal immigration the country was facing. As expected, Albania protested strongly to Greece and to many international bodies against the deportations which it characterised as gross violations of human rights, accusing Greece of ill-treating the deportees and declaring its determination to eradicate any attempts made by Greek chauvinistic circles to 'hellenise south Albania' (Antonopoulos 1995: 153). In the following days the USA and the Council of Europe urged Greece to show self-restraint; the Council of Europe also asked for the halting of deportations on the grounds that Albanian's economy was very much sustained by its illegal migrants. On 2 July, Greece reiterated its willingness to allow Albanian immigrants to work seasonally in the country, on condition that the rights of the Greek minority would be consolidated. It stated again that the deportations were irrelevant to the Maidonis affair.

On 14 July, Mitsotakis set Greece's conditions for the improvement of the two countries' relations. Apart from the return of Archimandrite Maidonis, he asked for the adoption of a number of specific measures that would have provided for more rights for the Greek minority.[9] Having put forward Greece's demands, the Greek Premier added that the country was ready to conclude an agreement with Albania for allowing a number of Albanian immigrants to work seasonally in Greece, provided that Albania would control its borders. He also emphasised that 'Greece would not accept illegal immigrants and the deportations will continue, *but not at the same pace*' (Antonopoulos 1995: 157, my emphasis). In relation to the Chams, Mitsotakis repeated what already had been said on that issue in the past. Albania rejected these conditions as unacceptable.

In September and early October the Albanian government proceeded to the closure of various Greek schools and to the radical change of the curriculum with respect to the ratio between the courses which were taught in the Greek and Albanian languages, at the former's expense. These developments made the spokesman of the newly-elected government of PASOK state that 'provocations and pressures, particularly in relation to educational and religious freedom, violate international law and undermine any attempt made for improving the relations of the two states' (Antonopoulos 1995: 165).

The new Greek Minister of Foreign Affairs Mr. Papoulias (who had been the prime mover of the rapprochement between the two countries in the mid and late 1980s when he was holding the same post), visited Tirana in mid-October. Central in his talks with the Albanian government were once again the issues of illegal immigration and the Greek minority. With respect to the former he declared the willingness of the PASOK government to regulate it, by issuing a considerable number of seasonal work permits to Albanian immigrants who were already working or who would wish to work in Greece, provided that Albania would take appropriate measures for the control of the illegal flow. In relation to the latter he asked for the reopening of the minority schools and for respect of the rights of the minority according to international law. For its part, the Albanian government admitted for the first time that the Greek minority existed not only in the designated minority areas, but all over the country. At the same time, it committed itself to the policy that human and minority rights as well as religious liberties would be fully protected within the pending Constitution. The Albanian side did bring up the Chams' issue, but not in an importunate manner as at other times. Mr. Papoulias' approach to that matter was similar to that of the previous Greek government.

The Papoulias visit was seen by both sides as a fresh start in the relations of the two states. As Sali Berisha said in early December, 'There will be better relations with Greece. The visit of Papoulias . . . was of great value to us. It will be of great benefit to Greek–Albanian relations' (Vickers and Pettifer 1997: 197).

The optimism, however, was to last only for a few months. On 10 April 1994, Albania announced that unknown individuals had attacked a military camp at Peshkepi (close to the border with Greece) and killed two soldiers. The responsibility for the attack was claimed by an organisation called MAVI (Front for the Liberation of Northern Epirus), which officially had ceased to exist since the end of World War II.[10]

This episode triggered the second and most serious crisis in relations between the two states in the 1990s (Antonopoulos 1995: 181–96; Doudoumis 1996: 92–4). Albania reacted by condemning Greek circles for the attack, deporting the Greek Consul-General of Gjirokastër, appealing to the UN Security Council and arresting ethnic Greeks. Greece's initial response was to deport the First Secretary of the Albanian embassy in Athens. Despite some attempts to defuse the tension, this was further escalated when on 20 May the Albanian government took into custody six members of Omonia on the charge of high treason. It accused them 'of secessional activities, in collaboration with various Greek foundations and Northern Epirus organisations, as well as with the Greek security forces; activities which in particular periods of time had been supported by Greek governmental authorities at a high level' (Antonopoulos 1995: 182).[11]

Following the commencement of the trial of the 'Omonia Five' – as they became known – on 15 August (the sixth member would be tried at a later date), the Greek government was swift to respond. Prime Minister Papandreou characterised the trial as a mockery and 'an offensive act against the Greek minority . . . [a] . . . thoughtless provocation against Greece which could not remain unanswered' (Antonopoulos 1995: 191). That answer was the blocking of $41 million aid from the EU, the stoppage of further progress on a bill for the seasonal work of Albanian illegal immigrants, the intensification of border controls and a significant increase in the number of those deported. Once again, the Greek government officials stated that the deportations were not connected with the trial of the Omonia Five, but routine measures for the control of immigrant criminality (Antonopoulos 1995: 913).

During the trial (21 August), the extremely provocative initiative of a Greek Group Captain brought the tension to new high. He flew over the cities of Vlorë and Sarandë and threw leaflets calling upon the minority to revolt and unify south Albania with Greece. Albania's reaction was a stormy one, accusing Greece of having put forward plans for the destabilisation of the country and for the annexation of half of it. On 1 September Berisha further berated Greece for vengeful deportations of Albanian immigrants.

In such a highly charged atmosphere, the trial concluded on 9 September with the conviction of the Omonia Five, sentences ranging from six to eight years imprisonment. The Greek Parliament issued a unanimous resolution condemning the trial and its outcome, while various international bodies which had sat in on the trial (such as Amnesty International, the Human Rights Helsinki Group, the Minnesota Advocates and others) issued critical statements in relation to the accusations, the way in which the trial had been conducted and its outcome. Equally critical were parties of the Albanian opposition. The sentences of the Omonia Five were slightly reduced at the Court of Appeal, but that did not have any effect on the Greek government's attitude which had hardened into a total refusal to have any contact with the Albanian side unless there was a significant improvement in the case. However, this tough stance did not modify Albania's intransigence: the latter set as conditions for the release of the tension, the consolidation of the immigrants' position, the demonstration of a positive attitude on the Chams' issue and the recognition of the existence of an Albanian minority in Greece.

A new problem was added in October with the proposed new Albanian Constitution, due to be approved by referendum on 6 November. According to Paragraph 4 of Article 7, the leaders of the big religious communities had to be Albanian citizens, born in Albania and permanent residents in the country for the last twenty years. This meant that Archbishop Anastasios (a Greek citizen) would be forced to leave his post. This was seen by Athens as a direct attempt to undermine the Orthodox

Church, deriving from the fact that the anti-religious policies of the communist era meant that there were not enough qualified Albanian clergy who could be considered able enough to replace the charismatic and learned Anastasios. This interference of the Albanian state in the internal affairs of the Church was further perceived as an effort to deprive the minority of its religious liberties. Despite Greece's protests and although the constitution itself and the referendum process were also under attack by the Albanian opposition, the government went ahead with its plans without making any compromises. To its surprise, 54 per cent of the electorate voted against the proposed constitution in the referendum.

On 28 November, and as a goodwill gesture, Greece lifted the veto it had exercised in the EU for the granting of the $41 million aid to Albania. A few days later (5 December), the sixth of the Omonia members was released on the basis of a broad amnesty given by the government. With a Presidential Decree issued the following day one of the remaining five was also released and the sentences of the other four were reduced.

This sudden leniency towards the members of the Omonia (which was to some extent the result of pressure exercised by the international community) was further demonstrated on 8 February 1995, when Albania's Supreme Court of Appeal released the last four of them on five-year suspended sentences (see Antonopoulos 1999: 158–60, 167–72; Doudoumis 1996: 95–7). Following that, a new visit of the Greek Minister of Foreign Affairs Papoulias was arranged for mid-March. On 28 February, however, which was the day on which a bill for the legalisation of the illegal immigrants would be presented to the press by the Minister of Labour Mr. Skoularikis, the latter announced the postponement of the presentation by saying that,

> there is going to be a visit to Albania of Mr. Papoulias and because a large part of the regulations concern Albanians, we judged that we have to wait for the return of the Minister of Foreign Affairs, in order to take into consideration some particular issues which most likely he will discuss with the Albanian government; it would not be proper for us to influence the discussions. (*Eleftherotypia* 1 March 1995)

Mr. Papoulias' visit to Tirana between 13 and 15 March met with success, largely due to the significant change in attitude of the Albanian government (Doudoumis 1996: 95–6). President Berisha – *inter alia* – expressed his thanks to Greece for the 'valuable' help it had offered to his country by hosting a large number of Albanian immigrants, proposed that the two countries sign a treaty of friendship and cooperation, and voiced his wish that their various differences be solved through dialogue and constructive collaboration. In that context, the Albanians mentioned the Chams' issue, but only incidentally. In more practical terms, the two sides agreed in principle on a variety of issues. Most importantly, Albania agreed to the opening of Greek private schools and to the free teaching of the

Greek language in all parts of the country where there were ethnic Greek students. For its part, Greece committed itself to tackling in a constructive way the issue of Albanian illegal immigrants (the issue which was at the top of the Albanian agenda), by legalising a large number of them and by creating a system of seasonal work permits. The elaboration and promotion of these agreements was left to mixed committees of specialists from the two countries. In the following months there was increased diplomatic activity, but nothing concrete or important came out of it.

On 31 August and 1 September, the Albanian Minister of Foreign Affairs Mr. Sereki visited Athens and held talks with his opposite number (*Eleftherotypia* 1 and 2 September 1995; *To Vima* 3 September 1995). On the agenda were two principal issues: the education of the minority and the regularisation of Albanian immigrants. For its part Greece had made clear to Albania beforehand that it would not proceed to a final agreement on the immigrants before Albania gave specific undertakings in relation to the minority's education. Due to lack of inclination on the Albanian side to do so, or to present alternative documented proposals, the negotiations reached a deadlock.

In January 1996, there was a change of Prime Minister in Greece: Costas Simitis replaced the seriously ill Andreas Papandreou. At the same time, President Berisha re-offered the invitation he had made in 1995 to his Greek opposite number Mr. Stephanopoulos to visit Albania. The new PASOK government accepted the invitation and the Greek President visited Albania on 21 March (Antonopoulos 1999: 176–7, 181–2; Doudoumis 1996: 97–8; Vickers and Pettifer 1997: 199–200). The results of this visit were particularly important for the improvement of Greek–Albanian relations. The two countries signed a Treaty of Friendship, Cooperation and Security of twenty years duration and ten initial agreements. Among these was one on the seasonal work of Albanian immigrants and the mutual control of illegal immigration, and one on the education of ethnic Greeks. The Greek President seized the opportunity to state – *inter alia* – that his country had no intention of using the minority against Albania and it was willing to further contribute to the latter's development, provided that the rights of the ethnic Greeks would always be respected.

A direct result of the Treaty was the signing on 17 May of the first piece of legislation with regard to immigrants from Albania – the 'Agreement on Seasonal Employment between Greece and Albania'. This was followed by the passing of Law 2434/1996, by which the process for the legalisation of undocumented immigrants was initiated.

Thus far, the discussion of Greek–Albanian relations in the years 1990–6 has shown that dealings between the two states were still governed by animosities and mistrust which had their roots well in the past, and that the migrant situation was repeatedly embroiled in political horse-trading. Right from the start, immigration became a major concern among several others awaiting to be resolved. However, as my discussion has clearly indicated, the existence of these other unresolved matters between the two states made the settlement of the immigration issue very difficult. The question we will now address is what influence the state of the relations between the two countries had on Greece's policy response to immigration in the years up to 1996. This discussion will primarily draw on the empirical evidence from the interviews I conducted in Greece.

There was a general agreement among the people I interviewed that the climate of Greek–Albanian relations did indeed influence Greece's stance on immigration and allied policies. Furthermore, it was noted that the presence of Albanian immigrants in the country was used by both the ND and PASOK governments as a bargaining tool for the attainment of other purposes, pre-eminently connected with the Greek ethnic minority. When Greece finally managed to secure better treatment for the minority, it then proceeded to put forward measures for the management of immigration. The former Minister of Foreign Affairs, Papoulias, was particularly revealing in this regard. He said that the immigration issue was a diplomatic instrument with many uses. In his own words:

> One way it was used by us was for exerting pressure on Berisha. [It was like saying to him that] you cannot behave in such a way and be uncompromising with respect to the minority, when we have in our country 300,000 illegal immigrants. Well, when [for example] there was this crisis and he wanted to pass a new Constitution according to his own taste and without backing down from his very tough views on the Hellenism of Albania, we decided to send him as a 'present' around 150,000 Albanians, who contributed to voting against the Constitution. Because all these people went to their villages and said, 'look what Berisha is doing to us; they are deporting us from Greece and we are losing our jobs and we will die [from hunger], only because he does not want to allow the functioning of the minority schools or because he does not want to grant rights to the ethnic Greeks'. Yes, it was used in such a way.

Similarly the representative from the Coalition party Mr. Kounalakis noted:

> It could be said that during the 'good' periods in our relations, we 'facilitated' [turned a 'blind eye'] this migratory wave to Greece and during the 'bad' periods we were making . . . massive arrests and deportations. All these were directly or indirectly connected to the state of our relations. Beyond any doubt the immigration issue has been used as a bargaining tool.

Another use of the immigration issue, according to Mr. Papoulias, was that

> during the crisis in the Greek–Albanian relations in Berisha's period – when the leading members of the Omonia had been arrested – you could say to third parties, the EU and the United States, that you [Greece] were sustaining Albania. And if you think about it that was true, when the 300,000 Albanian

immigrants were sending back around $350 million; the Albanian economy was heavily dependent on that money.

In this way, Greece was aiming to achieve three objectives. The first was to convince its Western allies that, for its part, it was doing its best to improve relations between the two states, and that it was up to Albania to further improve them by settling their differences over the Greek minority. In this context – the second objective – Greece was also aiming at increased pressure on Albania by third parties which had been involved as mediators, particularly the EU and the United States. The third objective was connected to the broader geopolitical interests of Greece. By underlining its contribution to Albania's economic survival, it wanted to demonstrate its goodwill towards a neighbouring country which was going through a difficult period, and in that way to establish itself in the eyes of the international community as the main factor of stability in the troubled post-communist Balkans.

However, negotiating with Albania to find a mutually acceptable solution on the twin issues of immigrants and the minority proved a difficult task for Greece. It was noted by some of the interviewees that Albania's deep-rooted mistrust towards the minority, and towards Greece's intentions with respect to south Albania, constituted a major impediment in their talks on the minority issue and, by extension, those on immigration. It was also emphasised that, despite the change in recent years in Greece's attitude towards 'Northern Epirus', Albania remained unconvinced about Greece's good intentions, not least because of the activities of various nationalistic Greek circles that continued hatching plans for the 'liberation' of the region – an admission which certainly gives more credence and justice to the attitudes of the Albanian side. With such a background, the bringing up of the Chams' issue is seen by some interviewees as nothing else but an attempt made by Albania to present a similar 'counter-issue' to Greece's one on the minority for negotiating purposes.

Summarising, we can say that the state of Greek–Albanian relations did influence Greece's policy response to the large-scale immigration from Albania in the period 1990–6. The immigration issue was embroiled in the long-standing disputes of the two countries, and it was used as a bargaining tool by Greece for achieving other purposes, pre-eminently the protection of the rights of the Greek minority in Albania.

The period 1996–7

The procedure for the legalisation of the undocumented immigrants living in Greece was set out in Article 16 of Law 2434 of 1996. This article provided for the creation of a 15-member Committee (comprised of government, trade union and other officials) which was entrusted with the task of formulating two Presidential Decrees that would specify who would be entitled to be registered and then regularised, the procedure and means by which the whole process would be carried out, and for how long the successful immigrants would be granted permission to stay. Those entitled to be registered were given a 'Temporary Residence Card' (White Card) and if they could fulfil various conditions they were then given the Green Card – a 'Residence Card of Limited Duration'.

The Committee started its deliberations on 1 November 1996 and by early summer 1997 it had agreed on the final form of both Decrees. Unexpectedly, however, a Cabinet meeting on 27 June took the decision to exclude from the legalisation immigrants from countries neighbouring Greece (*Eleftherotypia* 1 July 1997). According to my interview material, the person who put forward that proposal and supported its adoption with extreme obstinacy was Minister of the Interior Papadopoulos, who was aiming at the exclusion of the Albanian immigrants. According to the interviewees, his action can be explained by the fact that he is from Thesprotia (an area that, as we saw earlier, is closely associated with the Chams issue), which is also his electoral base. For instance, Member of Parliament Dr. Katsanevas said:

> Yes, it was Papadopoulos [who reacted to the legalisation]. He personally has a problem with that, because he is elected in Thesprotia and he was afraid that there will be problems with the Chams and things like that. There was a personal problem for his area . . .

Similarly the representative of SOS Racisme said:

> Papadopoulos' main fear was the alteration of the composition of the population by the Albanian immigrants, as it seems he had the view that if they were legalised they would not go back to their country . . . Generally there is this idea that immigrants from neighbouring countries, and particularly from Albania, can create problems in the long run, by forming minorities.

The Cabinet's decision startled everybody, particularly the participants in the 15-member Committee. The reactions it triggered were immediate and strong. The special adviser to the Minister of Labour, Mrs. Zalaora, said to the author:

> We [the Ministry of Labour] did not want that. All the drafts of the Presidential Decrees were without such discriminations; alas if you are going to have a legalisation and you include such a differentiation in the legal framework, I do not believe there is any meaning in doing this. And especially when you exclude citizens of countries from which the problem [of immigration] is most intense [namely from Albania] and who constitute more than half of the population of the target group you are aiming to regularise.

In the same vein, the powerful and politically influential General Confederation of Greek Workers (GSEE) addressed a letter directly to the Prime Minister in which it expressed its astonishment over the decision taken, asking him to withdraw this decision (*Eleftherotypia*, 1 July 1997). Reactions also came from representatives of immigrant organisations, who made it clear that they would not participate in the legalisation process unless all immigrant nationalities were allowed to do so (*Eleftherotypia*, 5 July 1997).

Irrespective of the views and objectives of Papadopoulos, the question still remains as to why the government went ahead and adopted his proposal, contrary to what the Committee was proposing and – it must be said – to common sense. It is certain that if the legalisation had proceeded in such a way, its outcome would have been far from satisfactory, to say the least.

Officially, the government justified its decision by saying that if citizens from neighbouring countries were included in the legalisation, there was a great possibility that this would trigger a new migratory wave towards Greece, given the political and economic instability those countries were experiencing (Antonopoulos 1999: 297). This argument cannot be considered a strong one. Moreover, the General Secretary of the Athens Centre for Workers and Employees said in his interview that soon after the GSEE had sent its letter to the Prime Minister, Mr. Simitis had replied by saying that the government was not planning to go further with that decision, insinuating that the whole issue had to do with Greece's foreign policy. I believe that there is enough evidence to support the view that the underlying factor was once again Greek–Albanian relations.

In June 1997, Albania was still convulsed by the crisis that had broken out in January when the so-called 'pyramid' investment schemes collapsed. As a result of this financial scandal, a large part of the Albanian population lost their savings, which in many cases consisted of money earned through work abroad. The state had basically disintegrated through the ongoing widespread violence and destruction (particularly in the south), and the government's inability to control the situation. This was due to the fact that, for a big segment of the population, it had lost its legitimacy to rule, as it was held responsible for the economic devastation the 'pyramids' had caused. After intense negotiations among the Albanian political parties, and with the involvement of the international community, elections had been called for 29 June. The main opponents were on the one hand the Democratic Party of President Berisha and, on the other, a coalition of three opposition parties under the leadership of the President of the Socialist Party, Fatos Nano.

Greece's favourite candidate in these elections was clearly Mr. Nano. As emerges from the interview material, he – unlike Berisha – was held in high esteem by the Greek side. It should not escape notice that Nano was by origin Orthodox Christian from southern Albania, whereas Berisha was a northern Muslim. Berisha was variously described by my interviewees as 'unreliable', 'confrontational', 'ruthless' and 'power-hungry'. Nano, on the other hand, was considered a responsible politician and the person most suited to lead Albania during a difficult period. He was also thought to be a reliable interlocutor with whom there could be a better understanding over the issues that created friction between the two states. These were two reasons why, in March of that year, Greece had officially asked the Albanian government to release him from prison, where he had been since 1994, sentenced to 12 years for allegedly squandering public money (Antonopoulos 1999: 121, 161–2). That same month President Berisha granted him a pardon and in early May – after pressure exercised by the international community – he was permitted to participate in the forthcoming elections.

Greece's favour towards Nano was clearly demonstrated in June, when he was allowed to speak to a big crowd of Albanian citizens at a pre-election rally in one of Athens' central squares. The police did not interfere and no arrests of illegal immigrants were made. During the visit Nano held talks with Prime Minister Simitis, the Minister of Foreign Affairs, and also visited PASOK's headquarters. The Greek side reassured him that it would keep the promise it had made a few days earlier to facilitate Albanian immigrants who wanted to vote by granting them special permits of one month duration in order to travel to Albania for the elections and return back to Greece without any problem (Antonopoulos 1999: 289–95). Nano and his coalition won the elections by a landslide. Berisha resigned office on 23 July.

The good climate that had developed between PASOK and the newly-elected Albanian rulers became evident very soon. During the visit of PASOK's Secretary General Skandalidis on 26–27 July the Albanian side showed an extremely friendly attitude. Nano received the Greek politician by saying among other things that PASOK and his party 'are the two halves of the same political body, which have common programmes, ideas and principles, and they believe that in this new phase a new climate of confidence will be created between the Greeks and the Albanians'. On his part Skandalidis stated that Greece 'has decided to put aside all those things that divided us in the past and to concentrate on all those that unite us' and also that 'the new Albania will find in us the allies, the friends, the helpers, in its path towards democracy, in re-establishing its institutions and in its re-organisation, and even more so, for its accession into the European family [meaning the EU]' (*Eleftherotypia*, 28 July 1997).

Following Mr. Skandalidis' visit, a large Ministerial delegation headed by the Minister of Foreign Affairs Mr. Pangalos, went to Albania in August (Antonopoulos 1999: 304–07). In a very warm atmosphere the two sides signed a Protocol which put in place the Agreement on the Seasonal Employment of Albanian citizens in Greece, while the Greek Deputy Minister of Labour Mr. Protopapas set out plans for the regularisation of illegal immigrants by also announcing that the two Presidential Decrees will cover all of them, including the Albanians. The Albanian government expressed its full satisfaction in that decision. For his part Mr. Pangalos emphasised that if Greece was implementing the existing laws to the letter, there would have been no possibility that 300,000 Albanians would be living and working in the country; but he also added that, with the help of the Albanian government, this unlawful situation had to come to an end. In this context, the Greek Minister of Public Order agreed with his opposite number that the Greek police would help in the creation of an Albanian border police unit by providing supplies and expertise.

The final decision for the participation of all illegal immigrants in the legalisation process was taken in early September, at a meeting comprising the Ministers of Labour, Interior and Public Order, with the Prime Minister as chair (*Eleftherotypia*, 3 September 1997). The decision was approved by the Cabinet three days later.

The main element, therefore, that comes out of my discussion in this section is that the Greek government, once again, chose to use the immigration issue as a means to achieve its foreign affairs objectives with respect to Albania: the main one of which was, at this stage, to support its favourite Prime Ministerial candidate, Fatos Nano. Greece believed that with him as a Prime Minister two things would be achieved: first, that the ongoing crisis in Albania would be defused (preventing therefore the country from collapsing, but also safeguarding the well-being of the Greek minority, as the southern areas were those which were experiencing the most explosive situation); and secondly, that it could settle in a mutually satisfactory way the differences that existed between the two states. It seems, therefore, that by temporarily excluding Albanian immigrants from the legalisation, Greece wanted to exercise similar pressure on the Albanian electorate to that it had exercised in 1994 (when the referendum on the Constitution was held). The strategy was to offer the legalisation of Albanian immigrants as a goodwill gesture to a prospective Nano government which would thereby gain support internally, as it would be seen by the Albanian people as a big diplomatic success on his part.

Conclusion and postscript: migration and Greek–Albanian relations post-1998 – towards a normalisation in their affairs?

The purpose of this chapter has been to explore to what extent Greece's policy response to the migratory wave from Albania has been influenced by the state of the relations between the two countries and by Greece's foreign policy objectives towards Albania. The analysis has concentrated on the years 1990–7, because it was during that period that the interplay of migration and international politics had the most profound effect on events, attitudes and policy decisions. My discussion has shown that the tension that existed in Greek–Albanian affairs during that time and Greece's foreign policy objectives – above all the desire to protect the rights of its ethnic minority in Albania – played a decisive role in Greece's policy-making on migration. Migration in turn became a very important foreign policy instrument for Greece in its affairs with Albania.

Since 1998, the situation has changed, and Greece has shown much more restraint in using migration as a tool of 'high politics'. The status of Albanian immigrants is conditioned by the policy framework that regulates the presence of all immigrants in Greece. This framework includes – *inter alia* – the provisions of the legalisation programme of 1998 and the new law on migration enacted in 2001 (Law 2910) that introduced a second legalisation procedure (on the current Greek legal framework see International Organization for Migration 2003). In both legalisations, Albanians constituted the majority of those who came forward to be regularised (Fakiolas 2003).[12] Moreover, the Greek government has showed willingness to resolve problems that emerge with regard to the immigrants. For example, responding to the strong protests of the Albanian government concerning the serious discomfort experienced by thousands of regularised Albanian immigrants in August 2002 when they were stuck for hours at the border-control points on return from their summer holiday, the authorities accelerated the construction of a new (third) border crossing which was opened in December of the same year (*Eleftherotypia*, 27 August 2002; 23 December 2002).

Without any doubt, Greece's changed attitude towards migration from Albania is a reflection of the improved state of affairs between the two countries that is evident since the governmental change in Albania in 1997. Although problems continue to exist and periods of tension have occurred, the two sides have managed to avoid degeneration of their differences into ugly confrontation. In the last few years co-operation has increased significantly, with Greece dedicating considerable effort and resources towards this end. Greece has put forward a number of bilateral agreements to assist Albania in transforming its institutions into democratic and efficiently run bodies (International Crisis Group 2001a: 14). Its contribution to improving Albania's policing capacity and effectiveness has been quite extensive and has included both logistical support and know-how. As the area of law and order is one of the most problematic in Albania, the two states have signed a protocol for joint sea patrols in the Corfu-Albania strait, in order to control illegal migration and the smuggling of arms and drugs (International Crisis Group 2001a: 14).[13] Greece's economic aid has also been substantial. In 2002 for example, Greece allocated €50 million to Albania from its programme on Economic Restructuring of the Balkans (the programme has an overall budget of €550 million, distributed to the six Balkan countries over five years). With respect to private economic activity the presence of Greek companies is second only to that of Italy. At present, there are around 200 companies in operation in Albania, which have invested an estimated €250 million (International Crisis Group, 2003: 14).[14] At a multilateral level, Greece has also been actively involved in the deliberation of projects concerning Albania in the context (for example) of the Stability Pact for South Eastern Europe (International Crisis Group 2001a: 14; Tsardanidis 2000), while it strongly supported the initiation of preliminary negotiations in February 2003 between the EU and Albania on a Stabilisation and Association Agreement.

From all the above, therefore, it can be seen that Greco-Albanian relations have advanced significantly in the course of recent years. However, there are still issues that could be potential sources of tension in their affairs. On the one hand, Greece would like to see further improvement of the minority's well-being and the consolidation of its rights. Although there is an improvement in the standing of the minority, concerns remain over educational and property rights and the advancement and adequate representation of the minority in the state's structures (for instance in the police and the armed forces).[15]

On the other hand, it must be said that any demands for the advancement of the minority's rights must take into account the severe depopulation of the minority areas and realistic estimates as to its actual size.[16] With regard to education for example, and as things stand now, state education in the Greek language is provided only in the minority regions, while for the creation and functioning of minority schools there have to be at least 20 pupils (Tsitselikis 2003: 177, 191, 205). But since 1990 there has been a considerable exodus of minority members who have left for Greece or moved to urban areas in Albania. According to recent estimates, the size of the minority in the minority areas seems to be around one third of what it used to be before 1990 (Baltsiotis 2003: 80), while minority pupils have decreased by three-quarters (Tsitselikis 2003: 188). Tsitselikis also notes (2003: 912) that some of the remaining minority schools operate with a much smaller number of pupils than that required by law. This has resulted in the closure of many minority schools; from the 108 that existed at the end of the 1980s, 50 remained in 2003 (Tsitselikis 2003: 185, 189). Migration to Greece will have also affected the minority's representation in the public sector, as the pool of potential civil servants has decreased; in any case, ethnic Greeks nowadays show little inclination to be employed in the public sector (Baltsiotis 2003: 70).

To what extent the departure of minority members to Greece is of a temporary or permanent nature remains to be seen, although it seems that many of them favour the latter perspective (Pavlou 2003). There is therefore an issue as to what the pragmatic demands by the Greek state might be in order to reflect the actual circumstances of the minority.

An issue that relates to the above is that in recent years Albanian citizens who can demonstrate adequate knowledge of the Vlach language or Vlach cultural heritage have been recognised by Greece of being of Greek origin.

They have consequently enjoyed privileged treatment by the Greek consulates in the issuing of visas. Some have argued that this might represent an attempt by Greece to introduce 'new blood' to the minority in order to compensate for the loss due to migration (Tsitselikis and Christopoulos 2003: 30–3). Though some Vlachs can claim descent from Greece (Baltsiotis 2003: 109; Winnifrith 2002: 26, 164), it is not clear that Greece is trying to create a 'new minority'. For instance, in the 2001 Albanian elections Greece did not display interest in the electoral procedure in areas with Vlach-speaking population (Baltsiotis 2003: 110). Furthermore, it has been argued that many of those who have presented themselves as 'Helleno-Vlachs' have done so in order to have access to various benefits (such as working visas and scholarships) rather than because they have a distinguishing Greek identity (Baltsiotis 2003: 89–109; Christopoulos 2003: 147–8; Schwandner-Sievers 1999).[17] Although it seems that many of these 'Helleno-Vlachs' are more interested in the benefits they would attain from Greece rather than the minority rights they might enjoy in Albania, this issue could represent a potential problem in Greek–Albanian relations, as the Vlachs are recognised by Albania as a distinctive language community 'fully incorporated in Albanian society' (Baltsiotis 2003: 157).

Another issue that is of particular concern to Greece is Albania's apparent inability to adequately control illegal migration and criminality. Despite increased collaboration in the field of law and order, issues of border security and organised crime continue to create tension in bilateral relations. On the other hand, although (as stated by the Albanian Minister of Foreign Affairs Mr. Meta in 2002) Albania 'appreciates the Greek government's efforts to improve the condition of the immigrants . . . ' (*Eleftherotypia*, 29 October 2002) and recognises the right of the Greek government to expel irregular immigrants (*Eleftherotypia*, 10 July 1999), it has also expressed on several occasions its great concern for the ill-treatment of expellees.

Finally, with respect to the Cham issue – a source of significant tension in the Greek–Albanian relations in the 1990s – Albania has in the last few years expressed again its desire for reaching an agreement with Greece over their property rights.[18] Athens, however, has again refused to discuss this subject as it considers it a 'closed issue' (International Crisis Group 2000b: 10–13, 25; Tiropoli 2000: 67; Vickers 2002).

So, given that there are still matters that could create friction between the two countries, is there a possibility that Greece could use migration again as a foreign policy instrument in its affairs with Albania? The most probable answer would be yes, but not in the same way as in the 1990s. On the one hand, as migration by its very nature involves states, external relations most probably will continue to influence policy decisions concerning immigrants. For example, Greece could connect the adoption of educational measures for the children of Albanian immigrants with educational issues for its minority in Albania. On the other hand, the existing more comprehensive legal framework places the whole migration issue in Greece in a different context from the pre-1998 one. Furthermore, Athens has expressed on numerous occasions its strong desire for the Greek minority and the Albanian immigrants to become a link between the two countries which can help them reinforce their friendship and co-operation (International Crisis Group 2001a: 15). It seems that there are good chances that such a desire could become reality, as there is also a growing realisation on the part of the Albanian political elite that establishing strong ties with Greece is of great importance to Albania's development and prosperity (International Crisis Group 2001a: 2, 9; 2000b: 25). Through this, not only will the country continue to derive benefits at a bilateral level, but also it will help Albania to fulfil its prime national objective of integrating itself into the Euro-Atlantic structures.

Notes

1 Greek historians point to the important Greek coastal colonies that were established in the area during the fifth century BC – such as Dyrrachium (Durrës) and Apollonia (near Fier) – and they claim that the Epirot tribes that lived in southern Albania were Greek, with Illyrian tribes living to the north. Albanians – who claim direct descent from the ancient Illyrians – have argued that the Epirot tribes were Illyrian who spoke Greek due to the influence of the colonies (Kondis 1994: 9; Pettifer 2001: 4; Vickers 1997: 1–4; for a good analysis of the different interpretations of ancient texts see Winnifrith 2002). The control of the area by the Byzantines, and the existence of many Greek-speaking and Orthodox Christian people, is for some historians a testimony of the continuing Greek presence in the area (Winnifrith 2002: 23, 71–95).

2 This argument had of course various shortcomings. During Ottoman rule a degree of identification of non-Greek groups with the Greek state had existed, due to common membership of the Orthodox Church and the prestige Greece enjoyed because of its close and privileged relationship with the Orthodox Patriarchate (Baltsiotis 2003: 48, 85). The common cultural element of Orthodoxy, however, does not seem to have balanced the scale towards Greece, as many Orthodox Albanians played an important role in the creation and establishment of the Albanian state (Baltsiotis 2003: 57, 74; Divani 1995: 274–5). Although language was not considered as the decisive element in the determination of the Greek origin, the existence of many Greek schools during the Ottoman period was regarded as a sign of Greek consciousness (Baltsiotis 2003: 52). This view overlooked, though, that by being the language of culture, religion and trade, Greek was the 'lingua franca' of the time (Baltsiotis 2003: 52–3, 57; Winnifrith 2002: 105, 108). Many people therefore spoke more than one language. Furthermore, it has been suggested that the important factor for the pro-Greek attitude of some non-Greek Orthodox during the early 1900s was not their Greek consciousness, but grievances due to the bad economic situation, their under-representation in the administration of the new state (compared to that of the Muslims) and the general insecurity of the period (Divani 1995: 217; Winnifrith 2002: 130–1). 'Most of us want

Albania, but we want a good Albania. If we cannot have a good Albania, we prefer Greece', a Christian resident of Korçë said in 1923 to the League of Nations (Tsitselikis and Christopoulos 2003: 30).

3 It is worth mentioning that the territory Greece claimed in 1919 corresponded (roughly) to the areas south of an imaginary line from Vlorë to Pogradeç. This was an area in which the Orthodox Christians were claimed to be the relative majority (Veremis *et al.* 1995: 12). The Greek Prime Minister Venizelos who put forward this claim had said that 'a significant part of this population had Albanian as their mother tongue and was probably of Albanian origin. But the decisive parameter [for determining their ethnic consciousness] was their culture and religion, and these were Greek' (Divani 1995: 261).

4 As the Chams' issue will come up again later in the chapter, it is useful to say a few more things about them. The Chams were living in the north-western part of Greece, mainly in the region that now constitutes the prefecture of Thesprotia. Most probably they had migrated to the area during the thirteenth and fourteenth centuries and their religion was Orthodox Christian, but many of them were forcibly Islamised in the seventeenth and eighteenth centuries. Following a 1923 agreement between Greece and Turkey on a compulsory exchange of population (based on religion), Greece attempted to include in the exchange also the Chams but with little success, due to the intervention of the League of Nations. From the 20,160 Chams who according to the LoN inhabited the area in 1925, only 2,993 left for Turkey. In the inter-war period their relations with the Greek state remained problematic, mainly because of their dispute over land expropriation. In the late 1930s their relations deteriorated further, when – with the encouragement of Italy – irredentist elements in the Cham community became more vocal. During Greece's occupation in World War II, the Chams had set up their own administration and militia at Thesprotia and collaborated closely with both the Italians and – when Italy capitulated – the Germans. Although the mopping up operations of 1944 were an Allied war plan, the reprisals by the partisans continued after 1944 (when the Cham troops left with the Germans) and well into 1945. Since their eviction, the Chams' main demands are their return to Greece, to be compensated for wealth loss and the restitution of their properties. (On the Cham issue see Antonopoulos 1995: 141; Kallivretakis 1995: 36–40; Kondis 1995: 159–62; Vickers, 2002).

5 An alternative viewpoint suggests there is no strong evidence that the population transfers constituted part of a deliberate plan of the regime to dilute the minority. Baltsiotis argues that in most cases the transfers have to be appreciated in the context of the 'rationale of the regime to develop new settlements near big public works, factories, etc., without any consideration of where the population really wanted to live' (Baltsiotis 2003: 80).

6 It must be said that since 1974 (after the fall of the dictatorial regime), none of the Greek governments had raised any official claim to south Albania. According to Antonopoulos (1995: 38), the right-wing New Democracy party (ND), which ruled the country from 1974 to 1981, had itself considered lifting the state of war and for that purpose had even drafted a relevant bill. This plan was never put forward, due to speculations by this party of the possible strong reactions of right-wing and ultra-nationalistic organisations and individuals involved with the 'Northern Epirus' issue, that constitute part of its electorate.

The socialist PASOK, on the other hand, had no such concerns, nor political connections to these groups.

7 Like other communist regimes, the one in Albania considered emigration the result of the capitalist system's inability to provide labourers with assured permanent employment in peripheral geographical regions, so that workers have to seek employment in the main centres of capitalist production, where they experience extreme exploitation at the hands of employers (King *et al.* 1998: 161). In this context (and as it believed that it was providing its people with satisfactory employment), the communist regime regarded emigration as a criminal act, a treason against the state which could be severely punished (even by death). An important difference, however, between Albania and the rest of the communist world was that Hoxha – in his effort to safeguard the true spirit of communist ideology – isolated his country not only from the capitalist world, but gradually from all other communist states as well. So, by 1990, the Albanian people had spent nearly 50 years in isolation from the outside world.

8 The alleged significant contribution of illegal – and particularly Albanian – immigrants to an increase in criminality in Greece constituted one of the most heated debates in the country with respect to immigration throughout the 1990s. On this issue see Karydis (1996).

9 Among them were: the return of the Orthodox Church's property; the establishment of public and private Greek schools in all areas where ethnic Greeks were living and not only in the declared minority regions; the teaching of the Greek language at all levels of education; the free development of minority educational, cultural and community organisations and the return to the minority communities of their properties; the halting of harassment and of the arbitrary dismissal of minority members from the civil services; and the granting to them of equal opportunities for advancement in the country's administration.

10 In March 1995 the Greek police arrested near the Greek–Albanian border five Greeks and two ethnic Greeks from Albania carrying military weaponry. The detainees were also found to be in possession of propaganda material with the acronym of MAVI. They were charged with a number of felonies (among which, participation at the Peshkepi incident and intentionally exposing Greece to the danger of war). These accusations were not proven in the subsequent trials and in 1997 the accused were given three to four year suspended sentences for misdemeanours (mainly for being in possession of weaponry).

11 By Northern Epirus organisations (NEOs), the Albanian authorities were referring to those mentioned in note 6. With the fall of communism, NEOs started being very active in promoting, distributing and broadcasting nationalistic propaganda and irredentist views on 'Northern Epirus' (Baltsiotis 2003: 111–14; Greek Helsinki Monitor 1994: 15). Some of the most prominent ones have been the Co-ordinating Student Committee of Northern Epirus Struggle, the Research Foundation of Northern Epirus at Ioannina, and the Panhellenic Association for the Struggle of Northern Epirus. The Greek Orthodox Church and particularly the Bishopric of Konitsa in northern Greece have been regarded as important agents for the 'promotion' of the 'Northern Epirus' issue. They might have also seen the accession to power of the ND party in 1990 as an advantage in promoting their agenda, given that

in the past this party was sympathetic to their views. It can be argued that there was indeed some form of collaboration between ND and NEOs. The support for example offered by ND to the Democratic Party in the 1991 Albanian elections (on the principle of 'ideological similarity') was matched by some NEOs, despite the fact that the Omonia minority party was also an electoral contestant (Vichou *et al.* 1995: 64–9, 81). Regarding the alleged Greek governmental support to secessional activities performed jointly by the secret service and NEOs, it has been argued that circles in the secret service had been supportive of the NEOs' irredentist views, while members of the Greek diplomatic corps were found to be in possession of irredentist propaganda material (Baltsiotis 2003: 111–12; Human Rights Watch 1995: 7; Vichou *et al.* 1995: 81). However, there has not as yet been concrete evidence to support governmental involvement – either by ND or PASOK – in recent years in secessional activities that might have been committed by organisations or individuals. It must be said though, that even if they did not support, the Greek governments have tolerated the nationalistic activities of the NEOs.

12 During the first legalisation, of the 369,629 immigrants who registered with the authorities, 65 per cent were Albanians (239,931). Detailed data from the second legalisation (concluded on 4 July 2003) have not yet become available. But from the 153,282 immigrants who submitted their application in the broader Athens area, 52 per cent (79,737) were Albanians (the total number of applicants for the whole of Greece was 351,110). It is estimated, however, that of the immigrants who did not come forward to be regularised (their number could be anything between 200,000 to 350,000 people), the majority are from Albania.

13 The co-ordination of the joint sea patrols is managed by the harbour-master of Corfu, where the Albanian officers have undergone training. The patrols are maintained on a 24-hour basis; the pursuit of suspected vessels can continue in Albanian territorial waters; and if their passengers reach the Albanian coast the pursuing crews – after informing the Albanian police and with its collaboration – can continue the chase in Albania.

14 Greek entrepreneurs had started investing in Albania in the early 1990s (Kondis 1995). They were actively encouraged by the Greek state which offered considerable investment initiatives in the form of grants, allowances and tax reductions that would cover ventures all across Albania. Until the mid-1990s, 50 such ventures had been approved with a total capital investment of €23 million from which the state offered as grant €4.4 million. Most of these ventures were located in south Albania and were in the industrial sector. In the last few years the scope of Greek enterprises has also expanded into the tertiary sector. Although Greek capital penetration can be seen as having an overall positive effect on the development of Albania, the domination of some companies in specific activities (such as the mobile phone industry) has raised concerns for the creation of monopolies.

15 Positive developments for the minority included, for example, the participation of the Human Rights Union party in the governmental coalition in Albania and the improvement of the institutional framework for education in the Greek language (Tsitselikis 2003). Related to the latter point, Albania has adopted a considerable number of international legal instruments for the protection of human and minority rights, the adequate implementation of

which though has thus far been regarded as problematic (Christopoulos 2003: 150–1; European Commission against Racism and Intolerance 2001; Tsitselikis and Christopoulos 2003: 34–7).

16 According to the 1989 census in Albania, the Greek minority numbered 58,758 people (around 2 per cent of the total population). This number took into account only those who resided in the designated 'minority zones'. Most widely accepted is an estimation of a Greek-speaking population of between 100,000 and 150,000 (Human Rights Watch 1995: 5–6; Kallivretakis 1995: 44; Pettifer 2001: 4).

17 For the same reasons, many ethnic Albanians have presented themselves as Greeks by changing their names and ethnicity into Greek, by acquiring counterfeit identity cards 'proving' their 'Greekness' or by using intermediaries to attest their Greek origin (Baltsiotis 2003: 64; Greek Helsinki Monitor 1994: 19; Pavlou 2003: 275).

18 Since 2000, there has been a 'qualitative' change in how the Cham issue is approached by Tirana. As has been said earlier in the chapter, for most of the 1990s Albania had used the Chams as a 'counter-issue' to that of the minority in its negotiations with Greece. Following Berisha's fall, the issue was not really raised until 2000, but since then both Prime Ministers Meta and Nano have voiced a strong desire for settling the question of the Chams' properties with Greece. However, the underlying political factor for the re-emergence of this matter seems to be internal politics (International Crisis Group 2000b). There is a growing feeling in Albania that now that the Kosovo problem has – to an extent – been addressed, the government should turn its attention to the other national issue, the Chams. An increasing number of Albanians see this matter as another 'historical injustice' to the Albanian nation which has to be rectified, and this is creating pressure on the government to be seen as responding to this popular demand.

References

Antonopoulos, E. A. (1995) *Albania and Greek–Albanian Relations, 1913–1994.* Athens: Okeanida (in Greek).

—— (1999) *Greece, Albania, Kosovo, 1912–1998. Brief Chronological Overview.* Athens: Okeanida (in Greek).

Athens Centre for Workers and Employees (1995) *All Different, All Equal. Research on the Illegal Foreigners and Employment.* Athens: Athens Centre for Workers and Employees (in Greek).

Baltsiotis, L. (2003) The Greek minority in Albania: an effort of approximation in a transitional society, in Tsitselikis, C. and Christopoulos, D. (eds) *The Greek Minority of Albania.* Athens: Kritiki Publications – Research Centre for Minority Groups, 45–125 (in Greek).

Christopoulos, D. (2003) The institutional regime as an ideological mechanism for the assimilation of the minority, in Tsitselikis, C. and Christopoulos, D. (eds) *The Greek Minority of Albania.* Athens: Kritiki Publications – Research Centre for Minority Groups, 127–64 (in Greek).

Divani, L. (1995) *Greece and Minorities. The System of International Protection of the League of Nations.* Athens: Nefeli Publications (in Greek).

Dodos, D. (1994) *The Electoral Geography of Minorities. Minority Parties in the South Balkans: Greece, Bulgaria, Albania.* Athens: Exandas (in Greek).

Doudoumis, G. E. (1994) *Balkan Developments*. Athens: Dodoni Publications (in Greek).
—— (1996) *Balkan Developments II*. Athens: Dodoni Publications (in Greek).
European Commission against Racism and Intolerance (2001) *Second Report on Albania*. [http://www.coe.int/T/E/human_rights/Ecri/1–ECRI/2–Country-by-country-approach/Albania/PDF_CBC2%20Albania.pdf]
Fakiolas, R. and King, R. (1996) Emigration, return, immigration: a review and evaluation of Greece's postwar experience of international migration, *International Journal of Population Geography*, 2(2): 171–90.
Fakiolas, R. (1997) *Recent Efforts to Regularise Undocumented Immigrants*. Dublin: European Foundation for the Improvement of Living and Working Conditions, Working Paper WP/97/40/EN.
—— (2003) Regularising undocumented immigrants in Greece: procedures and effects, *Journal of Ethnic and Migration Studies*, 29(3): 539–61.
Georgiou, V. (1994) *Northern Epirus. The Continued Ethnic Tragedy*. Athens: Rigas Publications (in Greek).
Greek Helsinki Monitor (1994) *Greeks of Albania and Albanians in Greece*. [http://www.greekhelsinki.gr/pdf/ghm-greeks-albanians.PDF].
Human Rights Watch (1995) Albania. The Greek minority, 7 (4): 1–20.
International Crisis Group (2001a) *Albania: State of the Nation 2001*. [http://www.crisisweb.org/projects/europe/albania/reports/A400299_25052001.pdf].
—— (2001b) *Albania's Parliamentary Elections 2001*. [http://www.crisisweb.org/projects/europe/albania/reports/A400399_23082001.pdf].
—— (2003) *Albania: State of the Nation 2003*. [http://www.crisisweb.org/projects/europe/albania/reports/A400917_11032003.pdf].
International Organization for Migration (2003) *Informed Migration*. Geneva: IOM.
Kallivretakis, L. (1995) The Greek community in Albania from the angle of historical geography and demography, in Veremis, T., Kouloumbis T., and Nicolakopoulos, E. (eds) *Hellenism in Albania*. Athens: Sideris, 25–58 (in Greek).
Karydis, V. (1996) *The Criminality of Immigrants in Greece*. Athens: Papazisis (in Greek).
King, R., Iosifides, T. and Myrivilli, L. (1998) A migrant's story: from Albania to Athens, *Journal of Ethnic and Migration Studies*, 27 (1): 159–75.
Kondis, A. (1995) The economy of Albania and the Greek minority, in Veremis, T., Kouloumbis T., and Nicolakopoulos, E. (eds) *Hellenism in Albania*. Athens: Sideris, 103–46 (in Greek).
Kondis, V. (1994) *Delicate Balances. Greece and Albania in the 20th Century*. Thessaloniki: Paratiritis (in Greek).
Lazaridis, G. (1996) Immigration to Greece: a critical evaluation of Greek policy, *New Community*, 22(2): 335–48.
Pano, N. (1997) The process of democratization in Albania, in Dawisha, K. and Parrott, B. (eds) *Politics, Power, and the Struggle for Democracy in South-East Europe*. Cambridge: Cambridge University Press, 285–352.
Pavlou, M. (2003) The Greeks of Albania in Greece, in Tsitselikis, C. and Christopoulos, D. (eds) *The Greek Minority of Albania*. Athens: Kritiki Publications – Research Centre for Minority Groups, 265–308 (in Greek).

Pettifer, J. (2001) *The Greek Minority in Albania in the Aftermath of Communism*. Sandhurst: Royal Military Academy, Conflict Studies Research Centre, No. G97.

Schwandner-Sievers, S. (1999) *The Albanian Aromanians' Awakening: Identity Politics and Conflicts in Post-Communist Albania*. Flensburg: European Centre for Minority Issues, Working Paper No. 3.

Tiropoli, M. (2000) Albania, in Dokos, T. and Pierros, F. (eds) *The Balkans after the War in Kosovo*. Athens: Sideris Publications, 54–80 (in Greek).

Tsardanidis, H. (2000) Peripheral cooperations in south-east Europe, in Dokos, T. and Pierros, F. (eds) *The Balkans after the War in Kosovo*. Athens: Sideris Publications, 287–312 (in Greek).

Tsitselikis, C. (2003) The education of the Greek minority in Albania, in Tsitselikis, C. and Christopoulos, D. (eds) *The Greek Minority of Albania*. Athens: Kritiki Publications – Research Centre for Minority Groups, 165–223 (in Greek).

Tsitselikis, C. and Christopoulos, D. (2003) The Greek minority of Albania: snapshots of uncertainty as ethnic verities, in Tsitselikis, C. and Christopoulos, D. (eds) *The Greek Minority of Albania*. Athens: Kritiki Publications – Research Centre for Minority Groups, 17–44 (in Greek).

Veremis, T., Kouloumbis, T. and Nikopakopoulos, E. (1995) Introduction, in Veremis, T., Kouloumbis T., and Nicolakopoulos, E. (eds) *Hellenism in Albania*. Athens: Sideris, 9–17 (in Greek).

Vichou, M., Dodos, D., Kafetzis, P. and Nikolakopoulos, E. (1995) The political presence of the minority, in Veremis, T., Kouloumbis T., and Nicolakopoulos, E. (eds) *Hellenism in Albania*. Athens: Sideris, 59–102 (in Greek).

Vickers, M. (1997) *The Albanians. A Modern History*. London: I.B. Tauris.

—— (2002) *The Cham Issue. Albanian National and Property Claims in Greece*. Sandhurst: Royal Military Academy, Conflict Studies Research Centre, No. G109.

Vickers, M. and Pettifer, J. (1997) *Albania: From Anarchy to a Balkan Identity*, London: Hurst.

Winnifrith, T. J. (2002) *Badlands–Borderlands. A History of Northern Epirus/Southern Albania*. London: Duckworth.

4

The Albanian migration cycle

Migrants tend to return to their country of origin after all

LOIS LABRIANIDIS AND PANOS HATZIPROKOPIOU

Many migrants dream of returning to their homeland, at least when they set out. The hope of eventual return engenders courage, 'justifies' difficulties and hardship, and is a crucial determinant in migrants' lives in the host country (Wiest 1979). Today, as the migratory phenomenon evolves new characteristics and melds with the broader trends of societal transformation described under the general label of 'globalisation', the return of migrants continues to become an integral part of the ongoing migration process (King 2000). However, emigration is still considered a one-way trip, especially when it is happening and particularly from the point of view of the destination countries; return migration remains a plan, realistic or not, of the migrants themselves, and a xenophobic wish in some host societies. We regard return migration as the invisible side of a unified duality, often underestimated or neglected in policy making, academic analysis and public discourse in the host country.

The primary concern of this chapter is to highlight the return of Albanian emigrants as an aspect of this particular case of migration that has been largely overlooked. Some basic quantitative findings are presented, mainly regarding the labour market performance of the Albanian emigrants who returned, but also in respect to questions surrounding their living conditions and socio-economic integration abroad and back home. The study is based on a comparative analytical framework: the different characteristics of Albanian migrants in Italy and Greece and their labour market performance while abroad and after their return are compared. We explore the trajectories of those Albanians who emigrated and later returned: from their situation immediately prior to migration to the conditions they faced in the host country and then to their experiences upon return. Hence, the complete 'cycle' of migration is discussed. Analysis of these trajectories leads to some interesting conclusions and raises important questions regarding the following:

- the characteristics of returning Albanian emigrants;
- the different levels of development and the social structures of the two host countries, which to some extent determine both the migratory population they attract and the characteristics of those returning (in terms of geographic origin, education and skills, savings and remittances, entrepreneurship, etc.);
- the effects of emigration and return on the economy and developmental process of Albania;
- the more general dynamics of Albanian migration and return.

Albanian emigration is a fairly recent phenomenon and since the possibility of a trend towards return has only just emerged there has been little research into this 'counterstream'. Previous studies take for granted that return is largely a temporary option (Kule *et al.* 1999; Mancellari *et al.* 1996); they do not, however, focus on the particularities and implications of return. Earlier survey work by Barjaba and Perrone (1996) and the International Organization for Migration (1995) should also be noted, but these studies are now dated. We were therefore compelled to collect our own data and to base this study exclusively on fieldwork research. Our empirical analysis is based on a recently concluded research project with wider objectives than the issues discussed in this chapter. The project was about identifying gaps in supply and demand of labour in Albania and the formulation of policy guidelines for the reintegration of return migrants into Albanian society.

The questionnaire survey

Deriving from this broader research, the primary data source for our analysis here consists of 324 questionnaires gathered from Albanian former emigrants.[1] In addition, we interviewed 15 'key informants', mainly policy-makers and businessmen. Since the total number of Albanian returnees remains an 'unknown' population and since much of the migratory movement, especially between Albania and Greece, consists of flows back and forth, the only way to take a more-or-less random sample was to employ the snowball sampling method. In order to achieve greater consistency and representativeness amongst those interviewed, we selected our questionnaire sample from people who:

- were over 18 years old;
- had stayed for more than one year abroad as emigrants;

- had returned to Albania and lived there for at least one year at the time of the interview;
- had been emigrants in either Greece or Italy; and
- originated geographically from various parts of Albania and from a variety of urban and rural backgrounds.

Nevertheless, we have to acknowledge the existence of possible biases in the selection of the sample, since the characteristics of the total population of returnees in terms of age, sex, family status, geographical distribution and labour market integration are unknown. In that sense, it would be dangerous to attempt generalised responses to questions such as 'who goes back'. A more integrated analysis might include some comparison between those who return, those who stay on abroad, and those who never emigrated. We are aware that our research offers a partial view of the impact of migration on labour market developments in Albania, addressing only the trajectories of those who went abroad and came back again. However, we do believe that our empirical findings provide a basis for generalisation regarding the economic performance and labour market integration of returnees, their relevance to the development of Albania, and the general dynamics of migration and return.

These dynamics, we argue, are determined to a significant degree by the factor of *proximity* and the consequent *'back and forth'* character of movements, particularly between Albania and Greece. To this respect, certain *transnational* features are apparent in the case of Albanian migration to neighbouring countries (Mai and Schwandner-Sievers 2003). On the one hand, migration and return appear not to be permanent, but rather *reversible* options for a significant number of Albanian people. On the other hand, many Albanians, especially among those who went to Greece, manage to live effectively *between* the two countries, either by coming and going for temporary work, or by organising their lives in both places of origin and destination, with the latter providing the material resources for the acquisition of income and the improvement of the 'home' conditions. Our findings suggest that emigration is not always a long-term life choice and it may be reversed at any time, especially for those who work in neighbouring countries.

Background characteristics of the migrants

We attained a sample of 300 men and 24 women who had been migrants in Greece (239 respondents) and in Italy (85) for at least one year. We should stress that we calculated the period abroad on the basis of the year of *first* emigration, while many of those who had been in Greece actually followed a circular or shuttle path of repeated migrations. Most of the emigrants to Greece had lived there for 5–8 years, those to Italy for 6–8 years. The return waves peaked during 1999–2000 for emigrants to Greece and during 2000–1 for emigrants to Italy. About 92 per cent of all returnees were married and the great majority (77 percent) was between 26 and 45 years of age at the time of the interview.

Regarding geographic distribution, two-thirds of the respondents were from Central Albania (62 per cent among emigrants to Greece, 81 per cent for those returned from Italy), 31 per cent were from the South (36 per cent for Greece, 15 per cent for Italy), while only 3 per cent were from the Albanian North. In total, 78 per cent originated from urban areas, with the principal urban regions being Tirana (24 per cent in total, 19 per cent among emigrants to Greece and 39 per cent among emigrants to Italy), Durrës (17, 9 and 39 per cent respectively), and Sarandë (15, 18 and 9 per cent respectively). In general, the migrants returning from Greece show a greater diversity regarding their geographical origin, with a stronger presence of people originating from rural areas and from the South of Albania, compared to the emigrants returning from Italy (see table 4.1). Finally, return migration accompanied by internal migration has been observed in relatively few cases. As expected, it has the form of a rural-to-urban movement: about 5 per cent have moved from villages to the prefecture capital, while another 3 per cent moved from small to bigger towns (half of them to Tirana).

Table 4.1 Place of origin of returning migrants to Albania (per cent)

	All returnees (n=324)	From Greece (n=239)	From Italy (n=85)
Region			
Northern Albania	2.8	2.5	3.5
Central Albania	66.4	61.1	81.2
Southern Albania	30.9	36.4	15.3
Top seven prefectures			
Tirana	24.1	18.8	38.8
Durrës	17.0	9.2	38.8
Sarandë	15.4	17.6	9.4
Bulqizë	9.0	10.9	3.5
Tepelenë	7.7	10.5	—
Librazhd	6.2	8.4	—
Gjirokastër	5.6	7.1	1.2

Source: Authors' survey.

The questionnaire was structured on the basis of the three distinct stages which make up the typical migration cycle: before emigration, during migration and after return. This reflected our attempt to profile the 'trajectories' of Albanian emigrants throughout the migration cycle, where each stage is crucially determined by its precedents. Most of the questions elicited quantitative, 'measurable' information about the performance and experiences of the people interviewed. Although economic conditions and labour market performance were the focus of our survey, data were also collected regarding the housing experiences and living conditions of the interviewees before, during and after emigration, as well as several aspects of their social integration in the host countries and into Albania after return. Some final questions involved subjective understanding and evaluation of the respondents' migration experiences.

In the discussion that follows we 'treat' emigrants to Italy and to Greece as two different groups. This is done for the purposes of analysis only. The phenomenon of re-emigration has been common amongst Albanians who, having spent some time in Greece, then set out for Italy or some other country. Research by Kosic and Triandafyllidou (2003) and King *et al.* (2003) provides evidence of Albanian migrants to Greece who later moved to Italy and the UK respectively. Unfavourable economic or social conditions in Greece and frequent problems with the police partly explain such movements, together with various factors attracting migrants elsewhere, ranging from positive legal provisions (e.g. the prospect of regularisation) to ambitious life prospects or to the role of the social networks. It is worth mentioning that some migrants have this in mind from the very beginning: in a recent survey of Albanians in Thessaloniki, about one third of the (male) respondents saw Greece as a 'transit' country, a first step before emigrating somewhere else (Labrianidis and Lyberaki 2001). This further confirms one of our arguments in this paper – that migration to Greece mostly arises as 'an option out of necessity', a solution in order to cover immediate needs, where movement is facilitated by proximity, land borders and relative ease of entry.[2]

The chapter continues with an overview of Albanian migration to Italy and Greece, discussing some of our survey and key-interview findings on the basis of theoretical insights about return migration. We then give an account of the experiences of the migrants abroad, comparing the characteristics of migrants to Greece with those to Italy. The next section focuses on the employment and living conditions of returnees; through comparisons with the previous migration stages we attempt to evaluate the migration experience as a whole. We then discuss the implications of our findings for economic development in Albania. Finally, we summarise and argue that Albanian migration has to be understood within a transnational framework of mobility.

Albanian migration at the turn of the millennium: what are the implications for return?

As shown in the opening chapter of this book, the case of the emigration of Albanians during the last decade of the last century is a rather unique example of massive population outflow. The 'Great Albanian Exodus' became probably the most 'celebrated' case in the new era of East–West mobility that emerged in post-1989 Europe. Recent estimates suggest that the number of Albanian migrants at the turn of the millennium equates to one quarter of the total population of the country, meaning that practically every family in Albania has at least one of its members working abroad (King 2003). Such figures prove not only that migration emerged as a principal survival strategy for many Albanian households, but also that it has become an important feature of the Albanian economy and society as a whole.

However, in our interviews with key informants, a degree of complacency was observed regarding the effects of emigration on the Albanian economy: the country's political and economic authorities seem to recognise only the positive effects of emigration. In particular, the dominant idea is that emigration is a way of 'exporting' unemployment and of importing undeclared wealth through remittances and accumulated savings. At the same time, migrants are believed to attain certain employment skills abroad, which may be useful to them and the country's economy upon their return.

Little concern is shown for the outflow of human capital, particularly the brain-drain phenomenon, which may undermine the future development potential of the country.[3] The flow of remittances may also appear problematic in the long run: in general, as King (1986) has observed, the tendency to remit declines as the period of stay abroad increases. Furthermore, the question of whether emigrants do acquire useful employment skills while abroad is highly debatable, especially with respect to economic development (King 1986, 2000; Swanson 1979). Overall, our impression is that neither research nor policies regarding the return of emigrants to Albania are currently among the priorities of the country's authorities, and certainly not from the perspective of economic development. This obviously results from the fact that return migration is a very recent phenomenon, still limited in terms of numbers and significance.

Albanian migration is a unique case for another reason too: it has been directed almost exclusively towards two neighbouring countries, Italy and Greece. The total number of Albanians in Greece is estimated at between 450,000 and 550,000, whilst 150,000–200,000 are thought to be in Italy.[4] While the proportion of Albanians in the total migrant population in Italy is about one in ten, in Greece it rises to about 60 per cent (King 2003).

The pattern of Albanian migration to Italy is marked by the developmental gap dividing Northern Italy from the South. More than half of the Albanian migrants in Italy are located in the North, about one third in the Centre and the rest in the South. King and Mai (2004) have studied Albanian migrants in two Italian cities, Lecce and Modena, characteristic of the Italian South and North respectively. They find that Albanians in the North tend to work mainly in construction and manufacturing, while construction, agriculture, handicrafts and labouring are the principal sectors of immigrant employment in the South. There is a percentage that is employed in the service industry, mostly in low-status service jobs, and in the North of Italy some Albanians also work in the lower ranks of the administrative-clerical sector. Services are of greater importance for female immigrant employment, especially cleaning and care activities. Employment of Albanian migrants in the Italian North is also characterised by higher wages and social insurance, as well as by greater upward socio-economic mobility. The general picture is that Albanians are better off financially in the North, but they are to a greater extent excluded from social life, while in the South they have better opportunities for social participation and interaction but much less access to registered and well-paid employment.

In Greece, the geographic patterns of integration differ, due to the dominance of Greater Athens in the country's economic geography and the more diverse development map in the rest of the country. Albanians in Greece are concentrated mainly in the large urban centres of Athens–Piraeus and Thessaloniki (about 40 per cent and 6 per cent respectively). Very evident are the contradictions between rural and urban areas, or between different sectors of the economy. In regional cities like Thessaloniki Albanian immigrants appear to be in a relatively good socio-economic situation and they enjoy living standards comparable to those of some sections of the local population (Hatziprokopiou 2003; Labrianidis and Lyberaki 2001). In agricultural districts migrants tend to 'adjust' to the characteristics of the local context, contributing to the survival or modernisation of agricultural enterprises, to the maintenance of rural population levels and, in some places, to the preservation of the traditional way of life, for instance by reintroducing 'long forgotten arts' like carpentry and stone-building (Kasimis *et al.* 2003). In general, 'permanent' migrants who arrived with the first wave of the early 1990s tend to have more stable employment and better-quality housing and are more likely to have attained legal status, in contrast to the more vulnerable position of 'sojourners' who come for temporary and seasonal work and go back again. The principal sectors of migrant employment in urban areas are construction, services and small manufacturing, while in rural settings they tend to work mostly in agriculture and construction. The predominance of the micro-enterprise in Greek productive structures and the high share of self-employment are of particular importance for Albanian migrants' employment in all sectors and areas in Greece. Here too, Albanian women are employed to a large extent in the lower strata of the service sector, but in cities there are also significant numbers working in small-scale manufacturing (mostly clothing). However, the late implementation of regularisation measures (only started in 1998) and the overall problematic reception of Albanians by the state in Greece, with numerous cases of police brutality, have made life more difficult for migrants in this country (Fakiolas 2003).

What the two countries certainly have in common, regarding the patterns of socio-economic integration of Albanian migrants, is the predominance of the underground economy (somewhat stronger in the case of Greece) and widespread 'Albanophobia' as a unique expression of racist hostility towards a specific migrant group (which also appears to be sharper in Greece). On the positive side, the time factor is of great importance: King and Mai (2004) and Labrianidis and Lyberaki (2001), for Italy and Greece respectively, suggest that as the years of residence in the host country pass, the migrants' socio-economic position improves.

The possibility of return itself is time-dependent: as the period of stay abroad is extended it is reasonable to assume that the likelihood of the migrant returning diminishes. In addition, migrants often make plans at the beginning of their journey; but, over the course of time, intentions are modified by actual experience. Therefore, the potential impact of the period of stay abroad on migration plans seems to be rather ambivalent. On the one hand, integration in the host society is subject to time, and the more a migrant stays abroad, the less likely it is for him/her to return. On the other, the capacity of some individual migrants or households to achieve their initial aims and then go back certainly depends on the time spent in the host country. But in the Albanian case, marked by a large-scale population outflow directed mostly to neighbouring countries, migration has been more or less a necessary strategy for survival, with proximity shaping mobility patterns and facilitating transnational practices and flows back and forth.

Patterns of mobility

Earlier we noted that, in the sample of Albanian returnees, the average period of stay abroad is about seven years. The main reason for return mentioned by respondents was positive economic factors (more than one third), which can be interpreted as achievement of their initial aims and ensuring better conditions upon return. About 37 per cent of the participants in our survey actually planned to return from the beginning, but only 20 per cent had intended to stay abroad for more than six years. The overwhelming majority mentioned purely economic reasons for their decision to emigrate; such reasons included the necessity to maintain/supplement the family income, to improve living conditions, or to find start-up capital to establish a micro-enterprise upon return. About half of the respondents regularly sent money to their families while abroad (in most cases just for support) and one third of them told us that they had attempted to establish a business even before returning home.

All this suggests that, in the Albanian case, migration emerges as a solution to the urgent problem of survival and limited life prospects which in most cases can only be solved by moving to a neighbouring country to seek work. Particularly in the Greek case, movement is facilitated by mountainous land borders which are difficult to patrol and are therefore easily crossed. In this respect it is worth noting that 55 per cent of the total respondents to our questionnaire had crossed the land or sea border illegally. In addition, 28 per cent had migrated to Greece more than once (compared to less than 4 per cent of emigrants to Italy): proximity and ease of entry determine movement back and forth and this is very likely to continue in the future. This means that, although all respondents had been living in Albania for more than a year at the date of the interviews, re-emigration may emerge as an option when things at home do not go well. While about 70 per cent declared that they had returned for good, 56 per cent would consider emigrating again if that was necessary. During their period abroad, 40 per cent of the respondents used to visit Albania once a year, and another 29 per cent were making more frequent return visits per year.

It was pointed out above that many of the respondents had actually planned their return from the beginning and that a significant proportion returned after achieving their initial aims. Additional reasons for return were family obligations (19 per cent), psychological reasons (13 per cent), or simply the desire to be home (8 per cent). About 17 per cent had been encouraged to return by friends and relatives, and 41 per cent had received help from friends and relatives upon return. It is obvious that in the case of return migration the motives are not the clearly socio-economic ones that inspired the decision to emigrate.

In our question regarding the respondents' own evaluation of their migration experience, 44 per cent said that it had been generally 'good', while only 6 per cent said that it had been 'bad'. In addition, 62 per cent mentioned that they managed to achieve their financial aims, and 62 per cent said their migration experience helped them to find employment back in Albania. Finally, the percentage who felt that they had generally benefited from their migration experience was 87 per cent.

Theorising Albanian return

It appears rather difficult to 'fit' the Albanian case within a theoretical model of return migration. Given the relative absence of any theoretical underpinning for the study of return migration (King 2000), most attempts at generalisation propose a series of typologies, drawn from different cases of migration and return (Gmelch 1980; King 1986, 2000). Gmelch (1980) has proposed a typology related to the contradiction between actual and intended migration duration, distinguishing between:

- migrants who intended to migrate temporarily and return after they had satisfied their initial aims;

- migrants who intended to return in the beginning, but for various reasons they settled abroad forever;
- migrants who intended to stay permanently abroad, but then decided to return back to their country; and
- migrants who left without any intention to return and actually stayed abroad forever.

Our findings show that the majority of Albanian emigrants returning from Italy and Greece fit the first case in Gmelch's typology. They intended to migrate temporarily and they did return after fulfilling their original plans.[5]

Another typology, combining the actual migration duration with factors such as the reasons of return and economic integration abroad and back home, is that of Cerase (1974), who studied Italian migrants returning from the United States. Cerase distinguished between return because of *failure* or *conservatism*, return for *innovation* or for *retirement*, and *no return*. Each of these five types is based on a progressively longer period abroad. The Albanian case is marked by a relatively short period of time spent in the host countries, therefore it would seem to fit in one of the first two cases. However, the factor of proximity, the contacts maintained with the homeland while abroad and the shuttle movements of many migrants make the Albanian case quite unique in exhibiting certain transnational features that cannot be described within past conceptualisations of movement. In addition, for many of our respondents the option of return became viable when they evaluated that their material conditions had been significantly improved or when they had attained their financial aims. In other words, our findings suggest return because of 'success', while the possibility of working abroad in the future remains open.

With respect to the old debate about whether returnees are 'successes' or 'failures' (see Gmelch 1980), this question may involve more than one answer, not least because definitions of success and failure are very relative (King 1986). We are aware, once again, of possible bias in the selection of our sample and keep in mind, for instance, the sad stories about Albanian human tragedies that occasionally appear in the Greek and Italian press. Nevertheless, it is reasonable to generalise from the findings that the majority of those *who did return* have benefited from the experience of migration. We come back to discuss this later on.

The experience abroad

In this section the findings regarding the employment and general economic characteristics of the Albanian emigrants abroad are presented. The key aim here is to compare the conditions and performance of emigrants who went to Italy with those who lived in Greece. This will help us to capture the selectivity of migration in terms of 'who goes where', and to discuss the differences between the two host countries. Our main finding is dual: not only did those who migrated to Italy have a 'better' socio-economic background, but also their labour market integration and other aspects of their social life were generally 'better' compared to the conditions faced by those who migrated to Greece. From this, one might argue that the characteristics of migrants attracted to a country, and their socio-economic integration, reflect to an extent the economy and society of the host country. On the other hand, two further factors seem relevant to the comparison: first, only the relatively wealthy could afford the extra cost of migrating to Italy (including paying smugglers' fees); and second, we need to bear in mind the fact that many migrants to Italy have already been to Greece (so that any attempt to differentiate between the two migrant streams on the basis of migrant characteristics is potentially problematic).

A first general comparative observation is that the overall education level of all emigrants was relatively high – something which has to be partly attributed to the educational system in Hoxha's Albania. About 40 per cent of the male respondents had finished high school, 30 per cent had some technical/professional education and 18 per cent were university graduates (the figures for women were 60, 7 and 15 per cent respectively). However, those who migrated to Italy were in general better educated: the percentage of people who were not high school graduates is significantly lower than those who had been to Greece, while there were more people who had technical or university education in the stream to Italy. Among women especially, the education level of those who went to Italy compared to Greece is higher by 14 per cent for university graduates and by 7 per cent for women with technical education.

A similar pattern applies to the employment background and the respondents' pre-migration financial situation. Italy has attracted lower percentages of people who were unemployed in Albania before emigrating, far fewer people who were working in agriculture and relatively more skilled workers, entrepreneurs and self-employed (table 4.2). In addition, those who migrated to Italy were in a better financial position in the post-migration period than those who went to Greece: none was receiving an annual income less than 100,000 lek (while about 25 per cent of those who went to Greece were).[6] The urban origin of the majority of the people who went to Italy, about 75 per cent from Tirana and Durres, offers a partial explanation for this. After all, the residents of these two cities have been exposed to TV images from 'beautiful Italy' for years before their emigration (Mai 2001). In addition, given the relatively easier and cheaper access to Greece, compared with a more expensive boat trip to Italy, it is reasonable to assume that most of the 'better-offs' had the option to emigrate to Italy, while necessity pushed the majority to seek work in Greece.

Table 4.2 Employment of returning migrants by sex, country of origin and stage of emigration (per cent)

	pre-emigration		abroad		post-return	
	men	women	men	women	men	women
All returnees (n=324)						
Business Owner	1.9	1.7	1.2	0.6	36.0	16.0
Self-employed	18.0	0.9	16.0	—	23.0	4.7
Professional	6.5	6.0	1.6	—	8.1	5.1
Farming	2.8	2.6	3.4	1.2	2.5	1.6
Manufacturing	9.9	5.1	20.0	5.5	7.5	3.5
Building/construction	20.0	—	34.0	0.6	5.3	—
Services (tavern, fast-food etc.)	6.8	3.4	11.0	21.0	2.8	9.0
Cleaner/dishwasher/ kitchen maid	—	13.0	0.3	53.0	0.3	6.6
Farm worker	4.4	6.8	8.7	1.8	2.2	3.1
Unemployed	11.0	44.0	0.3	14.0	5.0	39.0
Other	20.0	17.0	4.3	1.9	7.5	11.0
Returnees from Greece (n=239)						
Business Owner	1.3	1.2	0.4	—	29.0	17.0
Self-employed	5.1	4.1	1.7	—	9.2	2.9
Professional	17.0	0.6	14	—	24.0	3.9
Farming	3.8	3.6	3.4	1.7	3.4	1.9
Manufacturing	8.5	5.9	16.0	4.2	7.6	3.9
Building/construction	20.0	—	36.0	—	5.9	—
Services (tavern, fast-food etc.)	7.2	3.6	14.0	24.0	3.4	10.0
Cleaner/dishwasher/ kitchen maid	—	12.0	—	55.0	0.4	7.2
Farm worker	5.1	8.9	11.0	1.7	3.0	3.9
Unemployed	13.0	46.0	0.4	12.0	5.9	38.0
Other	19.0	15.0	2.9	1.7	8.0	12.0
Returnees from Italy (n=85)						
Business Owner	3.5	3.1	3.6	2.3	55.0	14.0
Self-employed	10.0	11.0	1.2	—	4.9	14.0
Professional	20.0	1.5	20.0	—	20.0	8.2
Farming	—	—	3.6	—	—	—
Manufacturing	14.0	3.1	30.0	9.3	7.3	2.0
Building/construction	17.0	-	27.0	2.3	3.7	0
Services (tavern, fast-food etc.)	5.8	3.1	2.4	12.0	1.2	4.1
Cleaner/dishwasher/ kitchen maid	—	17.0	1.2	49.0	0	4.1
Farm worker	2.3	1.5	2.4	2.3	0	0
Unemployed	4.7	38.0	0	21.0	2.4	47.0
Other	22.0	22.0	8.4	2.3	6.1	6.1

Source: Authors' survey.

In regard to the labour market experiences of migrants abroad, the findings are similar: emigrants in Italy were relatively better off than those in Greece. As we can see from table 4.2 again, the majority of male respondents (from both destinations) had worked in construction (34 per cent), manufacturing (20 per cent), agriculture (12 per cent) and services (11 per cent), while an important proportion (16 per cent) had been self-employed. Women's principal sector of employment abroad was low-status services, where they worked as cleaners or in taverns, fast-food outlets, etc. (74 per cent). It is clear that such jobs require a minimum of skills and do not offer any significant professional experience. Two key differences can be noted between the working experiences of those who had migrated to Italy and those who had been to Greece. First, the rates of self-employment and entrepreneurship were higher in Italy. Second, a greater percentage of Albanian migrants of both sexes in Italy had been employed in manufacturing, and a lower share of them had been working in agriculture.

Similar differences also existed between the general living conditions of emigrants in Greece and in Italy. Obviously, a central aspect of living and working abroad was the issue of illegality. In the Greek case the opportunity for legal residence came relatively late, since it was only in 1998 that the government launched the first regularisation programme. Apart from condemning migrants to informal work, 'illegal' status also caused problems in their everyday lives: 37 per cent of the respondents had been arrested by the police (66 per cent of them more than once) and 24 per cent had been expelled and then re-crossed the border. The majority of the respondents, though, had legal documents in the immediate post-return period (about 70 per cent).

Albanian emigrants in Greece were, if anything, in a slightly better situation than those in Italy regarding social security and public health insurance: 36 per cent had social security stamps in their last job in Greece (31 per cent of those in Italy) and 31 per cent owned a health book (cf. 29 per cent in Italy). However, if one looks at other indicators of the migrants' living conditions abroad we see that those who had been to Italy found things easier than returnees from Greece. Regarding housing, not only had emigrants to Italy enjoyed a greater living space (fewer persons per room), but also a larger share of them lived on the more prestigious upper floors. Also, in Italy a higher percentage of Albanian emigrants had basic household equipment such as a fridge (97 per cent, compared to 89 per cent of those in Greece) or a washing machine (83 per cent versus 63 per cent). The possession of motorised transport while abroad was also more frequent among those who had migrated to Italy (25 per cent, compared to 15 per cent for Greece). Furthermore, a greater share of emigrants to Italy used to go for holidays in Albania or in the host country. Participation in collective institutions (immigrant/ethnic associations), although at a very low level, was higher among Albanian migrants in Italy (about 6 per cent, compared to 2 per cent in the case of migrants in Greece). In Italy, emigrants found it easier to socialise with locals. This reflects, we believe, the general situation regarding their 'reception' by the locals: only 13 per cent in Italy reported problems of discrimination, while more than 40 per cent of the emigrants in Greece had faced such problems.

Contact with Albania was not lost during the period abroad. Two-thirds of the emigrants would visit Albania at least once in a year and more than one third used to vote in Albanian elections while abroad. About 15 per cent had a bank account in Albania and 8 per cent had some investment. Many used to remit regularly in cash, mostly directed to family support and only minimally for productive investment.

The experience upon return

Next, we compare the pre-migration and post-migration periods and, on the basis of the respondents' experiences, we evaluate the migration experience as a whole. The overall experience of migration appears to have been positive for both sets of returnees, especially in the sense of ameliorating their socio-economic situation and living conditions. We also observe that contacts with the host countries are not lost after return. Various links sustain transnational relationships, and this seems to be crucial in understanding the patterns of Albanian migration to Italy and Greece.

Employment

Our questionnaire findings regarding the employment status of returning migrants in the three stages of the migration cycle are summarised in table 4.2. A first observation is the overall decrease in the proportion of unemployed, which for male respondents has dropped to about half the rate it used to be before emigration. The large number of unemployed women probably hides the fact that many women were simply housewives before emigration and still continue to be so after return, having worked abroad. No problems seem to exist regarding the process of labour market integration after return. Thus, 27 per cent found a job immediately (some had pre-arranged their employment), while only 6 per cent were unemployed for more than five months after return. Those returning from Greece appear to have been more adaptive than those returning from Italy, as 87 per cent of them (compared to a 68 per cent returning from Italy) found a job in less than three months.

Important increases have taken place in entrepreneurship and self-employment, as well as an overall rise in the proportion of professionals after return. Less than 2 per cent of the sample were business-owners before emigrating. Those who owned a private business after emigration reached 36 per cent among men and 16 per cent among women. Self-employment expanded too, from 18 per cent for men and 1 per cent for women to 23 and 5 per cent respectively.

On the other hand, the proportion in all other occupations declined: farmers and farm workers, workers in manufacturing and low-status service employees (workers in restaurants and fast-foods, cleaners, etc.). The most dramatic decrease took place among those who had formerly worked in the construction sector: from 20 per cent in the pre-migration stage to 5 per cent post-migration.

This is hardly surprising, since these were exactly the jobs most returning emigrants were performing in the host countries. Two possible hypotheses can be advanced for returnees to 'reject' the jobs they did abroad. First, Gmelch (1980) and King (2000) offer a psychological explanation. After years of savings and hard work in the host countries, former emigrants want to live peacefully in their homeland, avoiding drudgery and preferably working in their own businesses.

The second explanation relates to the many changes in the economy of the source country. For instance, Ilahi (1999), in his study of Pakistani return migration, explains the phenomenon as a rational response to opportunities and constraints while abroad and after return: the economic conditions that returnees find in their country upon return are crucial to their labour market integration. In the case of Albania, the most notable employment change in this period of very rapid transformation has been the significant decrease in the importance of the public sector in economic life, including employment in state-owned companies. One third of the respondents were employed in the public sector before leaving Albania, but only 12 per cent after return. The Albanian Institute of Statistics (INSTAT) recorded the number of people employed in the public sector as dropping from 850,091 to 188,965 during the decade 1991–2001.[7] According to the same source, employment in absolute numbers dropped in almost all sectors between 1991 and 2001, with the most dramatic decrease taking place in total industrial employment, although the proportion of employment increased in some sectors such as electric power and the water industry, as well as trade. However, if we take a look at the sectoral employment of the questionnaire respondents, the most notable rise has been among those working in industry/manufacture (from 16 per cent before up to 23 per cent after emigration).

So, the employment mobility of Albanians who go abroad and return is not only determined by their own wish to work independently, possibly on the basis of savings from their migration, but it is also an indicator of the changes brought about by transformations in the Albanian economy. These involve ongoing privatisation and limited access to formal paid employment, which makes the options of self-employment and entrepreneurship more of a 'necessary choice' for individuals and households.

Now, if we compare the labour market performance of former emigrants to Italy and Greece after they have returned to Albania, we find again that those who have been to Italy are in a relatively better situation (table 4.2). A lower percentage of them tend to return to the jobs they were doing before emigration, or to perform tasks similar to the ones they were doing abroad. None have returned to agriculture-related work. In addition, a much greater share have become business-owners. Thus, the argument developed in the previous section goes further: the strengths or the malfunctions of the host country's economy have the potential to influence migrants' performance in their own country after return. Of course, differences in the economic and social capital of the people who migrated to Italy and those who went to Greece also have a role in labour market integration back home. But migrants' employment and economic practices back home reflect a strong influence from the years they spent abroad and their different experiences in the two host countries.

It is also essential to see what types of businesses are started up by returning migrants. Most run service businesses, tourist-related enterprises and trading companies (see table 4.3). The most common types are small trade companies (garments, construction materials), fast-food outlets (pizza, souvlaki), grocery shops, confectioneries, bars, petrol stations, haulage (especially of agricultural products), small workshops (carpentry, aluminium windows and doors, metal gates, workshops repairing shoes), while manufacturing mainly concerns subcontracting in garments (returnees from Greece) or in shoes (returnees from Italy) and paint factories.

Table 4.3 Businesses established by return migrants in Albania, by sector and country of emigration

Economic Sector	All returnees	Returnees from Greece	Returnees from Italy
Agriculture	1	1	0
Manufacturing and cottage industry	5	3	2
Trade	24	16	8
Tourism	24	14	10
Services	55	32	23
Other	3	2	1
Total	111	67	44

Source: Authors' survey.

Many of these enterprises seem to be 'replicas' of the ones their owners used to work in abroad. This might appear contradictory with our previous statement about the tendency of returnees to avoid jobs they were doing as emigrants. However, one should take into account that this involves a shift from dependent waged worker to self-employment and entrepreneurship. Former emigrants use the skills and 'know-how' they acquired abroad; in some cases they also benefit from contacts and collaboration they maintain with friends, relatives or previous employers in the host countries.

What is generally observed in other cases of return migration – that is, the tendency of returnees to invest in small companies and non-productive activities (King 1986; 2000) – also applies in the Albanian case: only 9 per cent of the business owners in our questionnaire run companies employing more than 11 persons, while 58 per cent have a maximum of 5 employees.[8] Bearing in mind that emigration has been above all a household survival strategy for Albanians, we can assume that most of the businesses owned by returnees also provide employment for other household members or relatives (note that more than half of the respondents find work with the help of friends and relatives). In general, most of the returnees' micro-enterprises have a family character and depend on extremely hard work by the owner and other family members. The rewards are modest, which means in practice that the majority of entrepreneurs will never become rich. They choose to establish a business in order to provide an additional income to the household and avoid paid employment, in the absence of feasible or attractive alternative options.

Living conditions

So far we have seen that, in terms of work and household survival, the experience of migration was generally positive. The majority have found a better job or started a business, and their remuneration is higher than before emigration. All this certainly provides higher living standards for the returnees. First of all, household income in general has been improved. The respondents' annual income before emigration was, on average, between 100,000 and 300,000 lek per year. Now it exceeds 400,000 lek per year; for 12 per cent it even exceeds 800,000 lek per year.[9] According to INSTAT, the average annual household income in urban areas was about 370,000 lek in 2000. Again we observe a difference between emigrants to Italy and Greece: a greater number of migrants returning from Italy achieve higher levels of household income.

We can also note some general trends in Albania's economic transformation reflected in the returnees' economic behaviour. Such trends include the broader use of money as a means of exchange and the development of financial services. Two-thirds of the respondents now have a bank account, and 43 per cent have various forms of investment.

In regard to the housing conditions of returning Albanian emigrants, the proportion of property-owners has risen from 85 per cent before emigration to 92 per cent after return. Although few respondents said that the money sent from abroad was 'invested' in housing, we can assume that in reality significant amounts of remittances and accumulated savings were used to buy new property or repair/extend existing accommodation. As can be seen in table 4.4, more people now live on the more prestigious upper floors[10] or even in individual houses, and the housing space is increasing too (in parallel, perhaps, with diminishing household sizes).

Table 4.4 Housing conditions of returnees by country of migration and stage of migration (per cent)

	In Albania		Abroad	
	pre-emigration	post-return	in Greece	in Italy
Property type				
Own	85.2	92.3	—	—
Rented	9.0	4.6	79.5	61.2
Dependent member, guest	5.9	3.1	9.2	35.3
Employer's place	—	—	11.3	3.5
Floor				
Ground	39.2	27.8	62.3	55.3
1st	25.0	24.1	22.6	24.7
2nd	15.1	17.0	6.3	4.7
3rd	10.8	15.7	5.0	4.7
4th and above	8	13.3	3.4	9.4
Individual house	1.9	2.2	0.4	1.2
Persons per room				
<1	17.0	29.0	18.0	21.2
1–2	67.3	68.5	59.8	57.6
2–3	13.6	2.5	18.0	20.0
>3	2.2	—	4.2	1.2

Source: Authors' survey.

In addition, more people now own certain household goods: before emigration, 86 per cent of the respondents had a fridge and 63 per cent a washing machine, while the possession of such products has risen now up to almost 100 per cent. Also, more than half of the people interviewed now own a motorised means of transport (48 per cent a car), compared to only 5 per cent before emigrating. Comparing the characteristics of the returnees with the general situation in Albania regarding the same indicators according to the 2001 Census (INSTAT 2002), we can observe that former emigrants enjoy a much more comfortable life than their compatriots: 74 per cent of Albanian households possess a refrigerator and 39 per cent a washing machine, while only 8 per cent have a car.

Regarding the social reintegration of the former migrants back in their homeland, in contrast to what is often written about problems in the socialisation of the returnees (e.g. Gmelch 1980), we found that more than 90 per cent of the respondents did socialise with either old friends, or relatives, or both. Clearly, this is explained by the fact that the people who participated in our survey had lived abroad for a relatively short period and most kept contacts and bonds with their country through frequent visits. However, membership of associations, trade unions, etc. remained low (7 per cent); this probably reflects a certain distrust in collective institutions as a result of bad experiences during the communist regime.

If we now look at the contacts that returnees kept with their host countries we can further support the argument that proximity and the relative ease of movement between Albania and Italy or Greece facilitate and enhance the mobility of people, goods and other resources in a newly-formed transnational space. After all, 12 per cent of the respondents still had family members working abroad and 18 per cent travel to the host countries at least once a year (to visit family members, or for tourism or financial/business activities). In addition, 57 per cent of the respondents maintain relationships with friends and relatives still in the host countries, while 13 per cent have professional contacts with local partners in Greece and Italy. Finally, 23 per cent of the respondents buy goods from their host countries, of which 60 per cent relate not to consumer goods but rather to business equipment and trading commodities.

Migration, return and development

We now proceed to interpret our survey findings in relation to the development of Albania. The increased prosperity of former emigrants may reduce social imbalances and boost consumption, but it does not necessarily create sustainable economic development (King 2000). The impact of return migration on the country of origin is subject to many factors. According to Bovenkerk (1974: 45–9), such factors include: (a) the number of people going back and the time when return takes place, (b) the length of stay in the host country, (c) the place where returnees settle, (d) the social class, profession and education of the returnees, and (e) the degree to which the returning wave is organised and the returnees are supported regarding their reintegration.

In theory, return migration can contribute to the development of the source country in two basic ways: the economic impact of financial capital entering the country (remittances and savings), and the transfer of human capital (skills and professional experience acquired abroad).[11] In regard to the first, remittances and savings can be directed towards consumption, the buying of land or property, or productive investment. We have already mentioned that the majority of the money remitted was used for the support of family members (consumption). Clearly, even when they are not invested, migrant remittances constitute a crucial supplement to the domestic income of many households. And although in theory the benefits are disputable, the impact of remittances on the Albanian economy seems to have been generally positive. Korovilas (1999) attributed the high growth rates of the Albanian economy in the mid-1990s to the inflow of migrant remittances. Holzner (2002: 3) reports that the inflow of remittances covered a substantial part of the huge trade deficit. According to Mancellari *et al.* (1996), emigration and migrant remittances have contributed to the reduction of unemployment, the rise of productivity in some sectors (construction, agriculture) and the creation of new jobs in Albania. In 1997, the International Monetary Fund estimated remittance flows at 15–20 per cent of GDP. In a recent survey, about half of 700 Albanian returnees reported sending back money in cash while abroad: 53 per cent was directed to consumption, while the rest was saved in banks (16 percent) or invested in financial institutions or property (7 per cent in each); only 7 per cent was invested in some form of business activity, with the remainder (10 per cent) used for other activities (Kule *et al.* 1999: 8). According to the same source, 17 per cent of 200 Albanian companies surveyed had used migrant remittances in order to get established. So, part of the returning capital is invested, although not always in productive activities. The negative side of the unproductive investment of remittances manifested itself in the 1997 crisis in the pyramid investment schemes: the proliferation of pyramid schemes was closely linked to the inflow of remittances (Korovilas 1999). However, remittances are believed to have fuelled growth again since 1997, especially in the service and construction sectors. Further analysis of the contribution – actual and potential – of remittances to Albanian economic development is offered by Piperno's chapter in this volume.

The second important issue is related to the extent to which returning migrants bring with them new skills and abilities applicable at home. The majority worked in unskilled or semi-skilled jobs abroad. In that sense, the migrants' employment experience abroad tends if anything to have a deskilling effect. This, however, is not necessarily prejudicial to Albania's own productive base, since this is changing anyway. And in any case, returnees prefer not to continue in the type of employment they had as emigrants. However, although this may be true for paid employees, it does not apply in the case of business-owners: as has been mentioned already, the types of enterprises that returnees run are sometimes copies of the types of companies they used to work in abroad. Kule *et al.* (1999: 10) claim that the period spent abroad enhances the prospects of finding a job or starting up a business upon return. In their survey of Albanian companies, they found that about half the business owners considered emigration an advantage for finding employment at home, while 40 per cent believed that former emigrants had better chances of finding a job and two-thirds thought that emigrants were better equipped to establish a firm at home. All these findings imply that, despite the deskilling effects of employment abroad in terms of the educational/professional qualifications of the migrants, Albanian returnees seem to have generally benefited from their migration experience at this level, in some cases by having acquired useful skills to start a business on their own.

Conclusion

In this chapter the issue of return migration from Italy and Greece to Albania has been discussed in the light of empirical material collected through a questionnaire survey. Our findings confirm that return migration from neighbouring host countries back to Albania is a *reality*, undeservedly neglected by academic research and policy-makers. We have provided evidence from survey data, facilitating a preliminary understanding of the characteristics of the return flow. Furthermore, our data has allowed us to compare the experiences of emigrants abroad and to conclude that, for several reasons, the developmental level and employment conditions in the host countries produce a selectivity in the migration process and also influence the performance of former emigrants after return. In this respect, Italy seems to have attracted a higher proportion of educated and skilled Albanian workers, mostly of urban origin, and also offered relatively better working conditions.

We have also elaborated some of the principal issues regarding the relationship between Albanian migration, return and economic development. On this basis, we have highlighted the importance of micro-enterprises, both for the returnees themselves and for the country's economy. Although characterised as 'the engine of growth', the development of such small enterprises faces financial, fiscal (high taxes and contributions) and institutional constraints, tending to drive their activities into the informal sector of the economy (Hashi 2003). Supporting small businesses and providing conditions conducive to their legitimate development should, therefore, be one of the priorities of government policy. It would also be much wiser for Greece, Italy and other developed countries wanting to support development in Albania, to give a helping hand to micro-enterprises in conjunction with setting up other forms of aid schemes.

However, there is another important matter arising from the analysis of the dynamics of Albanian migration and return, and this is the issue of *proximity*. Closeness may reduce the inclination to *permanent* return, at least in the short term; the accessibility of the country of origin makes contacts easier and allows frequent visits, thus eliminating the immediate psychological/family motives for return as long as economic and life prospects are better in the host countries.[12] On the other hand, proximity may facilitate the possibility of *short-term* return, since the option of seasonal or occasional movements for temporary employment remains open and there is always the possibility of emigrating for a second time.

In the past fifteen years, following the demise of the Iron Curtain, population mobility in Europe has had much to do with cross-border and shuttle movements between neighbouring countries, especially in respect to East–West mobility patterns. As King and Mai (2004) put it, 'although international migration is seen as an increasingly globalising phenomenon, much transnational mobility remains local or regional in scale'. Recent Albanian migration underlines the statement, 'geography matters'. Proximity has shaped the patterns of emigration from Albania and there is reason to assume that it will equally determine the waves of return migration in the coming period.

In general, labour movements from Albania to Italy and Greece seem to be embedded within a wider framework of mobility which also involves flows of goods, services, capital, as well as information, signs and images. Italy and Greece are Albania's main trading partners (Mancellari *et al.* 1996: 477). In 1998, one fifth of the 1270 Greek investment projects in Eastern Europe were concentrated in Albania, reflecting a high demand among Greek enterprises for cheap and flexible labour which is available either in Greece (via immigration from Albania), or abroad through direct investment in Albania (Labrianidis *et al.* 2004). Furthermore, 'Western' images and values have also 'travelled' to Albania with Italian television (Mai 2001) and through the experiences of emigrants returning or visiting relatives back home.

Rogers' (2000: 8, 10) analysis of European expressions of transnationalism suggests that in Eastern Europe there has been a history of 'borders moving across people and their communities'. What actually takes place now is not a 'flood' from East to West, but 'a much wider field of mobility', the majority of movements being short-distance, cross-border flows between neighbouring countries. In the Albanian case one can observe several kinds of flows moving 'back and forth' and communities of people expanding beyond national borders. Geographic proximity and ease of entry, especially regarding Albanian migration to Greece, have shaped migration patterns. Obviously, there are those returning for good, as well as those who will permanently settle (or have already done so) in Greece, Italy, or somewhere else. But for an Albanian who has been an emigrant, let us say, in Greece, who knows the language and has friends and relatives who are still there, perhaps also business or personal relationships with Greeks, it is not at all difficult to get a coach from Tirana or Sarandë and go down to Athens, Larisa, or wherever.

In the newly-emerged transnational space linking Italy, Albania and Greece, population movement seems to be becoming easier and easier despite national barriers, while other forms of mobility (of capital, information, traded or smuggled goods, etc.) have also become more frequent. In that sense, as Glick-Schiller *et al.* (1992: 5) have written, 'constant back and forth flows of people could not be captured by categories of "permanent migrants", "return migrants" or "sojourners"'. These informal migrant social networks link people who live in different places and, as we have seen, such links continue to exist after migrants return: either with relatives and friends still abroad, or with Greek or Italian friends and colleagues. In some cases, migrant networks constitute a form of social

capital, since certain resources (like other forms of capital) can be mobilised through certain types of social groups and relationships (Ammassari and Black 2001: 21–2). This trend, easily observed in the Albanian case, might be more widespread in coming years, as transnational structures become more consolidated.

Notes

1 Fieldwork took place during March and April 2002. Questionnaires were administered by a group of students from the University of Tirana working under the supervision of Kosta Barjaba, Alfred Kocollari and Brikena Brahimi.

2 Cases whereby the sequence of countries is reversed are rare but by no means unknown. In our sample of 324, three involved migrants going first to Italy and subsequently to Greece.

3 Even in instances where the brain-drain phenomenon is studied, the question of return of the highly skilled Albanians who work abroad is given less attention than other issues, such as the amount of money they remit or the general description of the characteristics of this particular section of the emigrant population (Gedeshi 2002).

4 These figures combine officially-recorded migrants with estimates of the undocumented. For Albanians in Greece, two particular facts need noting: first, a significant part of the Albanian migrant population in Greece belongs to the ethnic Greek minority of southern Albania or has mixed ethnic origin; secondly, much of the Albanian migratory wave to Greece has to do with seasonal and temporary cross-border movements. For further discussion of Albanian migrant numbers in Greece and Italy, which includes reference to more recent (and possibly more speculative) higher estimates, see Barjaba and King's account in Chapter 1 of the current volume.

5 But, of course, our methodology of interviewing only returnees automatically misses out the second and fourth types of possible return or non-return.

6 100,000 lek equals approximately 780 euros or £520.

7 INSTAT web page www.instat.gov.al; various tables.

8 These figures are consistent with the overall size distribution of private enterprises in Albania after shutting down or selling off large public companies. According to INSTAT, among a total of 35,477 registered active enterprises in 2000, 96.6 per cent employed 1–10 employees, while less than 1 per cent were companies with more than 50 employees.

9 However, it has to be acknowledged here that the amounts of money stated have not been adjusted for inflation; therefore the actual difference between pre- and post-migration periods is probably far more modest in some cases.

10 Until the early 1990s, the 'nicest' floor to live on was the second (Albanians say 'third'). Later, when multi-storey blocks came to be built in ever-larger numbers, the best floors for living became those from the third upwards.

11 There is a substantial literature on this: see Swanson (1979), Wiest (1979) for earlier surveys; Ammassari and Black (2001) for a more recent overview.

12 Statements about proximity and mobility are more applicable to Greece that to Italy, especially with regard to 'illegal' immigrants in Italy.

References

Ammassari, S. and Black, R. (2001) *Harnessing the Potential of Migration and Return to Promote Development: Applying Concepts to West Africa*. Brighton: Sussex Centre for Migration Research, University of Sussex, Working Paper 3.

Barjaba, K. and Perrone, L. (1996) Forma e grado di adattamento dei migranti di cultura albanese in Europa (Italia, Grecia, Germania): 1992–5, in Barjaba, K., Lapassade, G. and Perrone, L. (eds) *Naufragi Albanesi: Studi Ricerche e Riflessioni sull'Albania*. Rome: Sensibili alle Foglie, 123–68.

Bovenkerk, F. (1974): *The Sociology of Return Migration: A Bibliographic Essay*. Nijhoff: The Hague (Publications of the Research Group on European Migration Problems, 20).

Cerase, F. P. (1974) Migration and social change: expectations and reality. A case study of return migration from the United States to Italy, *International Migration Review*, 8(2): 245–62.

Fakiolas, R. (2003) Regularising undocumented immigrants in Greece: procedures and effects, *Journal of Ethnic and Migration Studies*, 29(3): 535–61.

Gedeshi, I. (2002) The Albanian brain drain. Paper presented to the International Conference *Albanian Migration and the New Transnationalisms*, University of Sussex, 6–7 September 2002.

Glick-Schiller, N., Basch, L. and Szanton-Blanc, C. (1995) From immigration to transnational migration: theorizing transnational migration, *Anthropological Quarterly*, 68(1): 48–63.

Gmelch, G. (1980) Return migration, *Annual Review of Anthropology*, 9: 135–59.

Hashi, I. (2003) Financial and institutional barriers to SMEs' growth in Albania: results of an enterprise survey, *Economic Policy in Transitional Economies*, 11(3): 221–38.

Hatziprokopiou, P. (2003) Albanian immigrants in Thessaloniki, Greece: processes of economic and social incorporation, *Journal of Ethnic and Migration Studies*, 29(6): 1033–58.

Ilahi, N. (1999) Return migration and occupational change, *Review of Development Economics*, 3(2): 170–86.

International Monetary Fund (1997) *Albania: Recent Economic Developments*. Washington DC: IMF.

INSTAT (2002) *The Population of Albania in 2001. Main Results of the Population and Housing Census*. Tirana: INSTAT.

International Organization for Migration (1995) *Profiles and Motives of Potential Migrants from Albania*, IOM web site at www.iom.int.

Kasimis, Ch., Papadopoulos, A. and Zacopoulou, E. (2003) Migrants in rural Greece, *Sociologia Ruralis*, 43(2): 167–84.

King, R. (1986) Return migration and regional economic development: an overview, in King, R. (ed.) *Return Migration and Regional Economic Problems*. London: Croom Helm, 1–37.

—— (2000) Generalisations from the history of return migration, in Ghosh, B. (ed.) *Return Migration: Journey of Hope or Despair?* Geneva: IOM/UN, 7–55.

—— (2003) Across the sea and over the mountains: documenting Albanian migration, *Scottish Geographical Journal*, 119(3): 283–309.

King, R. and Mai, N. (2004) Albanian immigrants in Lecce and Modena: narratives of rejection, survival and integration, *Population, Space and Place*, 10(6): 455–77.

King, R., Mai, N. and Dalipaj, M. (2003) *Exploding the Migration Myths*. London: The Fabian Society/Oxfam.

Korovilas, J. P. (1999) The Albanian economy in transition: the role of remittances and pyramid investment schemes, *Post-Communist Economies*, 11(3): 399–412.

Kosic, A. and Triandafyllidou, A. (2003) Albanian immigrants in Italy: migration plans, coping strategies and identity issues, *Journal of Ethnic and Migration Studies*, 29(6): 997–1014.

Kule, D., Mancellari, A., Papapanagos, H., Qirici, S., and Sanfey, P. (1999) *The Causes and Consequences of Albanian Emigration during Transition: Evidence from Micro-data*. London: European Bank for Reconstruction and Development, Working Paper 46.

Labrianidis, L. and Lyberaki A. (2001) *Albanian Immigrants in Thessaloniki*. Thessaloniki: Paratiritis (in Greek).

Labrianidis, L. Lyberaki, A., Tinios, P. and Hatziprokopiou, P. (2004) Inflow of immigrants and outflow of FDI: aspects of interdependence between Greece and the Balkans, *Journal of Ethnic and Migration Studies*, 30(6): in press.

Mai, N. (2001) Italy is beautiful: the role of Italian television in the Albanian migratory flow to Italy, in King, R. and Wood, N. (eds) *Media and Migration: Constructions of Mobility and Difference*. London: Routledge, 95–109.

Mai, N. and Schwandner-Sievers, S. (2003) Albanian migration and new transnationalisms, *Journal of Ethnic and Migration Studies*, 29(6): 939–48.

Mancellari, A., Papapanagos, H., Sanfey, P. (1996) Job creation and temporary emigration: the Albanian experience, *Economics of Transition*, 4(2): 471–90.

Rogers, A. (2000) A European space for transnationalism?, *Transnational Communities Programme Working Paper Series*, WPTC-2K-07. *ESRC* Transnational Communities Programme, Institute of Social and Cultural Anthropology, University of Oxford.

Swanson, J. C. (1979) The consequences of emigration for economic development: a review of the literature, *Papers in Anthropology*, 20(1): 39–55.

Wiest, R. (1979) Anthropological perspectives on return migration: a critical commentary, *Papers in Anthropology*, 20(1): 167–87.

5

Albanian migrants' remittances

A development opportunity?

FLAVIA PIPERNO

The objective of this chapter is to analyse the main constraints and opportunities for the valorisation of remittances in Albania. The chapter is part of a study on possible strategies for the use of remittances as a vector of local development in emigration countries.[1] This issue is seen as particularly relevant since, in recent years, the savings sent by migrants to developing countries have become a very important economic resource, contributing in many cases one of the main sources of financial revenue at the national level. In this context a crucial strategic role could be played by policies aimed on the one hand at channelling remittances through formal structures in the immigration countries, and on the other hand at promoting saving and investment in the countries of migrant origin. Such policies therefore target three core areas:

- the stimulation of saving by emigrants;
- the channelling of remittances through formal structures and their deposit in the countries of origin; and
- the facilitation of productive investment by emigrants in the countries of origin.

These measures are part of a double-level policy. In the migrant receiving countries a key objective is the re-orientation of money transfer flows from informal to formal channels. In the migrant countries of origin, a crucial issue is the setting-up or consolidation of centres for the collection of remittances (such as specialised savings and credit institutions); such remittance facilities should be able to increase their financial volume and direct them at the same time (through adequate incentives) towards socially productive investments with a multiplier potential for employment and local economic development (Falchi 1995). The effectiveness of these policies is obviously linked to the existence – in the countries of migrant origin – of financial structures (not necessarily banks) which can act as intermediaries in orienting credit towards productive purposes. Other important pre-conditions include the presence of dynamic entrepreneurs at the local level and the existence of a conducive economic environment (adequate basic infrastructure, good level of access to local markets, local supply and marketing capacity, and an effective regulatory system).

My research in this chapter aims to verify whether, in the specific Albanian context, a policy of profitably using remittances can be successfully pursued or, on the contrary, the minimal pre-conditions for the undertaking of such initiatives are lacking. The fact that Albania is often defined, within the policy debate, as the 'worst case' as far as the feasibility of such policies is concerned, is quite telling about the importance of this preliminary stage of the analysis. So, on the one hand, one can note that remittance flows to Albania have been increasing at a high rate during recent years (table 5.1). In 2001 emigrants' remittances ($620m) corresponded to approximately one seventh of the country's gross domestic product (GDP), and in 1999 was twice as large as foreign exchange revenues from exports, almost four times as large as the value of direct investments, and approximately 60 per cent larger then the revenue generated by industrial production (UNDP 2000: 43). But on the other hand, the weakness of the financial system and the very low productive capacity result in the almost exclusive use of remittances for the purchase of imported goods, lessening thereby the potentially positive impact of remittances on the local economic system.

Table 5.1 Remittance flows to Albania, 1992–2001

Year	Total remittances ($million)	As % GDP	As % comparison with exports	Total remittances per capita ($)
1992	150	—	—	47
1993	274	22.3	224.5	86
1994	377	19.4	267.4	118
1995	384	15.5	190.7	118
1996	499	18.6	237.3	152
1997	266	11.6	188.8	80
1998	452	14.8	219.0	134
1999	368	10.0	133.6	109
2000	530	14.3	205.4	170
2001	620	15.2	203.2	200

Source: Albanian Central Bank.

In the following my analysis will focus on the main obstacles to a policy aimed at the valorisation of remittances in Albania, but will also try to point at some elements that, despite all the difficulties, could make a case for some pilot attempts in this domain. My approach will concentrate on three aspects:

- constraints and opportunities related to the Albanian financial system;
- constraints and opportunities associated with the involvement of the Italian financial system in policies for the valorisation of remittances in Albania;
- opportunities related to some specific features of the socio-economic behaviour of Albanian workers in Italy.

The account is based on a body of evidence derived partly from secondary sources, but more particularly from 46 interviews with key informants. Four categories of persons were interviewed:

- directors and officials of financial institutions in Tirana (n=8);
- directors and officials of financial institutions in Rome (n=11);
- directors and officials of research centres and NGOs in Albania and Italy (n=12);
- leaders and representatives of Albanian community organisations in Rome, Milan and Turin (n=15).

Constraints and opportunities of the Albanian financial system

The traditional banking system

Notwithstanding some recent improvement in macro-economic indicators (growth of GDP, low inflation, decreasing unemployment, declining deficit, etc.), Albania still possesses a backward financial structure. The persistence of a wide 'grey area' in banks' corporate governance, management, credit practices, linkages to enterprises and government financing, entails inefficiencies and structural weaknesses in the banking sector. Moreover, banking authorities often lack the expertise, independence and sometimes even the enforcement ability to adequately perform the surveillance functions entrusted to them. The capital market is weak.

Following the crisis of the pyramid schemes in 1997, the Albanian authorities have adopted measures to strengthen the financial sector and to enhance the role of the private sector in the banking system. The operations of the smallest of the three state-owned banks, the Rural Commercial Bank, were suspended at the end of 1997 and the bank was liquidated in 1998. The process of privatisation of the second largest bank, the National Commercial Bank, was completed in 2000, and it is still underway as far as the third state-owned bank – the Savings Bank – is concerned. As of the end of 2001 the banking system consisted of 13 commercial banks, three of which were foreign banks' branches. In 11 banks private foreign shareholders held a majority stake. According to the Economist Intelligence Unit, the share of Albanian banking assets held by foreign entities rose from 60 per cent in 1999 to 84 per cent in 2001, whereas the state-owned banks' share dropped from 38 to 13 per cent (Economist Intelligence Unit 2002: 33–4).

Due to the weak legal infrastructure and to the instability of the productive system, loan policies are very risky and underdeveloped. These limits make capital trading negligible and limited to treasury bills and government bonds. The Savings Bank has invested disproportionately in government bonds; having also being subject to strict limits imposed on lending, it has not performed an effective financial intermediation role towards the private sector. On the other hand private banks have so far shown little propensity to extend credit to the private sector, largely focusing on trade financing and fee-generating activities. In fact, the credit provided by the banking system to the private sector was the smallest of all the South-East European countries, representing only 4.6 per cent of Albanian GDP.[2]

My interview with the officer of the Bank of Italy in charge of a study on the Albanian financial context brought into evidence the vicious circle between the lack of a credit policy and the small concern of commercial banks in fostering deposits. The banks' reduced commitment to loan policies make them minimally interested in attracting savings and consequently in channelling remittances: additional funds could not be profitably invested and would entail at the same time high management costs. Within such a context, a policy of capitalising on remittances is regarded as decidedly premature.

Such a picture was confirmed by the bank officials interviewed in Tirana (Tirana Bank, Fefad Bank, Italian-Albanian Institute, Central Bank of Albania). In absolute terms, banks appeared not to be interested in a policy of stimulating credit and savings, nor in strategies aimed at capturing part of the remittances market. The interest rates and repayment terms are deeply unattractive.

Albanian banks can channel emigrant workers' remittances through the intermediation of 'correspondent banking institutes' in the host countries. The emigrant who wants to send money home can do it from any institute in the host country by specifying the corresponding institute to the Albanian bank where he wants to put his money, but this is quite a complex system involving relatively high transaction costs. As a result, immigrants prefer to resort to the Italian-Albanian Institute, the only Italian banking institution active in Albania, which offers simpler transaction mechanisms but operates exclusively through its Tirana office.[3] This causes the beneficiaries of the remittances to be tied to the capital city, even if many Albanian banks have opened branches in some provincial towns.

In spite of these conditions, the banks' officials do not perceive the situation as problematic. The complexity of the remittances market discourages banks from spreading their local presence both in Albania and in the destination countries, as well as from signing agreements with foreign financial institutes or development actors to increase the remittance flow passing through their structure.

Given such a context, it is interesting to note that even the official of the Fefad bank, one of the few institutes offering credit services to micro- and medium-sized enterprises, declared that the institute he represents is 'on the edge of its possibilities' and for this reason is not interested in setting up collaboration agreements with foreign actors since it is unable to manage new financial inflows.

The difficulty of the traditional banking system to act as a vector for a more productive and effective use of remittances clearly emerges from all these considerations. A partially different scenario is pictured, on the other hand, by officials of some non-banking organisations which have been developing, over recent years, micro-credit and savings services.

The micro-credit sector

Since 1994 the micro-credit sector has developed in Albania as an alternative to the weakness of the traditional commercial approach to credit, both in rural and in urban areas. Even if micro-credit is still not completely self-sustainable, it has proven to be effective in serving clients that are too small or without sufficient collateral for commercial banks.

At present the three major institutions managing micro-credit in Albania are: the MAFF (Mountain Areas Finance Fund), set up by the International Fund for Agricultural Development (IFAD), which controls micro-credit organisations (Villages Credit Fund – VCF) in 64 mountain villages along the eastern Albanian border; the RFF (Rural Finance Fund), set up by the World Bank, which manages savings and credit associations (SCAs) in eight rural districts in Central Albania; and the Besa Foundation – also set up by World Bank – which covers eight urban areas (Tirana, Vlorë, Durrës, Shkodër, Pukë, Berat, Elbasan, Kavajë). VCF and SCAs finance chiefly the agricultural and trade sectors, while the Besa Foundation financing is mainly addressed towards trade and services and, to a limited extent, manufacture. The average per capita loans amount to $1,100 for SCAs, $900 for VCF, and $3,000 for the Besa Foundation. By way of comparison, it is worth noting that the Fefad Bank, which is one of the few commercial banks granting loans to small enterprises, offers $6,430 per capita average credit.

In this respect, it is also relevant to mention the success of two other micro-credit projects: the first is run by PSHM (*Partneri shqiptar ne mikrokredi*), an organisation founded on USAID financing, and the second by the DSCAMF (Development of Savings and Credit Association Movement Foundation), with funding from the Irish League. PSHM manages a portfolio of $2.4 million and has 1,800 members; in the last three years it issued 5,000 loans corresponding to a per capita average of $1,402. DSCAMF manages 40 SCAs and involves 2,912 members, 220 of whom have loans outstanding. The total savings amount to $219,000 and the total outstanding loans to $167,000; the average amount of per capita loans is between $500 and $1,000.[4]

Overall, as of July 2001, active micro-credit clients numbered around 10,540, 89 per cent of whom were based in rural and mountain areas of Albania.[5]

During the interviews, the officials of the cooperation agencies operating in micro-credit activities affirmed that their organisations, although not completely self-sustainable, present good levels of stability and are strongly rooted into Albania. The solid sense of ownership developed by micro-credit members is probably one of the factors behind the very high credit return rate (around 99 per cent in the World Bank and DSCAMF programmes and about 95 per cent for PSHM).

The experience of micro-credit and micro-finance in Albania could demonstrate important lessons for the hypothetical productive use of remittances. As revealed in a study by the NGO PRODEM[6] – which operates in Bolivia with micro-credit projects – the micro-finance institutions (MFIs) are particularly effective in providing money transfer services because they are distributed in areas where commercial banks do not have a presence; in other words they can reach people who otherwise would not have access to banking services. Furthermore, they are closer to their markets, know the communities they serve and interact with local residents, who feel at ease working with them. These factors are particularly relevant for the reason that – at least according to PRODEM experience – each region has its own peculiarities and idiosyncrasies; hence the promotion of the financial products and services must be done locally, in the same town where the branch is. Secondly, the closeness with the community residents offers the possibility to set up a relationship of security and trust with the clients. Finally, MFIs tend to be more socially-oriented and usually search for customer loyalty and social impact. They work with micro-entrepreneurs and small farmers, a segment of Albanian society that has strong links to migrant workers.

The officials of the organisations dealing with micro-credit in Albania whom I interviewed declared that so far they had not carried out any policies aimed at productively channelling remittances (for example through agreements with financial associations in the immigration countries), but that they would be very interested in the issue. In their opinion, gathering enough funds to maintain micro-credit activity is key to the sustainability of the organisations they set up, and in this sense a strategy oriented to attract remittance flows could constitute a tool for ensuring their self-preservation. Furthermore it could constitute a means to attract new clients and enlarge the micro-finance field of competence. According to one interviewee, the desk officer for Albania at IFAD, at a first stage remittances should be collected in the savings bank and from there branched out towards the single micro-credit associations. This process is likely to need a 7–15 days period. In this informant's opinion, the formalisation of saving remittances should constitute one of the core elements to be pursued. At the moment, remittance recipients are inclined to spend the money received on consumption, or save it outside official channels; they should be stimulated to deposit it into formal structures and the micro-credit associations could cope with this issue by offering such a service within 'unbanked' areas at an interest rate not above the official one (around 4 per cent).

The Italian banking system and policies aimed at the utilisation of remittances in Albania

The traditional banking system

A policy aimed at the productive utilisation of remittances in Albania is strictly related to the existence, in the destination country, of appropriate structures for collecting and transferring emigrants' savings through formal channels. For this reason part of the research was carried out in Italy through interviews with officers in the banking sector (Monte dei Paschi di Siena, Banca Italo-Albanese, Banca di Roma, Associazione Bancaria Italiana, Banca d'Italia, Banca Nazionale del Lavoro).

The flow of remittances from Italy towards developing countries has been growing at a fast pace over recent years: in 1998, for the first time, outgoing remittances exceeded incoming remittances. In 2001 the remittance outflow reached 749 million euros, recording a 27.4 per cent increase over the previous year. During the same year per capita remittances grew by 30 per cent passing from 424 euros in 2000 to 550 in 2001 (Caritas 2002: 318). According to Caritas the big expansion of remittance flows during 2000–1 was unexpected because it did not correspond to an increase in the stock of immigrants in Italy, which remained unchanged at around 1.4 million (documented immigrants). The explanation therefore has to do with the increase of immigrants' savings capability (Caritas 2002: 78). Remittance flows from Italy to Albania have also grown steadily through the 1990s (except 1997), reflecting to some extent growing confidence in the home country.

And yet, the Italian banking system reveals its backwardness as far as the implementation of policies specifically addressed to immigrant clients is concerned. Two studies, sponsored by the Lunaria association (Mazzonis and Naletto 2000) and the Giordano dell'Amore foundation (Libanora 2002) demonstrate the weakness in this field, even if a number of institutes (Banca Popolare di Milano, Banco Ambrosiano Veneto, Banca Toscana,

Credito Cooperativo di Roma, Monte dei Paschi di Siena, Banca Nazionale del Lavoro) have recently set up some ad-hoc services in this respect. According to Libanora (2002), in 1999 about 1.25 million (many of them full-time employed) out of a total of 1.7m foreigners (both 'legal' and undocumented) were 'unbanked'. Among documented immigrants only one third had access to the banking system. Udo Enwereuzor (2000: 419–50) shows that Italian banks are not usually inclined to focus their services on immigrant clients because:

- immigrants are mainly precarious workers,
- their transactions have low value and high management costs, and
- the media have created a widely negative image of them.

From the immigrants' perspective the relation with the banking system is made difficult by language-related obstacles (the application forms are normally written in Italian) and the excessive amount of papers to be presented in order to open a current account (usually identity card, permit to stay, and the national insurance/fiscal code number are required; often certificate of residence, pay-sheet, income declaration and guarantees by Italian or foreign citizens are also needed – see Libanora 2002). Moreover, immigrants are disinclined to send money through the banking system because the official exchange rate is normally less favourable than the one they get through informal transactions, and also because those who are supposed to receive the money rarely have access to the local banking system.

However, it must be noted that the above-mentioned constraints are not the main ones. The interviews carried out by the Libanora (2002) study with 90 unbanked immigrants revealed that the key problem is their perception of banks as 'alien entities'. Immigrants do not really 'know' banks, nor do they really need them. This focus on 'distance' in the mutual perception of immigrants and banks is important because it indirectly brings to the fore the importance of migrants' communities and associations as possible vehicles of a more fruitful relation. Better organised communities can play a key role by:

- informing migrants about the local banking system and thereby building a stronger relationship and reciprocal trust between community members and banks;
- lobbying individual banks to make immigrants' needs clear and hence to promote the provision of appropriate services.

According to an interview with an official of the Monte dei Paschi di Siena, immigrant clients should be served by specific agencies at the national level. These agencies should offer specialised ad hoc services and involve migrant communities' representatives and officials from foreign banks. According to the experience of the Monte dei Paschi di Siena, the usual marketing campaigns have, in fact, a low impact on the immigrant population. Promotional campaigns should better integrate the local community leaders; obviously, from this point of view, better organised communities are favoured. At present, the Monte dei Paschi di Siena is preparing for instance a specific service package as a result of pressure exerted by the Senegalese community. Another interesting example is provided by the Philippine community, which collects the members' remittances in a single fund and sends the capital home through a common current account opened at the Banca Nazionale del Lavoro. This contributes to simplifying the practices (both for immigrants and the bank) and lowering transaction costs.

Italian banks' views of Albanians as clients

Albanian clients present, from the standpoint of traditional banking institutes, specific problems. My interviews with bank officials and with Albanian community members in Italy brought to light three core elements that make banks disinclined to create ad hoc services for them.

- **The fragmentary nature of the Albanian community**

Interviews carried out in Rome, Milan and Turin with Albanian migrant representatives clearly revealed one of the fundamental characteristics of the Albanian presence in Italy – its highly fragmented nature. Albanians associate with each other in small groups, many of them family-based, and do not club together in big associations with recognised leaders. Fixed meeting-points do not exist, as they do for other migrant nationalities. The fragmentation of the Albanian community is a constraint on the circulation of information and, as said, it can constitute an obstacle to the establishment of a smooth relationship between immigrants and banks. It is significant to note that some interviewees did not even know that banks offered money transfer services.

- **The tendency to resort to informal channels for sending remittances home**

Albanians do not organise themselves in order to send remittances, as some other immigrant groups do; they prefer to use the intermediation of relatives or close friends who happen to be travelling back home to take cash instead. This almost exclusive use of informal channels by Albanians is borne out not only by my own small sample of interviewees but also by somewhat larger-scale studies. For instance, a recent comparative study of Albanians (n=145), Moroccans (105) and Tunisians (80) showed that 90 per cent of Albanians sent money home via friends and relatives, but only 20 per cent of the Moroccans and 10 per cent of the Tunisians (Barsotti and Moretti 2004). Analogous results were found by an even larger survey (n=1700) of immigrants of various nationalities carried out by Natale and

Strozza (2003) – the results are set out in table 5.2. Where personalised channels are not available, Albanians tend to prefer the services of specialised agencies such as Western Union, which charge high commissions but are fast and effective.[7]

Table 5.2 Remittance channels by nationality (per cent)

Channel	Albania	FR Yugoslavia	Poland	Morocco
Postal order	11.1	19.0	20.5	58.3
By banks	10.1	6.3	7.6	3.8
Relatives and compatriots	61.6	31.6	43.8	14.9
Personally	17.2	31.6	20.5	20.9
Other channels	0.0	11.4	7.6	2.1

Source: Natale and Strozza (2003).

- **The weakness of the financial and productive environment in the country of origin**

The extreme weakness of the financial and productive environment in Albania – even more the perception of such weakness – constitutes a third inhibiting factor for Italian banks to invest in the country. The opinions expressed by the interviewees can be summarised in three points. First of all, poor reliability: investments in Albania are judged to be risky because of the high rate of non-performing loans and the danger of money loss or diversion. Secondly, security: banks are worried about possible money recycling and about the general weakness of the regulatory framework in Albania and the weak enforcement capacity of the juridical structure. Finally, the backwardness of the productive sector and the weak development of trade links with Italy make Italian banks unenthusiastic about investing in Albania, for example by setting up new branches.

The ethical finance circuit: a possible opportunity?

In Italy, as in Albania, the financial frame is made more complex by the presence of ethical finance institutions (Banca Etica, Banche di Credito Cooperativo, Mag 2) aimed at reaching sectors of the population which are traditionally excluded from financial service provision. As a matter of fact, immigrants constitute an important part of ethical institutions' range of clients and various ad hoc pilot projects have been set up in answer to specific requests. These projects are based on the idea of offering services with especially favourable conditions to non-EU nationals living and working with regular permits in Italy. Such services include the opening of current accounts, loans for buying a first dwelling, personal credit and the purchase of insurance products. Some organisations have also offered reduced rates for travelling back home, free use of the Internet, renting flats at controlled prices, and the professional training of young people. In order to facilitate sending savings back home agreements have been made with Western Union and with individual current accounts to channel the remittances sent home at a lower than average cost.

These examples show how ethical finance banks can become potentially very important actors within the framework of strategies aimed at providing value to savings sent home, not only showing their sensitivity to social needs arising within the local area, but also their concern for the needs of immigrant clients. Even more interesting is the close relations which these banks have with the countries of origin of the immigrants, and especially the support they provide to the micro-finance associations operating locally. The importance of a network of this kind becomes obvious if we think – as was said before – of the decisive role which MFIs can play in developing countries.

As an example, Banca Etica supports micro-credit in developing countries, generally with support from Etimos, an organisation whose goal is to facilitate the channelling of funds towards micro-finance organisations. With funding by the regional governments of Tuscany and Emilia Romagna, for example, Banca Etica and Etimos have granted PSHM in Albania a sum of $20,000. The project – completed in May 2002 – has made it possible to grant 314 loans, for an average value of $1,294 and an average duration of 12 months. This project is supposed to be launched again through a fund (also amounting to $20,000) which the regional governments of Tuscany and Emilia Romagna will make available to PSHM as a guarantee fund. Thanks to this fund, 150 new small entrepreneurs will be able to have access to credit if assessed favourably. In this project, each entrepreneur must pay a share into the guarantee fund; also, for each dollar provided by co-operation, PSHM will allocate three for the loan. Questions remain, however, about the effectiveness of the size of the loan. Even in Albania, there is a limited amount an entrepreneur can do with $1,000 or $1,500.

The majority of measures taken to favour micro-credit are funded by ethical banks through savings deposits and the establishment of special guarantee funds. The policies adopted thus far generally use the savings of Italian clients; however, a careful study should identify interesting opportunities for strategies aimed at attracting, channelling and capitalising on immigrants' savings.

The officers of Banca Etica, of Credito Cooperativo and of Mag 2 who were interviewed believe that the institutions that they represent could pursue policies aimed at channelling immigrants' savings towards investment in their country of origin. Immigrants could for example be helped to set up businesses which could be managed by relatives in the country of origin. Ethical financial institutions could assist by evaluating the project, providing personal credit or setting themselves up as guarantors. A strategy of this kind could be associated with the migratory project of people who do not intend to go back home, but who would be willing to invest part of their savings in their country of origin. A different way of implementing the same strategy – as envisaged by the representative of Banca Etica – could involve the immigrants themselves as guarantors of the investments of their relatives who have stayed in the country of origin. The credit for the investment could be provided by local micro-credit institutions networking with ethical finance institutions in Italy. Measures of this kind would have the multiplying effect mentioned before, but would also have the advantage of respecting the idea of making the recipients of the loans take on responsibility. It would be the recipients of the credit – and not their emigrant relatives – who would pay back the debt they themselves contracted. Also, policies of this kind could easily be adopted by ethical finance institutions, since they would make it possible to keep the resources within the territory covered by such institutions, and would make use of a range of practices which have been fully tested.

The Albanian community in Italy: some opportunities

Analysing the opportunities implicit in the remittance flows from Italy to Albania also entails taking into account some key features of the Albanian community in Italy. The degree of immigrants' integration in the receiving country, their relation with banks and financial institutes, their linkages with the homeland and their propensity to invest there, are all factors which affect, in various ways, the size and characteristics of the remittance flow. The ensuing analysis, the result of qualitative interviews with key members of the Albanian community in Rome, Turin and Milan, will deal with these factors.

Aspects of the economic behaviour of Albanian immigrants in Italy

During the last ten years, Albanians have received much more than their fair share of coverage in the representation of the Italian media. Their image has been remorselessly and negatively associated with criminality and moral decay (Mai 2002). They are regarded as particularly unreliable, precarious and marginalised within the Italian society and this is one of the reasons behind the mistrust accorded to them by many banking institutions. A quite different picture emerges from the analysis of some figures that show how, after around a decade, the Albanian community appears to be increasingly rooted into the Italian social and the economic context (Piperno 2002). There has been a gradual ageing of the first generation of emigrants and no large-scale flows of emigrants returning to Albania. Many Albanians have achieved a progressively favourable inclusion in the Italian labour market and have settled in the host country with their families.

Several simple statistical indicators attest to this generally positive and progressively improving integration. On the labour market, Albanians' entries into employment have been at a higher rate than all the other major immigrant nationalities (Caritas 2002: 256). Albanians have a higher rate of family reunion than other immigrant groups (Caritas 2002: 78), and the number of Albanian children enrolled in the Italian school system is both higher than any other group, and the number is growing twice as fast as the overall total of immigrant children in Italian schools (Bonifazi and Sabatino 2003). Whilst Albanians rank second overall, after Moroccans, in the size of their 'community' in Italy (144,120 against 158,094, as of 31 December 2001), Albanian women outnumber Moroccan women (and all other nationalities) since 2000 (Caritas 2002: 98).

As far as remittances are concerned there is evidence that Albanians tend to send home large amounts of money (this tendency does not come out of official figures because of the widespread use of informal channels). In the research carried out by Natale and Strozza (2003), 65 per cent of the Albanian workers who managed to save a share of the income earned sent money home. The corresponding figures for workers from ex-Yugoslavia, Morocco and Poland were 55, 64 and 59 per cent respectively. Albanians also sent back, on average, higher levels of remittances than the comparator groups – an annual average of 2,852 euros, as against 2,762, 2,291 and 2,262 respectively for Poles, Moroccans and former-Yugoslavs (Natale and Strozza 2003: 338).

From this evidence it emerges that the majority of Albanians in Italy are not short-term immigrants but citizens who are stably settled in the host country. Many of them work, receive a regular wage, need to save and invest in Italy, and remit quite large sums of money to Albania. They consequently need access to the banking system and could be good clients for the banks. As a matter of fact, many Albanians send remittances through informal channels out of need and not by choice: the high costs involved in the 'official' process, the unfavourable exchange rate, the excessive length of the transactions, the minimal presence of banks in the Albanian provinces and finally uncertainty about the successful outcome of the process, have all hampered the migrants' resort to formal channels for sending remittances. Moreover, the crisis of the pyramid schemes in 1997, which in a few days wiped out the savings of hundreds of thousands of people (most of the savings deriving from remittances), the backwardness of the Albanian financial system and the ongoing process of bank privatisation constitute further reasons for continuing mistrust in the Albanian banking system.

Notwithstanding these difficulties and the apparent simplicity of taking money to Albania by hand (due to the geographical closeness between Italy and Albania), many immigrants are willing to use the formal channel for remitting their savings. Actually, taking money by hand is highly risky. First, there is the possibility that the money might be stolen, or confiscated at the border stations. Moreover there is a question of privacy: people would prefer not to bother their fellow-countrymen who happen to be going back, and at the same time they would prefer not to let them know the amount of their remittances. One key informant who is a keen observer of Albanian migrant society, pointed out how immigrants are often unable to resort to friends and relatives for sending money home because they no longer have close relations in the receiving country, or because there are quite long periods in which nobody happens to go back. Finally it is worth noting that many immigrants also need to utilise the official remittance channels because the migration law requires the receipts of such transactions as a formal precondition for the issuing of family reunion permissions.

As a result, policies aimed at channelling remittances through formal channels would respond to a real and grass-rooted requirement and would also meet with an open market as many Albanians would prefer not to resort to the money transfer agencies because of the high transaction fees charged. The lack of habit of resorting to official channels, the mistrust of the local banking system and the general lack of knowledge about microfinancing institutions in the country of origin are offset by the real need of sending money through official channels and could consequently be partially overcome by a good information campaign. Moreover, policies aimed at transferring remittances through official channels could interplay with, and be enforced by, practices encouraging the use of remittances for productive investments.

As a matter of fact, over the last few years the 'post-pyramids' Albanian economic revival has created new investment opportunities. All the immigrants interviewed declared that more and more Albanians are investing in the construction industry (and in its related activities), in trade (often between Italy and Albania), in agriculture and in the services sector; the manufacturing sector remains less developed.[8] Many investments are promoted by remittance recipients or by emigrants who entrust their relatives with the management of the activity. Also important is the dynamic interaction between investing remittances and savings and the process of return migration analysed by Labrianidis and Hatziprokopiou in the previous chapter.

During my own interviews, a widespread agreement was found in favour of supporting policies aimed at supporting the productive investment of migrants' savings in Albania. When I asked the immigrants how policies aimed at levering remittances from Italy towards local investment in Albania could cope with the persisting mistrust in the banking system, I was told that the strong interest in investing and saving money was already leading many Albanians to overcome such resistance. Policies aimed at orienting remittances towards investment in Albania could be based on credit incentives offered by Italian financial institutions, matching-funds issued by development actors or guarantee systems set up by ethical finance institutes possibly networking with local MFIs. The immigrants interviewed also declared that most of their fellow-Albanians are able to save money and would be interested in some sort of financial incentive that would help them increase their capital. Higher interest rates, for instance, would persuade many Albanians to deposit their money in formal financial institutes (also in Albania). This consideration seems to be confirmed by recent research carried out by Uruçi and Gedeshi (2002) on a small sample of 48 Albanian recipients of remittances. Also the survey carried out by Natale and Strozza (2003) found a relatively high propensity of Albanians to save remittances compared to selected other nationalities (table 5.3). Finally, according to estimates by the Central Bank of Albania, between 2000 and 2001 the level of deposits at a national scale rose by 20 per cent.

Table 5.3 Utilisation of migrants' remittances (per cent)

Category of use	Albania	FR Yugoslavia	Poland	Morocco	All countries
Short-term consumer goods	36.0	49.0	34.1	41.8	39.3
Long-term consumer goods	4.3	8.9	4.5	10.8	7.7
Housing	10.8	8.3	15.7	4.9	10.1
Savings	26.3	12.7	21.8	19.4	20.1
Education	8.6	11.5	14.5	8.8	10.6
Other	14.0	9.6	9.4	14.3	12.1

Source: Natale and Strozza (2003).

Aspects of the social behaviour of Albanian immigrants in Italy

Immigrants' propensity to send and productively deploy remittances can be heavily affected by their social behaviour patterns in the host country: for example, their degree of social organisation, their migratory plans and linkages with the homeland. In other migration contexts, the existence of immigrants' hometown associations in the host country has been shown to be crucial in the process of successful remittance utilisation. This is due to a number of reasons, such as the capacity of associations to promote banking services among their members and to lobby individual banks in order to get better conditions for remittance payments. Furthermore, immigrants' associations can act as promoters of local development in the home county by collecting voluntary donations among their members to finance social investment projects, for example small-scale infrastructure (roads, water and sanitation systems, health clinics, schools and churches).

In this regard, the fragmentary nature of the Albanian 'community' in Italy, noted above, is certainly a constraint. As the InteMiGra report[9] reveals, Albanians show a trend towards assimilation in the recipient country: they resort to Italian friends in order to get help and information to a much greater extent than the average; but on the contrary they demonstrate a weak propensity to organise themselves as a collective with specific requirements (they resort to home-town associations and to their conationals less than the average). Table 5.4 sets out a selection of data to highlight the unusual pattern of Albanian responses to the InteMiGra survey. Consequently they are not able to lobby Italian and Albanian institutions to achieve specific objectives. This pattern means that any strategy aimed at channelling and valorising remittances, even if it would be welcomed by the Albanian migrants themselves, must be promoted by an external agent such as a development cooperation or ethical finance organisation. The support of NGOs working in the field and able to be trusted by immigrants can be critical.

Table 5.4 Immigrants' strategies to resolve problems: comparisons by nationality (per cent)

	Albanians (n=406)	Former Yugoslavians (n=118)	Other East Europeans (n=150)	North Africans (n=223)	Sub-Saharan Africans (n=149)
Relatives	19.5	15.3	14.7	7.6	10.7
Conational friends	23.2	19.5	24.7	21.5	30.2
Italian friends	23.4	12.7	10.0	13.0	12.8
Italian voluntary sector	10.1	6.8	16.7	11.2	7.4
Conational assocation	2.0	0.8	0.0	8.1	6.7
Cooperatives	5.4	0.8	0.7	3.1	1.3
Public welfare services	8.4	14.4	8.0	13.5	12.1
Trade unions	1.2	5.1	2.0	7.2	4.7
Other	6.8	24.6	23.2	14.8	14.1

Source: Carchedi (2002).

Another important aspect that deserves attention is the close link between Albanian immigrants and their homeland, facilitated by the proximity between the two countries. This contributes to strengthening and stabilising the remittance flow and favours the consolidation of a trans-Adriatic social network that could trigger and channel local investment projects.

Research has shown that usually at the beginning of the migratory experience, the economic precariousness of migrants and the related difficulties in saving money severely limit remittance flows. At a second stage migrants, by now more integrated into the labour market, are able to send home a larger share of their earnings. Finally, at a third stage migrants are often joined by their families, and they try to settle down and upgrade their standard of living: this is likely to weaken the connection with the homeland and to reduce their inclination to send remittances home. In my opinion, this sociological model only partially explains the Albanian migratory pattern. In spite of the trend towards stable settlement, the Albanians whom I interviewed declared that they maintain strong ties to their homeland and send money to members of their family still in Albania even if they have their partner and children in the host country. On average, they go back once or twice a year. Often the older immigrants who are no longer able to work adopt a transnational migratory pattern spending long periods of the year in the homeland. Research by Barsotti and Moretti (2004) reveals that, compared to Moroccans and Tunisians, Albanians spend holidays in the sending country more frequently: 88 per cent spend vacations at home (cf. 87 per cent for Tunisians, 51 per cent for Moroccans).

Some suggestions

It is generally accepted that appropriate policies can encourage the deployment of remittances for longer-term growth and income security in labour-sending countries. In theory this should work in three ways:

- by redirecting remittances towards official channels;
- by encouraging migrants to hold savings in financial assets in the labour-exporting country in the shape of deposits or insurance products;
- by facilitating investment by migrants or their relatives in the country of origin.

The last part of my analysis is dedicated to pointing out some measures that can be taken in these three domains.

Redirecting remittances towards official channels

Shivani Puri and Tineke Ritzema (1999) note in a study commissioned by the International Labour Office:

> It is difficult to convert successful migrant workers/savers with no prior business experiences into dynamic entrepreneurs. It could be argued that it is more realistic to introduce financial intermediaries that capture migrant remittances as deposits and channel them to existing small and micro-business, rather than transforming migrants directly into entrepreneurs. In other words, rather than focussing on migrant-specific investment programmes, labour-exporting countries might wish to induce micro-finance institutions to capture remittances. The basic idea would be to design policies to transfer funds of the migrant workers through MFIs (micro-financing institutions) to entrepreneurs.

In this regard, networks linking financial institutes in Italy and MFIs in Albania dedicated to channelling remittances, for example through common current accounts, could constitute a first and simpler step in the process of remittance valorisation and could turn out to be a tool for indirectly financing local investments. Moreover ethical finance institutes could allocate part of the immigrants' savings to specific micro-finance institutions by using a range of practices which have already been tried out; for instance they could give the Albanian immigrants the possibility of opening a current account or undersigning special deposit certificates, the funds from which could be allocated to specific Albanian MFIs.

Another strategy could be to set up partnerships between development actors dealing with micro-finance in Albania and money transfer companies such as Western Union and Money Gram. Worldwide, Western Union and Money Gram channel about half of remittance flows. For migrant workers the use of a formal money transfer company represents a safe way to transfer funds in less than 30 minutes to their home town without legal restraints. The process is very simple and the client is not required to present personal documentation at the initiation of the process. The wide distribution system is another advantage that these companies offer – Western Union, for instance, has 85,000 outlets around the world.

Encouraging migrants to hold savings in financial assets in the labour-exporting country

The formalisation of remittances and their transformation into productive savings could constitute one of the core elements to be pursued by MFIs. The objective is to give the migrant workers (and their families in Albania) the possibility to have a savings account (also in areas not covered by the traditional commercial banks) where they can save their money and obtain satisfactory interest rates in return. As an example, MFIs managed by PRODEM in Bolivia are dealing with this issue, encouraging the recipients of the remittances to open a saving account that presents attractive conditions and allows them to access loans. Clients receive a 6.5 per cent annual interest on their money and the MFIs raise funds relatively cheaply and are consequently able to offer lower-priced loans to the benefit of local economies. Migrant workers' savings can also be managed in a manner resembling that of pension funds or insurance products.

Facilitating the investment by migrants or their relatives living in the country of origin

Financial institutes in Italy and development actors could pursue policies aimed at channelling immigrants' savings towards self-employment or businesses to be managed by relatives staying in the sending country. In the latter case, the strategy would take on board the migratory project of people not inclined to return but willing to invest part of their savings in the homeland. If the investment project is favourably valued, the ethical financial institutes could provide personal or collective loans or set themselves up as guarantors. A different way of implementing the same strategy could involve the immigrants themselves as guarantors of the investments, while the credit could be provided by local micro-credit institutions networking with the ethical finance bodies in Italy. The mediation of NGOs working in the field and able to be trusted by immigrants could also be critical for the sustainability of such policies.

Conclusion

Strategies to capitalise on migrants' remittances and their productive utilisation in Albania have to tackle several constraints but can also take advantage of some opportunities. Among the limitations related to the Albanian context, the weakness of the financial system is a key factor, and this also reflects the lack of any structured and consistent set of measures to provide financial support to the private sector (above all credit systems). The bank officials whom I interviewed in Albania did not show much interest in engaging with the remittances market, nor to establish cooperation agreements with Italian banking institutions or international aid actors, nor even to expand their activities across Albania and to Italy.

Among the constraints on the Italian side, the key issues are the weak (or in any case late) commitment of banking institutes to develop policies focused on the immigrant population, and in particular, their perceptions and difficulties in involving Albanians as potential clients. At the basis of this specific constraint is the unusually fragmented nature of the Albanian community in Italy, the widespread use of the informal channel for remittance transfers among its members, and (as noted above) the extreme weakness of the recipient financial system.

On the other hand, the less traditional finance organisations appear to be interested in devising strategies and mechanisms for channelling and valorising remittances. Attracting remittance flows, actually, could be to the advantage both of the micro-finance organisations in Albania and of the ethical finance institutes in Italy; the former could find in it a tool to make their credit activities more sustainable, and the latter could promote local development, at the same time attracting new clients.

Moreover, some specific features of the socio-economic behaviour of Albanian immigrants in Italy constitute points of potential strength. Albanians are increasingly stably rooted in Italian society and send home relatively large amounts of remittances. There is a need to guide and redirect remittances through official channels but several constraints relating to the guarantee of a secure, speedy and low-cost service to all parts of the Albanian territory must be overcome. There is the availability to save and invest in Albania and a relative propensity to 'respond' to financial incentives. Notwithstanding the well-advanced integration and settlement process, strong relations bind Albanians to their homeland; the existence of strong migratory chains make these linkages stronger, and many groups are available to collect funds for financing development projects in the villages of origin. Single members of the Albanian community present themselves as potential key actors in the development and promotion of initiatives in this field.

All these elements, that surely deserve further investigation, can make up important starting-points for pilot policy attempts in this area.

Notes

1 This is the 'Migraction' research project, carried out by CeSPI (Centro Studi di Politica Internazionale) based on funding from the Italian Ministry of Foreign Affairs. The objective of Migraction is to analyse Italian migration policy within a European context and, more specifically, to identify new strategies for strengthening the links between migration and development in some of the countries with the highest migratory pressure towards Italy, *viz.* Albania, Morocco and Tunisia. The chapter was written during a six-month internship at the Sussex Centre for Migration Research, University of Sussex, in 2002, and subsequently updated.

2 As against, for instance, 35 per cent in Bosnia, 16 per cent in Bulgaria, 41 per cent in Croatia, 19 per cent in Macedonia, 8 per cent in Romania and 40 per cent in Slovenia. Data from IMF: International Financial Statistics.

3 Recently an office has been opened in Vlorë.

4 These figures refer to 31 March 2002.

5 These figures derive from a report from 'Etimos', a not-for-profit micro-finance society composed of fair trade cooperatives, NGOs, associations and religious organisations. It collects savings in Italy via 'ethical' means and invests them in micro-credit projects in poor countries by networking with local partners.

6 See PRODEM–Fondo Financero Privado: *The role of micro-finance institutions gearing remittances towards productive investments*, Geneva, November 2000.

7 Some interesting details emerged in an interview with an official of the Italian-Albanian Institute, which channels about 90 per cent of the Albanian remittances which go through the official banking system. In at least half the cases of remittance transfers, bureaucratic difficulties get in the way and increase the costs involved. For instance, whenever the sender writes the receiver's address incorrectly or unclearly, the money is sent back to Italy and then remitted again to Albania. This triples the transaction costs. It is a common occurrence because of the lack of clarity of some Albanian addresses and because of frequent changes of residence amongst the Albanian population.

8 These impressions are confirmed by evidence in the Economist Intelligence Unit (2002) country profile: for instance the construction sector in Albania grew strongly, by 15, 18 and 15 per cent during 1999, 2000 and 2001 respectively.

9 InteMiGra was a research project on the integration of migrants in Italy, based on more than 1000 questionnaires to representative samples of the main immigrant groups in seven Italian regions. For the final report see Carchedi (2002).

References

Barsotti, O. and Moretti, E. (2004) *Rimesse e Cooperazione allo Sviluppo*. Milan: Franco Angeli.

Bonifazi, C. and Sabatino, D. (2003) Albanian migration to Italy: what official data and survey results can reveal, *Journal of Ethnic and Migration Studies*, 30(6): 967–95.

Carchedi, F. (2002) *La Ricerca: Sintesi del Progetto InteMiGra*. Teramo: InteMiGra.

Caritas (2002) *Immigrazione Dossier Statistico 2002*. Rome: Anterem.

Economist Intelligence Unit (2002) *Country Profile: Albania 2002*. London: EIU.

Enwereuzor, U. (2000) *Discriminazione e Razzismo*. Bologna: Il Mulino.

Falchi, N. (1995) *International Migration Pressure*. Geneva: IOM.

Libanora, R. (2002) *Immigrati e Servizi Bancari. Risultati di una Ricerca Condotta a Roma e Milano*. Rome: Giordano dell'Amore Foundation.

Mai, N. (2002) Myths and moral panics: Italian identity and media represenation of Albanian immigration, in Grillo, R. D. and Pratt, J. (eds) *The Politics of Recognising Difference: Multiculturalism Italian-Style*. Aldershot: Ashgate, 77–94.

Mazzonis, M. and Naletto, G. (2000) *Migranti e Banche in Italia e in Europa*. Rome: Lunaria.

Natale, M. and Strozza, S. (2003), Lavoro, reddito e rimesse degli immigrati stranieri in Italia: finalità, progettazione e realizzazione di un'indagine sul campo, in Acocella, N. and Sonnino, E. (eds) *Movimenti di Persone e Movimenti di Capitali in Europa*. Milan: Il Mulino, 289–367.

Piperno, F. (2002) *From Albania to Italy: formation and basic features of a binational migration system*. Rome: CeSPI, background paper for the CEME (Cooperative Efforts to Manage Emigration) visit to Italy and Albania, May 2002.

Puri, S. and Ritzema, T. (1999) *Migrant Workers' Remittances: Micro-finance and Informal Economy: Prospects and Issues*. Geneva: ILO Social Finance Unit, Working Paper 21.

UNDP (2000) *Albanian Human Development Report*. Tirana: UNDP.

Uruçi, E. and Gedeshi, I. (2002) *Remittances Management for Local Development*. Tirana, Centre for Economic and Social Studies (mimeo).

6

Albanian high-skilled migrant women in the US

The ignored experience

AIDA ORGOCKA

This chapter focuses on a little-studied migrant population: high-skilled women. It argues against a rhetoric that women migrants are primarily dependent on their spouses; this obscures agency in how their lives are constituted both in the sending countries and in the countries of reception. Although Albanian high-skilled female migrant experiences may have parallels with those of Albanian high-skilled male migrants, bringing women centre-stage may be significant in an important way. Because Albanian migration has been predominantly male, women have been subsumed as dependent and as individuals to be taken care of by spouses, relatives and/or families. Their migration experiences have been largely ignored. This chapter, instead, documents the perseverance and strong will of Albanian women to independently take opportunities to carve a professional life of their own. I borrow Amartya Sen's definition of an agent as 'someone who acts and brings about change, and whose achievements can be judged in terms of her own values and objectives' (Sen 1999: 19) to argue that Albanian high-skilled migrant women can be entrepreneurial and bold in finding and benefiting from opportunities to better their lives.

Unlike the other chapters in this book, which are mainly concerned with the Albanian migratory phenomenon within its regional context in Southern Europe (Albania, Greece, Italy), this chapter takes as its setting the most important non-European destination, the United States. Through an analysis of experiences of Albanian high-skilled migrant women in fashioning a professional career in the USA, I attempt to answer three questions:

- What has driven Albanian high-skilled women away from Albania?
- What are the challenges they face as they try to integrate in the USA?
- What factors would affect their eventual return to Albania in the short and long term?

The goals of my analysis are two-fold: to document and demonstrate that Albanian highly-skilled female migration is a visible reality that can hardly be ignored; and to offer an explanation of why this kind of migration has occurred, its nature and constraints and how it matters to Albania's intellectual assets. Presentation of these data is intended to serve as a launch-pad for the development of policies that foster a dialogue between the Albanian government and its high-skilled migrants.

Albanian migrants in the USA

Although Albanians have consistently chosen the USA as one of their important migration destinations in search of a better life (Trix 2001), they became visible in US media and politics only in the last decade of the twentieth century. Much of this is due to the disintegration of the communist regime in 1991, the collapse of the pyramid schemes in 1997 and the ensuing political turmoil in Albania, and the Kosovo war in 1999. The USA hosted 3,652 Albanian refugees between 1983 and 2000. While refugees settled in virtually all states, the main destinations were New York (1,130) and Michigan (485) (Office of Refugee Resettlement 2000). Albanians constituted 4 per cent of migrants coming from Europe, and ranked seventh after Russia, Ukraine, the United Kingdom, Bosnia-Herzegovina, Poland and Germany as of 2000. Seventy-six per cent of Albanian migrants came through the USA Diversity Visa Program. Homemakers, students, unemployed and the retired made up about 43 per cent of these migrants. Among the employed, 29 per cent were in the professional category, and 27 per cent in services (Immigration and Naturalization Service 2000).

In total, Census 2000 reports 113,661 Americans of Albanian ancestry; New York and Michigan are the states with the largest concentration of Albanian migrants.[1]

Despite their presence, Albanians are not a visible group in migration studies done in the USA. Francis Trix (2001) identifies four distinct stages of Albanian migration to the USA. The first one spans the end of the nineteenth century to 1939 and is characterised by an open flow of migrants between Albania and the USA. These migrants were predominantly male and came to the USA for economic reasons. Return of the first successful male migrants to Albania triggered a chain of male migration especially from south-east Albania. The imposition of immigrant quotas in the 1920s and the perceived improvement of conditions in Albania ended this first stage. Second, during the 1945–60 period, political migrants escaping the communist regime in Albania settled in the USA. Benefiting from the passage of the Hart-Cellar Act (1965), which abolished old country quotas, a third wave of Albanians, living outside Albania proper, immigrated to the USA between 1960 and 1980. Finally, in the early 1990s, the dramatic change of political systems and the re-establishment of diplomatic relationships between Albania and the USA brought more Albanians from Albania proper through family reunions, the annual diversity visa lottery, study scholarships and illegal migration. A considerable number of Albanian migrants to the United States were high-skilled. Since 1996, the USA has been the primary destination for Albanian professional migrants. As of 1998, 23 per cent of Albanian high-skill migrants had made the USA their adopted home (Gedeshi *et al.* 1999).

Albanians have continually seen the USA as a country that embodies freedom from political, religious and ethnic repression. It is no wonder that, before the most recent influx, migration of Albanians to the USA was associated with an intensification of national consciousness and organised political action. Historically, the Albanians of America supported the nationalist efforts to establish an independent Albanian state, lobbied for its territorial integrity and denounced the establishment of the communist regime (Jacques 1998; Trix 2001). The presence of Albanians in the USA is a reality of historical and political significance; their invisibility in America and in Albanian migration research is, however, not justified and needs to be problematised further.[2]

The study

My reflections in this chapter are based on a qualitative pilot study for a larger upcoming project on the experiences of Albanian high-skilled migrants in North America.[3] Very little research has been published on Albanian migrant women in the West, so the literature on which to build is sparse. To the author's knowledge, no other studies have explored why Albanian high-skilled women choose to emigrate, what they experience and how they acculturate, although Kelly's chapter in this book includes reference to Albanian student-migrants in Bologna. In my own study, approaching a relatively small number of participants facilitated the understanding of how events, actions and meanings were shaped by the individuals' circumstances in which they occurred. Moreover, these techniques gave voice to the women by focusing on preserving their individuality (Mauthner and Doucet 1998; Plummer 1995). A more formal approach would run the risk of relying too heavily on *a priori* hypotheses and not allow for inductive insights to be gained. While the findings presented below are restricted only to the researched group of Albanian migrant women, certain themes may be extrapolated for a wider understanding of the dynamics of acculturation for female high-skilled migration.

Only women who had travelled individually to the USA or had been primary applicants for a USA diversity visa (green card) lottery were targeted and included. The sample consisted of women who were primary decision-makers regarding migration. Twenty women (mean age 33, age range 19–49), living in the East Coast and Mid-West, mainly recruited through personal acquaintances and Internet discussion groups, participated. Randomness in sampling was not possible largely due to the fact that there is no accessible database from which to draw such a sample. Nor are the interviewees a stratified sample; there is no centrally gathered information on the proportions of Albanian female high-skilled migrants (and male high-skilled migrants) in different institutions, so any categorisation is liable to be arbitrary.

Participants had entered the USA between 1992 and 2001 as students (8 of the sample), as illegal migrants (7) or as green card holders (5). Seventy per cent of the participants (14) were single or divorced upon entry to the USA. They had the following characteristics in common: all claimed Albanian as their ethnic identity; they were mostly from the capital, Tirana, with a few participants coming from centre-south Albania (Korçë and Berat); they had received their early educational training in Albania; and all had migrated after the socio-political change in Albania. Although they differed in their method of entry to the USA, they were all pursuing or had completed graduate studies and were employed in their area of specialisation.

All participants in this study contributed their experiences in two separate methods of data collection: a general survey and a telephone interview, both conducted in Albanian. Initially, participants completed a questionnaire that elicited information on personal, academic and living experiences in the USA. Each participant then elaborated on the answers given in a follow-up telephone interview. These interviews lasted between 45 and 60 minutes. These data collection techniques were thought to be appropriate to an exploratory, relatively small-scale study of this kind.

Notes were taken during the telephone interviews. Where interviewee responses were vague, I asked participants to clarify. I also read back the responses noted to the interviewees and asked them to confirm whether I had noted the correct representation of their ideas. Data were then coded and grouped according to the information they elicited with relation to the study's key questions.

Findings reported in the rest of this chapter combine responses from both the general survey and the telephone interviews. Names are fictitious.

Leaving Albania

Decisions to emigrate to the USA were invariably influenced by the women's desire to advance their education and professional careers. This is not surprising given that more women than men enrol in universities in Albania annually.[4] My earlier study examining the future orientation of approximately 300 Albanian high school students found that female students had explored and were more committed to future education than male students (Orgocka 1997). The same study found that significantly more female students than male students saw more study opportunities abroad than in Albania.[5] Furthermore, women migrants in the present study mentioned that emigrating to the USA offered the opportunity of trying to live independently, away from the tutelage of the family. For women who had never lived alone, emigrating to the USA was the challenge of a lifetime. Associated with this, for half the participants the initial spur had also come from curiosity to go beyond Albania and discover the rest of the world.

Of concern, however, were two more serious reasons. About a third of the participants reported that in Albania women were not looked upon as professionals. Under the socialist system, emancipation put women on a par with men regarding educational and occupational opportunities, thus discouraging formal sex discrimination. During the 1990s, Albania's move into a market economy located women in a liberalised consumer culture, with an insistent stress upon glamour, excitement and sexual attractiveness. Looking for and obtaining a job implied that women had to provide sexual favours. Mira, a 30-year-old from Tirana recollected:

> A relative of mine once recommended that I go meet this programme director for a position in my line of training he had available. As soon as I entered, he closed the door. I didn't like it. I reminded him that he and my relative were good friends and that my family knew that I had come to meet him. He paced around the room for a few minutes, made a phone call and then opened the door and let me go. I so hated him. And then they say women are bad and immoral. Most of my women friends went through similar experiences.

Fifteen per cent of the participating women had done postgraduate work in the USA or in Western Europe and had initially returned to Albania upon completion of their studies. However, they discovered that the Albanian context was not entirely responsive to their individual choice to obtain training in the West; in fact they perceived that they were unwanted and unwelcome. Drita, a 32-year-old, commented:

> The 'you're overqualified for this position' sapped all energy I had. I couldn't get over the fact that I was overqualified for Albanian taste. Of course, you

> needed to know people to get a job. And a low-cut dress. That's when I decided to leave again.

Some women mentioned that their decision to move to the USA was associated with countering the image of the 'single woman' running away from the family grip. These women had to argue against a rhetoric that women do not need education beyond a university diploma, and that at their age (roughly 25–30), they needed to create their own family. Surprising as it may sound, however, most women reported that their decision to study abroad or emigrate was met with excitement from the family who thought that their daughters should seize this great opportunity. Two women mentioned that they were the first in their extended families to do postgraduate work, and their relatives thought of them as trailblazers and treated them with much respect.

While 15 per cent of the women mentioned that they had come to study in the USA thanks to the suggestions made by their friends, most attributed migration to their own initiative. While male high-skilled migrants are reported to migrate mainly because they have employment sponsorships, only a third of the women had entered the USA through a research or teaching fellowship from a host university. Even then, they had to go through a very competitive selection process that awarded fellowships to perhaps only a tenth of applicants. This finding is in line with other studies that conclude that, unlike other categories of economic migrants, professionals rely much more heavily on their occupational skills to come to the USA (Bagchi 2001).

As the interviews show, Albanian female high-skilled migrants emigrate for a wide variety of reasons, including the pursuit of greater freedom and self-development, dissatisfaction with domestic education options, and escaping social pressures. However, one motivation that does not feature prominently, especially in the interviews with single or divorced women, is emigration for economic reasons. There may be at least one fact that explains this. By choosing to emigrate alone these women are not following a conventional life path. The USA often may represent not an economic alternative but rather an *alternative way of living* that can free women from the constraints of life in Albania. They have ambitions to work and many succeed in it (as exemplified by their academic achievements and employment in professions they received training in), but work is seen not only in terms of making money but also as a means to self-fulfilment and a practical response to structures of patriarchal discrimination.

High-skilled work and integration in the USA

At the time of the interviews all women were employed either part- or full-time. All mentioned that their professional development was the best pay-off for their hard work. Postgraduate training had allowed them to navigate the professional world with a sense of security and confidence. However, most mentioned that this was due to perseverance in face of hardship. Women who had initially entered the USA illegally faced very poor prospects for locating employment after their arrival. Working in jobs below their level of education was coupled with 'You couldn't complain. They would just throw in your face the fact that you were illegal.' Most of the women described some form of discrimination that was not so much connected to being Albanian than being foreign. Mara, a 30-year-old, commented:

> It's their lot in life that they were born here. It does not make them better and me worse. There may have been a lag in the theoretical preparation when I first arrived here, but I have worked really, really hard. I can compete and do as good or a better job than natives.

Mara's comment that she viewed herself as similar or better than the natives in abilities, knowledge and skills in her profession is noteworthy because it may provide an explanation of how high-skilled migrants build confidence and adjust in the host society. Like other Albanian women in the study, Mara acknowledged that she arrived in the USA with a clear disadvantage in 'theoretical preparation'. She may have constructed a particularly positive self-image regarding acquisition of skills through hard work and perseverance, because these are the resources she drew on when she first decided to emigrate. That she was able to compete fairly with natives exposed to the same kind of training may be seen as a mechanism for enhancing her self-confidence in succeeding in an aggressive work milieu that may discriminate in terms of national origin.

Difference of culture and style of communication challenged integration in the professional life for 20 per cent of the women. Besa, a 45-year-old, recounted that the most unsettling feeling she still struggled with was that in her work, the mentality was: 'We are not interested in what you know, we want you to have command of what we are looking for.' Such a clash brought her close to losing her job, but:

> Children's parents who participated in the programme were on my side. They knew I was doing good work and they argued my case. I had more skills and education than my boss and she plainly told me, 'You're not getting a raise as long as I am here.' I stayed because I liked the work and I had a family to take care of. As soon as my boss left the agency, I was given a larger office, with windows of course, and they raised my salary ten per cent. I have always been a strong person, too bold maybe, and they probably hated my guts. But I work really hard.

While women overall did not consider that being female was a source of discrimination in their workplace, a few reported that they encountered problems from less-educated Albanian men. Ardita, a single 29-year-old recalled a painful story.

> After three years of hard work, I was interviewed and finally had the job I believed I could realise my potential in. One day, I was going past a hall and there were some Albanian men chatting. As soon as they saw me, one of them said, 'Look, here comes the tramp who has lovers who find her a job.' I could not believe my ears. Where were these lovers? Both the director and the programme chief for the position I interviewed for were women and certainly none of them had designs on me, I don't think. I was very indignant. But I couldn't do anything . . . And the one who said it, had come to me two months ago and I had helped his family find an apartment and his wife find a job. Of course, it has to do a lot with how well-educated these people are. But frankly, I do not think Albanian men have reached the point of looking at a woman as someone who can achieve something better than them. And they are far from knowing how to respect women.

Ardita's story illustrates how the international migration of high-skilled women may be a process of reconfiguration of gender relations. Similar to other countries in Eastern Europe, the process of political transformation in Albania was associated with a patriarchal revival in most areas of social life, including family relations, reproductive decisions, employment and income, political representation and civic participation. In her comparative work, Watson (1993) argues that exclusion and devaluation of women has been a fundamental – and not merely accidental – element of democratisation in the countries of Eastern Europe. In fact women are expected to sacrifice themselves for their men's chances of freedom and opportunity. The increasing emphasis of the private sphere strengthened the role of family and the definition of women as wives and mothers (see also Lobodzinska 1996; and the special issue of *Hypatia* 1993 on Eastern European feminism). That women migrate alone, gain access to valuable social and economic resources beyond the domestic sphere and achieve, illustrates their ability to mount a serious protest and reconfigure what patriarchy prescribes for them as destiny, thus seriously threatening the social order legitimised through newly-discovered pre-existing traditionalism.

Although professional life was important to women, they mentioned that it was constantly negotiated against a backdrop of other competing demands in life such as taking care of children and their family. For some of the single women, finding a partner and having their own family was also a concern. Of all the women that entered single or divorced in the USA, three quarters were still single and one quarter had married non-Albanian citizens. While some mentioned that marriage did not necessarily give them identity as a woman, they felt that having a family was as important as developing a successful career. Although a few mentioned that lack of connections and location did not allow for Albanian men and women to meet, others mentioned that living independently as a woman in the USA challenged Albanian men who went back to Albania to find twenty-year-old women to marry. Era, a single 30-year-old, commented:

> For each of us that has lived in America for a long time, in my case this is the sixth year, I am very convinced that if an Albanian man wants to enter a relationship with me, he has thought about this aspect, six years in America and nothing has happened to her. The idea that such a man thinks this way, irritates me. But this explains in a way the behaviour of Albanian men toward us. I see it with all the Albanian men I meet. All of them look at me thinking, 'You feel good there!' Because the concept of Albanians for America: it's a free country, you do what you want, they think that whatever happens, you're having fun, in the broadest sense of the word. So I am convinced that all of us have the 'brand'.

The integration of high-skilled women in the USA reflects the general character of international migration: a process of negotiating sameness and difference in ability and skills. A more gender-specific challenge, however, is that of coping with cultural expectations and a patriarchal ideology of sexuality that may take women to task for having developed a professional career instead of putting a premium on the ideal of domesticity. For Albanian highly-skilled migrant women, gain within a specific domain, i.e. professional achievement, has been accompanied by substantial costs. While taking pride in their achievements, these women have had to cope with unfounded stigma and criticism, hardly a feature only of Albanian communities. Scholars researching migrant women in general point to the fact that migration may not improve the status of women equally at home, in the community, and/or workplace.

Contemplating a return to Albania

That most of the women were well settled in a path toward completing their postgraduate studies and/or advancing their professional career in the USA does not mean that they had completed the cycle of calling the USA their adopted homeland, nor that they had definitely ruled out returning to Albania. Three-quarters of the participants thought of themselves as Albanians who observed all the rules and regulations of the host country and reported that being Albanian was a source of pride:

> I am not ashamed to call myself Albanian. Some instead of saying they are from Albania, say they are from Europe. It has never crossed my mind to deny where I come from even when other people have tried to put me in a tight spot because I am Albanian. I have always responded with pride that the love for my country has nothing to do with what has or has not happened there.

Women regularly kept contact with their families, relatives and friends through e-mail and telephone, read newspapers, books written by Albanians/about Albania, listened to Albanian music, attended events on Albania, and met other Albanians. Language, their past experiences and food were yet other ways that reminded them of their Albanian roots. Of particular interest was the active involvement of some of the women with the local Albanian community as well as with nationally-established organisms such as the Albanian American National Organization, the National Albanian American Council, the New Albanian Generation, and the Albanian American Women's Association.

Past work experiences in Albania had informed research on Albania for 30 per cent of the participants. Research ranged anywhere from occasional papers as class work to major postgraduate theses and dissertations. As one participant said, 'This is what we know. It's interesting and deserves to get some attention.' Their main motivation was 'to contribute a little and represent the voice of Albania in the world.'

However, doing research was associated with challenges of finding and obtaining authoritative information on Albania. Friends and colleagues in Albania remained an important source. Women who had done research on Albania reported on the lack of a database or databank with statistical indicators on Albania. Most mentioned that they needed to know people in the Albanian Institute of Statistics to be able to do meaningful work. The data published on the Internet were not substantial. Ana described her frustrations:

> In order to get material for these papers, you need to be *in* Albania and have very broad contacts and people in key positions in order to be able to access the information. Because such information as data on Albanian higher education (statistics, info. on curriculum development, financial management etc.) is not available on the web and easily accessible from here. I could have chosen to do a project on Higher Ed. in Nepal, let's say, and would have fared better since there is info about Nepal's Higher Ed. on the web, but I chose to write about Higher Ed. in Albania – national pride, I guess – and that really sunk me.

Participants also mentioned the lack of an authoritative publication venue beyond the option of a working paper series for presentation of their work. A prevailing concern was that 'Albania has no energy to heed its emigrants'. Lack of a concerted effort to bring high-skilled migrants' work back to Albania was attributed to absence of records regarding where Albanian professionals were (primarily because migration of high-skilled Albanians to the US is due to individual initiative and is not sponsored by governmental fellowships).

> I remember completing a questionnaire that the Albanian Open Society Institute mass-mailed to Albanian graduate students worldwide. But nothing

> happened afterwards. I thought it was wonderful that someone was thinking of us, but it turned out to be a one-time fluke.

Over 60 per cent of the participants considered returning and/or working in Albania short-term. All, however, pointed out that material rewards for years of hard work were in order. As Mara said, 'The whole idea of helping your country sounds so romantic to me. It is a job, and I will be committed to giving it my best shot. I have worked really hard to get this degree.' About 30 per cent of the women mentioned that either Albania was not yet prepared to see its high-skilled female migrants as successful professionals abroad, or that international development agencies that worked in Albania had considerable scepticism that Albanians could do satisfactory work:

> Consulting firms do not believe we can do a good job. There was this two-year contract to work in Albania and I was the perfect fit for it. My past work experience in Albania and my dissertation work focused on the same policy issues this international aid agency was committed to tackling. They ended up hiring an American that had marginal exposure to Albanian reality, a few months work in Kosovo. The new hire will need a programme manager and a translator to help understand Albanian reality and fashion a cooperation with government agencies. And I would not need these because I am so familiar with the topic, the government agencies and the country. It is an unnecessary waste of resources.

Although abroad for a considerable time and absent from the on-going processes of change in Albania, Besa's confidence expressed in the quote above is grounded in the shared ethnic identity with non-immigrant Albanians through commonality of language, a long socialisation process through socialism, a culture of music and cuisine (often cited by participants as sources of their identity), and work experience. Having obtained credentials from an educational institution in the West means that these graduates may also share a knowledge base, a language, a way of thinking and norms about how to practice expert skills that may complement the requirements of the work ethic in international aid agencies. It is therefore startling to find that Albanians may be discriminated on the basis of their ethnicity. Data and research on actual employment of returnees by international aid agencies in Albania are not available, thus precluding generalisation from the specific histories of participating women. However, this concern may point to the necessity of researching employment patterns of skilled returnees as it may shed light on the different factors that may bring Albanian professionals back to the country.

The desire and intentions of more than half of the women interviewed to return and work in Albania either short- or long-term were thus defined by a concern of balancing the individual's choice of personal security, professional satisfaction and economic benefits. Having received the training and skills necessary to help Albania develop, it is highly probable that they will return as entrepreneurs or agents of further economic and social development.

Conclusion

This chapter has made an effort to analyse how the experiences of high-skilled Albanian migrant women in the USA are embedded both in the processes of migration from the home country and in the processes of settlement in the host country. It located the motivation of Albanian high-skilled women to migrate primarily in the socio-economic circumstances of Albania. Women reported that the main reasons that triggered their motivation to migrate were professional advancement through education, interest in the world beyond Albania's borders, and the lack of attention to their professional training in Albania. Whilst on the one hand in the USA women had the opportunity to realise their intellectual potential, they also mentioned that part of the process was dealing with discrimination that resulted more from being a migrant and foreign than their gender. In the end, women reported that their professional training had given them adequate skills to contribute to Albania. The majority considered that working back in Albania could happen if the government would recognise their hard work through financial rewards.

Two basic insights follow from this analysis. The first is the general relevance of expanding migration research to include women's concerns in describing how high-skilled migration affects individuals' lives. Given that women represent almost half of international migrants (United Nations Statistics Division 2000), the invisibility of high-skilled migrant women is not justified. In the present state of affairs, Kofman (2000) observes that as households rely more and more on two incomes, and as women have entered higher education and gained greater independence, discussion of female high-skilled migration becomes crucial.

To be sure, women do not live and work in gender isolation, and their situations cannot be adequately analysed as if they were. Although the Albanian women I talked to recognised that women face specific problems, they viewed their lives as being affected by the same social, political and historical forces as men's. This could explain why, when talking about discrimination, the majority of women emphasised either their status as migrants in the USA or as Albanians when faced with potential barriers in trying to obtain a position with international aid agencies. Although gender-based research may emphasise women's additional constraints of sexual exploitation because of patriarchal ideologies that construe them as less valuable human beings, future directions could include analysing how high-skilled migration defines and affects the lives of women *vis-à-vis* men.

The second insight relates to the relationships to be established between high-skilled migrants and the Albanian government. The professional experiences of high-skilled migrant women suggest that it is incorrect to assume that Albania has lost the intellectual potential these women can offer. Although the vast majority of Albanian high-skilled migrants will be firmly grounded in the USA, some will continue to contribute to political, economic and social life in Albania and become part of the transnational communities that link Albania to the rest of the world. The interviews underscore the importance of moving beyond stating that the flight of Albanian intellectuals has resulted in a brain-drain calamity for the country. Given the interest and commitment of Albanian high-skilled migrants to contribute to their country, Albania should pay closer attention to encouraging a continuous dialogue with its citizens wherever they settle.

Acknowledgements

Many thanks to the Albanian migrant women, whose real names I do not mention here because of the oath of confidentiality. I also thank Edwin Silverman for his help with locating statistical information on Albanian migrants and refugees in the US; and Frosina Information Network, Tani Mezini and Kestrina Budina for help with locating participants. This chapter benefited greatly from the critical readings of Michel Cukier, Russell King, Nicola Mai and Stephanie Schwandner-Sievers. My thanks go to each of them.

Notes

1 These data were not segregated by age and gender.

2 A more general observation needs to be made here. Until the late 1990s studies on Albanian migration in general were sparse. Çobani (1997) explains that for Albanians international migration has been continuously considered a national calamity. During the communist regime international migration was treated as a serious wound inherited from the past that needed to be cured. The radical measures that the communist regime took to put an end to migration abroad had an impact on what could be treated a viable area for study by migration scholars. The only legitimate domain of research remained the Arbëresh of Italy who had emigrated from Albania proper in the fifteenth century; the rest of the diasporas were of interest to the Albanian communist diplomacy and the state security (Çobani, 1997: 62–3).

3 The project itself acknowledges the differences of migration experiences of high-skilled men and women and seeks to link these differences to (a) the roles, attributes and behaviours that both Albanian and USA society consider socially appropriate for women and men; (b) household dynamics including division of labour, access to and control over resources and decision-making; and (c) constraints, opportunities and needs facing Albanian women and men.

4 See Instituti i Statistikës (INSTAT) *Social Indicators*, at http://www.instat.gov.al (retrieved 10 May 2003).

5 Research with female overseas students from less wealthy countries lists academic reasons, unavailability of quality education and a motivation to make a

contribution to their own country through acquisition of advanced knowledge and technology (Goldsmith and Shawcross 1985).

References

Bagchi, A. D. (2001) Migrant networks and the immigrant professional: an analysis of the role of weak ties, *Population Research and Policy Review*, 20: 9–31.

Çobani, H. (1997) *Arkipelagu i diasporave shqiptare i parë nga Zvicra*. Tirana: Idromeno.

Gedeshi, I., Mara, H., Dhimitri, R. and Krisafi, K. (1999) *Emigrimi i elitës intelektuale nga Shqipëria gjatë periudhës së tranzicionit*. Tirana: Luarasi.

Goldsmith, J. and Shawcross, V. (1985) *Women as Overseas Students in the United Kingdom: It ain't half sexist mum*. London: World University Services.

Hypatia (1993) special issue on Eastern European Feminism, 8(4): 85–128.

Immigration and Naturalization Service (2000) *Statistical Yearbook of the Immigration and Naturalization Service*. Washington, DC: INS.

Jacques, E. (1998), *The Albanians: An Ethnic History from Prehistoric Times to the Present*. Jefferson, North Carolina: McFarland.

Kofman, E. (2000) The invisibility of skilled female migrants and gender relations in studies of skilled migration in Europe, *International Journal of Population Geography*, 6(1): 45–59.

Lobodzinska, B. (1996) Women's employment or return to 'family values' in Central-Eastern Europe, *Journal of Comparative Family Studies*, 27(3): 519–44.

Mauthner, N. and Doucet, A. (1998) Reflections on a voice-centered relational method: analysing maternal and domestic voices, in Ribbens, J. and Edwards, R. (eds) *Feminist Dilemmas in Qualitative Research: Public Knowledge and Private Lives*. London: Sage, 119–46.

Office of Refugee Resettlement (2000) *Annual Report to Congress*. Washington, DC: Office of Refugee Resettlement.

Orgocka, A. (1997) *Contextual Factors and the Future Orientation of Albanian High School Students*. Unpublished M.S. thesis, University of Illinois at Urbana-Champaign, Urbana Champaign.

Plummer, K. (1995) *Telling Sexual Stories: Power, Change and Social Worlds*. London: Routledge.

Sen, A. K. (1999) *Development as Freedom*. New York: Alfred A. Knopf.

Trix, F. (2001) *Albanians in Michigan*. East Lansing: Michigan State University Press.

United Nations Statistics Division. (2000) *The World's Women, 2000: Trends and Statistics*. New York: United Nations.

Watson, P. (1993) Eastern Europe: the silent revolution of gender relationships, *Das Argument*, 35(6): 859–74.

7

'Greece belongs to Greeks!'

The case of the Greek flag in the hands of an Albanian student

GAZMEND KAPLLANI AND NICOLA MAI

On 28 October Greece celebrates its 'no day'. This commemorates the refusal to allow Italian fascist troops to invade the country from their Albanian strongholds during the Second World War. Every such day all public schools organise a parade in which the most academically outstanding student holds the Greek flag. In October 2000, it happened that the best student of a school in the small town of Nea Michaniona, in the region of Thessaloniki, was Odysseus Cenaj, an Albanian citizen who had immigrated to Greece together with his parents in 1998. The possibility that an Albanian migrant might hold the Greek flag on the occasion of a 'national' celebration provoked harsh reactions from Greek parents and the case attracted much interest from the media, which immediately presented it in terms of a 'national *affaire*'.

The main arguments according to which the Albanian student should *not* have been given the right to hold the Greek flag, as they were reported and amplified by media discourse, were the following:

> No one can impose (on Greek citizens), on the day they celebrate Greece's victory against its enemies, to see the flag of their country in the hands of an offspring of an enemy country . . . even though we can not find any trace of the anti-Greek characteristics of the country of his origin in the amiable face of this particular student. (*Eleftherotypia*, 5 November 2000)

> Unfortunately a boy from Albania was the best student of his school and asked to hold the flag of his second homeland, as he said. [. . .] but the (Greek) flag must be held at least by those who believe that they are Greeks deep inside . . . In this case, we have heard on television people saying that these issues are not DNA-related . . . But it's exactly the opposite: these

> issues are indeed DNA-related and are registered in our collective memory. (*Eleftherotypia*, 5 November 2000)

> In no other EU country, nor elsewhere, could it happen that someone who is not a Greek (neither in his heart, nor in his papers) can hold the Greek flag in a national celebration (*To Vima*, 25 November 2000)

> Every nation has its own flag . . . One cannot poke his nose in the other's national holiday; it is simply not his business . . . (*To Vima*, 30 October 2000)

> Albanian nationalism is changing the borders in the Balkans, it treats the North-Epirotans violently . . . while in Greece the labour market has been disrupted and huge social problems have been created by massive, uncontrolled, illegal immigration. (*Eleftherotypia*, 30 October 2000)

> Greece is a nation sitting in a region full of national prejudices and . . . facing direct threats. Its national cohesion is one of its most important assets. For this reason, the most elementary political foresight would suggest facilitating the entry into Greece of immigrants from states which are not our neighbours and with which there is more cultural affinity (Russia, Poland, Georgia etc . . .). (*Kathimerini*, 3 November 2000)

Although the official position of the Greek Orthodox Church[1] was in support of Cenaj, some of its most powerful figures expressed contrary views which received a loud echo in the Greek media. For instance, the metropolitan of Alexandroupolis addressed the case by citing the famous national-populist expression by the Greek former prime minister Andrea Papadreou[2] – Greece belongs to Greeks (*Eleftherotypia*, 2 November 2000). And the metropolitan of the region of Kalavrita posed a rhetorical question: 'Are there not enough Greeks to defend the honour of the Greek flag? Are perhaps the Albanians governing us, unnoticed?' (*Ta Nea*, 1 November 2000).

Greek public opinion was split between those who maintained that an Albanian student *could* hold the Greek flag and those who opposed such a possibility, claiming that it would be a contradiction *vis-à-vis* concepts such as the 'nation' and 'history'. Although Cenaj received wide support from many leading figures in the public and political arena, including the Greek president, he eventually resigned and did not finally hold the Greek flag in order not to exacerbate the growing tension the case was creating within the local and wider Greek communities. In the immediate aftermath of this event, new legislation was passed allowing foreign students enrolled in public schools for at least two years to carry the Greek flag, should they be entitled to according to their merits. However, just three years later Cenaj was to experience the same conundrum, but this time ranged against him were not only the parents but also his fellow-students. On this second occasion his cause was subject to even more polarised reactions. Some 50 students occupied the school in Nea Michaniona on 21 October as a sign of protest, and were backed by the local parents' association. Once more, Cenaj was obliged to step down 'for the last time indeed' – as he said.

Given the large-scale immigration of Albanians and of other migrants in recent years, and the increasingly family-based structure of this immigration, the issue of foreign-national children in Greek schools is unlikely to subside. Indeed, as was pointed out by Barjaba and King in the opening chapter of the book, the number of non-Greek children in Greek schools is increasing fast and is a revealing indicator of the 'settling down' of the immigrant population in Greece. As of 2002, more than 98,000 foreign pupils were enrolled in Greek schools, accounting for almost 9 per cent of the overall school population. As regards nationality, 72 per cent are from Albania.[3]

Clearly, Albanians are not unknown to Greeks and the new relationships emerging from the contemporary migratory context can be seen as superimposing themselves onto a pre-existing trans-Balkan context. In this respect, Albanians are a 'new-old' presence for Greeks. Our aim in this chapter is to interpret and analyse the wider social discontent triggered by the notion of an Albanian student holding the Greek flag. The case of Odysseus Cenaj exposes the way the unprecedented Albanian migration of the 1990s, and the Greek reaction to that immigration, produced new-old patterns of inclusion and exclusion and ways of classifying 'otherness', this time within rather than outside national borders. For this reason we will first attempt a short review of the representations of Albanian immigration in the Greek media discourse. However, our aim is neither to simply record the cultural construction of the Albanian migrant nor to show how this is involved in multiple dynamics of social exclusion and stigmatisation. What interests us most is the significance of this cultural construction in relation to its inscription into the Greek socio-cultural imaginary. In this respect, perhaps the most important question this chapter is trying to answer points to the social and political implications of such cultural constructions.

Our analysis is organised in four parts as follows. First, we say a few general but important things about identity, ethnicity and the nation, and the role of the media in all this, especially in the Greek case. The succeeding section addresses the nature and rootedness of Greek nationalism in the process of historical (re)construction of a Greek national identity, working from some general principles of European nationalism again to the specificity of the Greek case. Then we turn to the arrival of large numbers Albanian immigrants in Greece, and their 'reception' by the Greek media as 'criminals', as the embodiment of 'poverty' and 'backwardness', and as the 'invader' and 'enemy'. In the final part of the chapter we try to explain how these representations were consistent with the reconfiguration of the main coordinates shaping Greek national identity under the pressures exerted by the dual processes of European integration and Balkan disintegration.

Media, identity and the nation

Since the role of the media is one of the main elements of our analysis in this chapter, we believe that a short analysis of the interconnection between media, (national) identity and the way they impact on migration-related dynamics is indispensable. The conceptualisation of identity we adopt is one which emphasises its processual and relational nature against the fixity and givenness through which identity formations were interpreted and analysed in the past (Hall 1996: 3). The main implication of a conceptualisation of identity in fluid, plural and performative terms is that it acknowledges how identity formations are constituted 'within, not outside representation' (Hall 1996: 4), thereby highlighting the importance of socially established practices of communication in their emergence and maintenance. Most importantly, it highlights the fictional character of any identity formation, which can only be positively asserted in the relation to a plurality of 'constitutive' others (Hall 1996: 5).

According to the anthropologist Michael Moerman, ethnicity is an emic category of self and mutual identification which is discursively sustained through social interaction, rather than based on any objectively existing factor of differentiation (Moerman 1965: 1215–19). Although sometimes ethnicity appears as the hegemonic way in which a migrant group describes itself, its members can still recognise themselves in relation to other components of their identity conditions. These can sometimes be subject to a dynamic of ethnicisation by hegemonic social actors in the host society as well as in the migrant group. Thus, when analysing the processes of transformation characterising any identity formation, one has to focus on the way specific discursive formations and social practices were brought into play by specific actors in order to deal with emerging social needs. In fact, ethnicity also involves 'an attribution of identity to a minority by the majority; a relation and process intimately connected to issues of power, hierarchy, stratification, indeed to the nation-state' (Campbell 1999: 11).

In this perspective, if nationalism is simply 'an ethnic ideology which demands the right to its own state on behalf of the ethnic group', then national identity could be seen as a special case of ethnic ideology (Eriksen 1995: 261–6). The very process of definition of a social group in terms of ethnicity rather than nationality can be seen as an arena of political struggle between different ethnic minorities within a national political community. At the centre of the analysis of any nationalist ideology must be the relationship between its majorities and minorities, the latter being defined as groups who are 'politically non-dominant, and which exist as an ethnic category' (Eriksen 1995: 267). When analysing any national(ist) identity formation it is important both to understand according to which power dynamics and strategies different ethnic groups exercise their cultural and political hegemony, and to know through which narrative practices their privileged entitlement to power and control is legitimised, for which 'sames' and against which 'others'. Thus, rather than as given and fixed cultural entities, ethnic and other 'national' identities can be better understood as the fluid outcome of different competing attempts to exercise power and control. Such identities are the product of a political engagement with the world. In this respect, when analysing any politics of identity and representation, the key task, as Floya Anthias (1998: 519) suggests, is to identify who, within social groups, has the power to 'promote dominant characterisations' of ethnicity.

This issue leads us to the last point of this first theoretical section of the chapter – the relation between media and the emergence of a national consciousness. In his analysis of nationalism Benedict Anderson defines the nation an 'imagined community' (Anderson 1991: 6) which is both 'limited and sovereign'; he stresses the role of the development of large-scale means of communication and cultural homogenisation in the emergence of national communities. According to Anderson, nations emerged as spaces and places of identification as a consequence in particular of 'print capitalism' which 'made it possible for rapidly growing numbers of people to think about themselves, and to relate themselves to others, in profoundly new ways'. (Anderson 1991: 36, 46). Likewise, according to Marshall McLuhan there are very strong links between the emergence of nationalism and the spread of typography, to the point that this was named the 'architect of nationalism' (McLuhan 1987). The advantages in adopting a conceptualisation of national identity in these media-related terms are that it is consistent with a definition of identity in the processual and fluid terms set out above and that it acknowledges how the emergence of new communication technologies was linked to the advent of new forms of national consciousness and belonging.

As far as the relation between media and the emergence and maintenance of a national consciousness is concerned, there are two main theoretical and philosophical approaches. These are grounded into different positions within the founding sociological debate on the relation between structure and agency. The first claims that people believe they learn what happens in the world, whereas in reality they simply learn what happens in the newspapers (Wieviorka 1998: 115–16). This approach is underpinned by a conceptualisation of the relation between texts and audiences which denies the possibility for the latter to play an active role in the process of construction of meaning. On the other hand, there is an opposite approach emphasising the highly active role of the viewer/reader in constructing meaning out of visual and narrative texts. According to this second theoretical perspective, the audience can actively choose among the pictures and texts encompassing it, and the 'impact' of television, for instance, would be the outcome of a whole creative relationship between the viewer and that which they are watching (Willis 1990: 36–7).

The difficulty in finding an adequate analytical framework to assess the 'impact' of media on people's cultural construction of the world surrounding them is that none of these two theoretical poles is sufficient in explaining the complexity of the dynamics involved. In the words of Demertzis:

> the conditions shaping the impact of the media are exceptionally complex and dynamic (. . .) the public is not passive and prone towards unconditional manipulation. However, the media has the power to impose the issues of public debate and to influence decisively the recipients regarding issues in which it does not have experience or for which it hardly can shape a concrete representation. (Demertzis 1999: 383)

Beyond the intrinsic complexity of the relation between texts and audiences, one also has to acknowledge the importance of the link between political power and the media. Although the nature and coerciveness of this interconnection varies from country to country, there are at least three main factors influencing the way media can affect the processes of construction, reconstruction and/or deconstruction of national identities:

- The circumstances in which specific events take place. In times of crisis, media tend to be more keen on mobilising fantasies of national supremacy and on being receptive to official discourses, when compared with less tense circumstances.
- The open or the closed character of the national communication system. In societies where media are directly accountable to the state and their institutional autonomy is not ensured, they will tend to rely on official briefs and narratives, whereas in a more open and plural communication environment there would be more space for independent sources of information. However, the existence of independent and competing media does not guarantee the plurality of any national information system. Especially when an event is framed in terms of a national crisis, media can compete in spectacularising it and framing it according to the same discursive and visual narratives, rather than offering a range of different interpretations. This latter point leads us to our last consideration:
- The place of nationalism in the political culture of the country. The extent to which stereotypical representations of ethnic and other diversities prevail over other narrative strategies depends on the type of nationalism that predominates in a country and on its overall rootedness into the national identity. Whereas in a political culture of pluralism and tolerance nationalist-bound narratives will have to compete with other discourses in framing reality, in opposite conditions they would be the main (and often the only) way of representing 'the Other' (Demertzis 1999: 377–9).

As far as the first two factors are concerned, research carried out in the

1990s shows how Greek print and electronic media, especially in their interaction with public rituals, contributed to the rise of Greek nationalism (Sofos and Tsagarousianou 1994). This became particularly evident in the case of the so-called 'Macedonian question'[4] which coincided with the evolution of the Albanian migration to Greece. During this crisis period, through the adoption of a series of narrative techniques and ideological strategies, Greece was presented as a 'brotherless nation', as a 'righteous victim' that had been hunted almost everywhere and by everyone, a nation that had to defend its historical rights to friends and foes alike and a nation that did not fit into any international community or alliance. Consequently, since 1991 a shift from a defensive to an offensive nationalist discourse took place in both media and political agendas (Demertzis *et al.* 1999: 32). Finally, as far as the third consideration listed above is concerned, the Greek press can be seen as having developed simultaneously with the Greek state. Greek newspapers have a long history of polarisation and division along party-affiliation lines (Demertzis *et al.* 1999: 30–1).

A brief genealogy of Greek national identity: caught between homogeneity, Western Europe and 'the Balkans'

One of the first scholars to analyse the different experiences of nationalism across Europe was Hans Kohn (1945). According to Kohn, whereas in England, France and America it was the middle classes who elaborated a voluntaristic type of nationalism, in Central and Eastern Europe, including Germany, in the absence of the middle class, it was the intellectuals who promoted an organic, mystical and often authoritarian nationalism. In other words, because of the lack of social differentiation in many non-Western societies, nationalism found there its first expression in the cultural rather than in the social and political field. Moreover, Kohn underlines the ambivalence of the relation between the sources and the recipients of national discourses and ideologies. In this perspective, as an outcome of an ambivalent reaction to Western cultural hegemony, elsewhere national ideologies sought and found legitimacy in the celebration of the past and 'extolled the primitive and ancient depth and peculiarities of . . . traditions in contrast to Western rationalism and to universal standards' (Kohn 1945: 18–20). Although Kohn's distinction between 'Western' and 'Eastern' European forms of nationalism was criticised for being essentialist, some of his main arguments are found to reappear in much later analyses of nationalism.

For instance, the influence of Kohn's analysis is tangible in Peter Sugar's analysis of nationalisms in Eastern Europe. According to Sugar, these shared with Western nationalisms the revolutionary drive to transfer power to 'the people'; but they also translated anti-clerical, constitutional and egalitarian political concepts and ethno-linguistic claims into a 'national' idiom which was strongly influenced by the religious and state traditions of the area. Sugar's analysis of the 'bureaucratic' character of the Greek nationalist movement is particularly interesting for our analysis.

> While the Greek Movement started among the merchants and other middle-class elements, this group lacked leadership, was dispersed all over Europe, and was unable to shape events during Greece's war of independence. . . . Under these circumstances only the government and the bureaucracy could make their voices heard effectively everywhere in the country. The foreign dynasties and their military and civil servants, both foreign and domestic, were anything but popular and were in need of an issue that could unite the factions of the population and reconcile it with the government. Irredentist nationalism offered the solution for these needs and developed into the main domestic and foreign propaganda that was in the hands of the government. (Sugar 1969: 46–54)

Other scholars elaborated on Kohn's analysis of the ambivalence between emulation and hostility embedded in the process of cultural translation of nationalist ideology from 'Western' to 'Eastern' contexts. Amongst these is John Plamenatz, according to whom 'Eastern' nationalism is 'both imitative and competitive' and is bound to become 'illiberal'. Plamenatz finds that 'the desperate attempt to "catch up" with others, and therefore to imitate them extensively . . . , in order to assert yourself against them by finding your own unique place in what has hitherto been their world, their civilization, is profoundly disturbing' (Plamenatz 1976: 33–5). Following the same historically deterministic line, Liah Greenfeld stresses the ambivalent relationship of emulation and perceived inferiority generated by the process of 'importation' of nationalist ideology by using the concept of *ressentiment*. In Greenfeld's own words:

> Every society importing the foreign idea of the nation inevitably focused on the source of importation – an object of imitation by definition – and reacted to it. Because the model was superior to the imitator in the latter's own perception (its being a model implied that), and the contact itself more often than not served to emphasize the latter's inferiority, the reaction commonly assumed the form of ressentiment . . . , a psychological state resulting from suppressed feeling of envy and hatred (existential envy) and the impossibility of satisfying these feelings. . . . Ressentiment felt by the groups that imported the idea of the nation and articulated the national consciousness of their respective societies usually resulted in the selection out of their own indigenous traditions of elements hostile to the original national principle and in their deliberate cultivation. . . . Wherever it (ressentiment) existed it fostered particularistic pride and xenophobia, providing emotional nourishment for the nascent national sentiment and sustaining it whenever it faltered. (Greenfeld 1992: 7–9)

Finally, among the analyses reflecting Kohn's approach to nationalism, perhaps the most significant one for the purposes of this chapter is Miroslav

Hroch's study of nationalist movements in Central and Eastern Europe. Hroch (1996) stresses the importance of timing among these nationalist movements, as well as the different socio-economic context into which they were deployed. Thus, according to Hroch, nationalist ideology was able to give a political expression to social antagonism more successfully where society was already organised according to different and competing socio-political agenda. Unlike in Western Europe, where national agitation acquired a mass character only after the establishment of a civil society or a constitutional order, in the lands of the Ottoman Empire this happened already under the old regime. This means that national agitations in the Balkans took place in a context characterised by lack of political education and of any self-assertive experience of the subaltern ethnic groups because of the absolutist oppression under which they had grown up. In the absence of more articulate forms of political discourse, according to Hroch, social contradictions or hostilities tended to be expressed according to homogeneous national categories (Hroch 1996: 87).

Returning to the main argument of the chapter, we will now explore the way the considerations outlined above were mirrored in the historical emergence of Greek national identity. The notion of a Greek 'national' consciousness emerged with reference to the project, called 'the Great Idea', of unifying into the Greek state all the territories inhabited by Greek-speaking Christian Orthodox populations. This identity project can be seen as emerging from the fusion between the Ottoman association of religious and 'national' belonging shaping the local or *villayet*-based administrative system and the Enlightement-based narrative of national identification. Many scholars, following Kohn, argued that Greek nationalism has been more 'cultural' than 'political', as religion, culture and language, rather than universal citizenship rights, played a key role in the definition of the national identity. For instance, the Greek historian Thanos Veremis underlines how Greece was the first nation-state to emerge out of the Ottoman Empire and how its national identity and culture are characterised by the perception of a common cultural, rather then racial continuity (Veremis 1995: 101). Paschalis Kitromilides also seems to follow Kohn's approach when he points out how, unlike in Western Europe, in South-Eastern Europe the liberal anti-despotic legacy of the Enlightenment met powerful social and cultural resistances and produced a 'hybrid' form of nationalism, based on 'the mirage of enlightened despotism' (Kitromilides 1990a: 60). In Kitromilides' own words, in Greece, as in the rest of the Balkans, nationalism 'was geared both to the aggrandisement of the nation-state as well as to the preservation of power alliances and social structures in the state they existed at the time of national autonomy, which coincided with the twilight of the age of the Enlightenment' (Kitromilides 1990a: 66). In fact, in the second half of the nineteenth century 'the original ethnic definition proposed by the Enlightenment against Orthodoxy . . . was transcended to the point at which Orthodoxy was encompassed within the ethnic definition of Hellenism' (Kitromilides 1990b: 60).

As a result of the convergence of these heterogeneous doctrines and dynamics, 'Greekness became inextricably related to common ancestry, cultural traditions and religion, . . . (a) triple boundary distinguish(ing) Greeks from the non-Christian populations of the Ottoman Empire, on the one hand, and, on the other hand, from the South Slavs living in the Balkan peninsula who could not raise a claim in classical Greek culture' (Triandafyllidou and Veikou 2002: 194). Consequently, Greece is one of the most homogeneous societies within the EU, as more then 90 per cent of Greek citizens consider themselves ethnically Greek and have Greek Orthodoxy as a common religion (Tryandafyllidou 2002: 150–1).

On the one hand, this national homogeneity can be seen as the outcome of a series of historical events allowing the concentration of ethnic Greeks within the boundaries of the Greek state. On the other, it should be seen as the result of specific policies aimed at the assimilation of all aliens. These, as Christos Rosakis points out, were usually 'peoples sharing common characteristics with neighbouring countries' and who could be incorporated into 'the mainstream of those speaking the Greek language and professing the "official" religion of the Christian Orthodoxy' (Rosakis 1996: 97). Unsurprisingly, according to Kevin Featherstone, Greece's national identity is still characterised by the social primacy of the *ethnos* over notions of individual rights and the scope of dissent and by a strong and pervasive sense of what it is to be Greek in differentiation from foreigners (Featherstone 1996: 13).

The hegemonic position of the ideology of (Greek/Orthodox) homogeneity shaping Greek national consciousness can be seen as determining the problematic stance the Greek state has taken *vis-à-vis* its national minorities and the issue of the form of citizenship to be granted to its growing immigrant population. As far as the first issue is concerned, Greece only recognises the existence of the 'Muslim' (ethnic Turk) inhabitants of Thrace, thereby implicitly denying the existence of other ethno-linguistic and religious minorities, such as the Roma who make up 3.3 per cent of the total Greek population, ethnic Albanians (Arvanites) 2 per cent, members of the Macedonian minority 2 per cent, Vlachs 2 per cent and Pomaks 0.3 per cent (Triandafyllidou 2002: 151). Greece's resistance to the acknowledgement of these minorities can be seen as the result of the fact that most of them, notably the Muslim, but also the Macedonian and the Arvanites groups, have been identified with territorial claims coming from neighbouring countries with which geo-political relations have always been tense (Rozakis 1996: 98).

As far as the second issue is concerned, during the 1990s Greece became a desired destination for a number of migrant groups, mainly from Eastern Europe. For the first time in its history as a unified nation-state, Greece witnessed a massive presence of foreigners (*allogeneis*) in its territory.[5]

According to the results of the 1998 regularisation, the Albanians were by far the largest immigrant nationality in Greece, accounting for two-thirds of those who were regularised. Other important regularised groups also came from Eastern Europe – Bulgaria, Romania, Ukraine and Poland. A second regularisation took place in 2001; as of now, only the overall number of applicants, 367,860, is known. Although doubts have been raised over the accountability of the results of the second regularisation (see Fakiolas 2003), what emerges is that Albanians are by far the largest migrant group in Greece, perhaps as high as 500,000–600,000, equivalent to 5 per cent or more of the Greek population. Interestingly, both Pontic Greeks (ethnic Greeks from the Soviet Union) and ethnic-Greek Albanians were not included in these regularisation processes; they were offered a preferential treatment on the basis of their compatibility with the main co-ordinates of Greekness (Triandafyllidou 2002: 152).

As for the notion of *ressentiment* and its potential rôle in shaping the relation between Greek national consciousness and Western Europe, Greek national identity can be seen as emerging out of two contradictory dynamics. On the one hand there was a hegemonic reaction against the most radical and revolutionary implications of the Western experiences of nation formation. As a result, 'Greekness continues to be defined as a transcendental nation in Greek public discourse', in particular as regards its inextricability from religious Orthodoxy (Triandafyllidou and Veikou 2002). On the other hand, Greek national consciousness can be seen as having partially interiorised the conditions of culture offered by the 'Balkanist' discourse, an ambiguous Western interpretation of the 'nature' of South-East Europe which fuses 'otherness' with marginality and West-East interstitiality.[6]

In the next section of the chapter, we explore the way Greece seems to have interiorised the condition of inferiority posited by the Balkanist discourse in a distinctive way. More specifically, we show how the way Albanian migrants were represented by Greek media was instrumental in the disavowal and displacement of the features of 'failed Europeanness' and Ottoman-bound in-betweenness instituted by the Balkanist discourse. We will introduce as an heuristic device the notion of 'Albanism' (Mai 2003) as the discourse of a doubly articulated ambiguity inscribed within the already imputed ambiguity posed by the Balkanist discourse. In relation to discourses developed and circulated by Greek media, we suggest that Albania seems to be subject to a discourse of a doubly imputed ambiguity, as the ultimate 'Balkan in the Balkans'.

The cultural construction of Albanians in Greece

The end of the Albanian communist regime in 1991 saw a series of mass exoduses towards Greece, the main destination for Albanian migrants throughout the 1990s. As a result, for the first time in the twentieth century, Greek media and the public discourse were forced to address the existence of large numbers of 'aliens' within the national territory. The penetration of Albanian migrants into the Greek social and cultural context triggered a proliferation of representations of 'otherness' in the Greek press, which is characterised by a high level of sensationalism (Tsoukalis 1996: 28). Despite the existence of significant differences among Greek newspapers in the prevalence of populist discourses and spectacularising representations of migration-related issues, on the whole Albanian migrants have been represented in very negative and stigmatising terms and became the primary targets of negative stereotyping by the Greek media (Triandafyllidou 2002). The most common discourses constructing the Albanian immigrant in the Greek mediascape can be divided according to three main overlapping strands.

The first of these projects **the Albanian migrant as the pre-eminent representative of criminal behaviour.** Typically, Albanian criminals are represented as committing crimes of an unprecedentedly violent nature, where the profit is often disproportionately small to the violence involved. These accounts usually explain criminal events as emerging from the Albanian 'cultural heritage' rather than as provoked by specific circumstances. In other words, the main characteristic of this discursive dynamic is the ethnicisation of criminal behaviour, whereby events are explained according to cultural rather than social or political factors.

The Albanian migrant as the embodiment of poverty and backwardness is the second overarching discourse. Among the tropes embodied in the Greek media's cultural construction of the Albanian, that of poverty has a special weight. Poverty is not only his bodily stigma. Even in his criminality, the Albanian is characterised by a 'syndrome' of poverty, wretchedness and misery, from which he cannot escape. Thus, not only is Albanianness equated to criminality, but to a certain kind of criminal behaviour which is itself constructed as poor and miserable, since Albanian migrants are portrayed as stealing 'worthless objects that Greek criminals don't consider worthwhile' (*Eleftherotypia*, 3 June 99). Usually, Albanianness is constructed as inextricably intertwined with backwardness and a kind of animal primitiveness, as the following excerpts convey.

> Albanians mess up even the churches. They steal the laundry . . . The place where they live has been transformed into a pigsty. (*Eleftherotypia*, 22 January 1991)

> PIGS! This is the first picture catching the eye of the visitor as he enters Gjirokastër. Pigs are everywhere . . . (*Eleftherotypia*, 3 July 1994).

In their representation of Albanian migrants, Greek media convey a symmetrical differentiation between incommensurable kinds of people.

According to these accounts, the 'Albanian Other' is not simply described in terms of cultural incompatibility, but as unfit for assimilation on the basis of his lack of civilisation: hence the irony of Albanian children coming top of their class at school. Poverty is for the Albanians something like their fate or their nature, as they are associated with an imagined 'civilisation of poverty'. These cultural constructions and associations can also be seen as very powerful tools in enforcing lived conditions of marginalisation and exclusion; they are consistent with policies and practices which limit and define the areas of society in which specific social groups are expected to position themselves and, most importantly, remain. Hence, these dynamics can be seen as playing a clear social function, that of symbolically policing the boundaries of ethnic homogeneity and purity which sustain Greek national consciousness. This latter observation points us to the third set of Greek media discourses constructing the Albanian migrant.

This sees **the Albanian as an 'invader' and as a 'traditional enemy' of Greekness**. According to this framing, Albanian migrants are presented as conscious agents, aiming at disrupting Greek nationality/sovereignty and social cohesion by their imposition into the national(ised) space as a 'minority'. An important role in fixing the image of the Albanian as a 'traditional enemy' and 'invader' of Greekness was played by the mounting tension, especially between 1991 and 1995, around the issue of Northern Epirus.[7] However, this issue was part of the national imaginary long before the Albanian immigrants arrived in Greece. The question of the treatment of the Greek–Albanian minority living in southern Albania became highly politicised during the 1990s and played a key role in the definition of a policy on migration, which became conditional to the quality of the (usually strained) relations between Greece and post-communist Albania. Finally, the Kosovo crisis of the late 1990s and the ensuing NATO intervention in Kosovo and Serbia offered themselves as further occasions for Greek media to construct Albanian migrants as enemies of Christian Orthodoxy and consequently, in their eyes, as potential external and internal threats to Greekness. Here, it is important to remember how, as mentioned above, in conditions of perceived emergency, negative stereotypes about the national 'constitutive other' coalesce with the fantasies of national superiority and tend to dominate both state propaganda and the wider public arena.

Because of the cultural construction of the Albanian migrant as the embodiment of irreconcilable difference, from the very beginning a very strict if not absolute dividing line was drawn between Albanianness and Greekness, both defined in the fixed and reductive terms outlined above. The founding symbolic opposition of 'criminal and ungrateful Albanians' versus 'honest and hospitable Greeks' was reinforced by the representation of social antagonism in southern Albania in terms of the ethnicised opposition between Albanian persecutors and North-Epirotan victims.

As a consequence of this association, in Greece the crimes committed by Albanians have often been vested with a national dress according to a symbolic syllogism which went something like this: in Greece the Albanians murder North-Epirotans while in Albania they brutally oppress them, because they want to kick them out of their ancestral lands. These associative dynamics expose the 'hierarchies of Greekness' (Triandafyllidou and Veikou 2002) according to which Greek national consciousness and policies addressing the presence of migrant groups within Greek society are articulated and managed. In all these dynamics of cultural construction, which were reflected also in the case of Odysseus Cenaj, the strategy of stigmatisation and exclusion is achieved through what Pierre André Taguieff calls the 'de-realisation of the individual', by which he means the process of the 'dissolution of individuality into a collective entity' according to categories such as 'race', 'nation', 'culture/civilisation', 'mentality', 'people' etc. (Taguieff 1987: 316).

When analysing the content of Greek media representation of Albanians it is easy to see how the two ethnic groups are constructed as irreconcilably different on ethno-national rather than racial/biological criteria, according to the main parameters of Greek national consciousness. This is the phenomenon which Etienne Balibar calls 'racism without races', a discursive apparatus which does not 'postulate the superiority of certain groups or peoples in relations to others, but "only" the harmfulness of abolishing frontiers, the incompatibility of life-styles and traditions' (Balibar 1988: 21). What lies behind the cultural construction of the Other in terms of absolute difference is the concept and practice of hierarchy: some civilisations are regarded as 'universalistic and progressive', while others are conceived and discarded as 'irremediably particularistic and primitive' (Balibar 1988: 25). In this respect, the Greek media's representation of Albanian (and other) migrants has involved two parallel socio-cultural operations. By culturally constructing Albanians as 'unfit for civilisation', Greek media simultaneously devaluated their identity and culture in order to symmetrically re-define a strategically opposite image of Greekness as the 'embodiment of civilisation'.

The next and final section of this chapter will explain why, among all migrant groups, Albanians became Greece's main 'constitutive other' at a time of heightened socio-cultural and geopolitical change. It will do so by underlining the way the regime of 'Albanophobia' circulated within the Greek mediascape was consistent with a perceived need to re-organise Greece's national identity in order to meet the triple challenge posed by the process of European integration, the post-1989 disintegration of the Balkan geopolitical scenario, and the arrival of an unprecedented number of Albanian migrants into Greek society.

Producing the absolute difference: suppressing similarities between Greeks and Albanians

During the 1990s, Greek national identity was subject to new and unprecedented pressures and underwent a process of re-articulation in response to new perceived threats and priorities. These correlated with a shift in Greece's positionality *vis-à-vis* the main symbolic oppositions and boundaries which have articulated its national consciousness historically: its ambivalent relation to Europe and the Balkans, the rejection of its Ottoman past and heritage, and the Greek experience of emigration and poverty. As far as the relation with Europe and Europeanness in general is concerned, throughout the 1990s Greece's disappointing economic performance and its often nationalist foreign policy in the Balkans became the focus of much criticism from many EU and international institutions and representatives. Consequently, although Greece recorded the highest level of support for the process of European integration, during the 1990s it gradually became perceived as the most problematic member of the EU (Pettifer 1996: 17). Moreover, with the collapse of the Soviet empire in the Balkans, Greece suddenly lost its privileged geopolitical function as the eastern bulwark of NATO (Veremis 1995: 99) and was faced with the potential re-actualisation of unresolved territorial disputes with Macedonia and Albania.

Significantly, these conflicts became inextricably tied up with issues overlapping ethno-linguistic minorities amongst all of the neighbouring countries involved. Finally, the massive arrival of a large number of Eastern European migrants following the collapse of communism in the Balkan region in the early 1990s exacerbated feelings of anxiety which emerged from the sudden blurring of the main moral and geopolitical boundaries of Greek national identity. This, as we have seen, has historically been articulated by discursive sets underlining Greece's territorial integrity, its ethno-linguistic and religious homogeneity and its privileged cultural proximity to Europe and to European and Western culture.

According to Triandafyllidou and Mikrakis, in the 1990s the mass arrival of 'illegal newcomers' generated a 'feeling of discomfort and anxiety' in Greek public opinion, as immigration came to be perceived as presenting a number of threats, 'all associated with the "purity" of the domestic culture' (Triandafyllidou and Mikrakis 1995: 178). Vasilis Vamvakas takes this point further when he claims that, because of the similarity between Albanians and Greeks, the arrival of the former group has produced a 'dizziness' rather than a mere crisis of identity. The way similarity, rather than difference, should be seen as the main factor sustaining the vehement stigmatisation of Albanian migrants has been pointed out by many Greek scholars. The historian Alexis Heraklides seems to corroborate this line of interpretation when he points out that 'detesting the Albanians and everything Albanian is (maybe) due to the pronounced interrelation and historical interaction of the two peoples, who have lived as mixed cultural groups for centuries . . . ' (*Ta Nea*, 7 December 2000). In the same vein, Vamvakas stresses how Albanians are reserved an absolutely negative status in Greek media discourse because, being indistinguishable from Greeks at a physiognomic level, they were associated with undesirable memories of Greekness such as poverty, experiences of social anomie and the necessity of internal and international emigration (Vamvakas 2000: 136).

In conclusion, as a consequence of the interlocking of the geopolitical and socio-cultural circumstances described above, because of their overwhelming numerical superiority over all other migrant groups and of their somatic and cultural proximity to Greek people, Albanians were identified with aspects of Greekness which have been selectively disavowed and rejected in the historical process of formation of the Greek national culture. This hypothesis seems to corroborate René Girard's argument that the conflict between different cultures is provoked not from the existence of (cultural) differences but from their erasure (Girard 1972: 77). In this respect, the ambivalent positionality that Albanian migrants find themselves assigned by Greek society seems to mirror the condition of the 'barbarian'. This figure, according to Taguieff, does not represent the embodiment of irreconcilable alterity, but the more threatening impossibility of differentiating 'sames' from 'others' (Taguieff 1997: 69).

Returning to the case under examination, we can argue that, in winning the entitlement to carry the Greek flag in front of his Greek fellow-students, the Albanian migrant named after Odysseus, the Greek classical hero *par excellence*, was perceived as breaking down the racialised (in culturalist terms) hierarchies of civic entitlement shaping Greek national consciousness. By transgressing the boundaries of otherness and sameness articulating the cultural and hierarchical difference between Albanianness and Greekness, Odysseus Cenaj triggered what Girard (1972: 81) defines as a 'crisis of difference'. In this respect, the controversy generated by the very possibility of the Greek flag in the hands of an Albanian student[8] can be seen as a manifestation of the 'fear of social degradation' described by Max Weber (quoted in Taguieff 1997: 64). In this case, an important role is played by *ressentiment* (resentment), which should be seen as the end-result of the overlapping dynamics of ethnocentrism and class contempt.

In this respect, it is very important to acknowledge the implications for our argument of Etienne Balibar's analysis of workers' interiorisation of the bourgeois racist and discriminatory discourses. In Balibar's own words, the 'tendency on the part of the working class to preserve gains that have been made . . . and to turn back against bourgeois society the signifiers of class racism' shapes its ambivalent desire to both 'escape from the condition of exploitation' and reject 'the contempt to which it is subject' (Balibar 1988: 214). According to Balibar, this ambivalent assimilation and rejection of stigmatising and racialising discourses explains the permanence of xenophobia within the working class. When workers project their resentment and fear onto foreigners in the face of competition for strategic resources, 'it is a hatred of themselves, as proletarians – in so far as they are in danger of being drawn back into the mill of proletarianisation – that they are showing' (Balibar 1988: 214).

Behind the violence with which Albanian migrants have been criminalised and stigmatised by Greek media one can trace the resurgence of discourses and categories of exclusion, marginalisation and racialisation which were partially internalised as a residue of Greeks' own past experience of migration, exploitation and hardship. In other words, because of their physiognomic and cultural proximity, Albanians reminded Greeks of their own near-past of poverty, social unrest, authoritarianism and emigration. In this respect, 'Albanophobia' can be seen as the by-product of the anxiety generated by the fear of having to regress culturally, socially and economically, according to a racialised, or rather, Balkanised, hierarchy of civilisation. This is structured according to perceived levels of Balkanisation, that is of incomplete Europeanness, which are defined as inversely proportional to the perceived level of Ottomanisation. According to this imaginary hierarchy, Albanians rank lower than Greeks. If we define *Albanism* as a discursive set constructing Albania and Albanians in terms of doubly articulated 'Balkan' in-betweenness and failed Europeanness, it is easy to see the way its emergence was consistent with Greece's desire to hold on to a position of cultural and moral superiority in times of geopolitical and cultural turmoil. Unsurprisingly, Greece's entitlement a privileged position was argued on the basis of its self-perception as the most civilised, i.e. least Balkanised and most Europeanised, state in South-Eastern Europe.

Notes

1 We refer to the position of the Orthodox Church because its place in the social and political development of Greek national identity has been and still is is very important. On many occasions the Orthodox Church has taken a leading role in political affairs. An important example of this relationship was the clash between the Greek Church and the Greek government on the question of the introduction of the new EU-standardised identity card, which does not mention religious affiliation. In 2001, the Orthodox Church reacted to the decision to adopt the new format by accusing the Socialist government led by Kostas Simitis of implementing anti-national politics which might undermine Greek civilisation. Not only did the Orthodox Church organise massive anti-government protests in Athens and Thessaloniki, but it also indicted an informal referendum appealing against the new identity card format, which was signed by the current Greek prime minister Kostas Karamanlis.

2 On Andreas Papandreou and his national-populist ideology, see Pantazopoulos (2001).

3 These data are from a survey carried out by the Institute for the Education of the Homogeneis Population and Intercultural Education. The figures given

here do not include the 31,000 *homogeneis* students, most of whom are ethnic Greeks recently immigrated ('repatriated') from the former Soviet Union. Sources: *Eleftherotypia*, 11 October 2003; Macedonian Press Agency, 30 June 2004.

4 This refers to the tension between Greece and the Former Yugoslav Republic of Macedonia (FYROM) on the issue of the name of the new-born state, which was initially named 'Macedonia'. As the Greek government perceived this to be a potential threat to Greece's territorial integrity, it pressured both the UN and the EU not to recognise the Macedonian state except under the name FYROM. In 1994, as massive demonstrations were staged in the main Greek cities, the Greek government went as far as imposing an economic embargo on the Macedonian state until it obtained the change of name into FYROM and the adoption of the current flag in 1995.

5 In Greece there are two categories of immigrants: the *homogeneis* and the *allogeneis*. The Pontic Greeks (ethnic Greeks from the former Soviet Union) and Vorioepirotes (Albanian citizens of Greek ethno-linguistic origin and Orthodox religion), although belonging to the first category, were treated differently in relation to their entitlement to Greek citizenship. Whereas the Pontic Greeks were given full citizenship, Greek-Albanians were only given special rights, such as a three-year permit to stay, while all other migrants (including 'non-Greek' Albanians) normally have yearly permits, renewed with great difficulty. The differential treatment given to the two ethnic-Greek groups can be seen as originating from the implication the entitlement to Greek citizenship would have on the survival of the Greek minority in Albania. As the concept of *genos* is very close to the concept of race (*homogeneis* = of the same race as us), what this distinction implies is that being Greek is a matter of 'blood'.

6 Elaborating on Edward Said's seminal work on 'Orientalism' (1978), Maria Teodorova analyses 'Balkanism' as a Western European discourse on South-Eastern Europe formed gradually over two centuries and consolidated around the first Balkan wars and World War I. Whereas the Orientalist discourse presents the West and the Orient as incompatible and oppositional entities, in the Western European imaginary the Balkans are seen as an historical and cultural area *between* East and West, Europe and Asia; hence 'Balkanism is a discourse about an imputed ambiguity'. For Teodorova the West's perception of the Balkans is one of 'an incomplete self . . . the shadow, the structurally despised alter-ego' (Teodorova 1997: 11–17).

7 Northern Epirus is the term used to refer to that part of Epirus which is part of southern Albania. Since this is also the region of Albania where the Greek–Albanian minority lives, the use of this word is seen by many Albanians as implying a territorial claim, while in the Greek context its use differs according to the 'intensity' of the nationalistic orientation. Thus, for Greek nationalist hardliners, who define as Greeks all the Albanian citizens of Orthodox faith, the region stretches as far as the River Shkumbin, just 70km south of Tirana, while for others it designates the provinces of Sarandë, Gjirokastër and Korçë, where the Greek minority is concentrated. For an analysis of the role of Greek territorial claims in the diplomatic relations between Greece and Albania see the contribution of Konidaris to this volume.

8 Of course, Albanians are not the only foreign or foreign-origin pupils in Greek

schools, and Greek-origin children are also present in large numbers in schools in Germany and elsewhere. In their study of migrant children's experiences in Europe, Ackers and Stalford (2004: 230) present the case of a German pupil at a Greek school who was verbally abused by her Greek classmates after she held the Greek flag in the Independence Day parade. They taunted her: 'How can a German hold our flag?' This demonstrates the depth of feeling of Greek nationalist sentiment; but the scale of victimisation seems much greater (and the publicity more widespread and indignant) when the hands holding the flag are Albanian.

References

Ackers, L. and Stalford, H. (2004) *A Community for Children? Children, Citizenship and Internal Migration in the EU.* Aldershot: Ashgate.

Anderson, B. (1991) *Imagined Communities.* London, Verso.

Anthias, F. (1998) Rethinking social divisions: some notes towards a theoretical framework, *The Sociological Review*, 46(3): 505–35.

Balibar, E. (1988), in Balibar, E. and Wallerstein, I. *Race, Nation, Classe: Les Identités Ambiguës.* Paris: La Découverte.

Bambakas, V. (2000) The Construction of Otherness in Public Discourse from the 1980s. Athens: Panteion University, PhD thesis.

Campbell, J. R. and Rew, A. (1999) The political economy of identity and affect, in Campbell, J. R. and Rew, A. (eds) *Identity and Affect.* London: Pluto Press, 1–36.

Demertzis, N. (1999) *The Discourse of Nationalism.* Athens: Sakkoula (in Greek).

Demertzis, N., Paparthanassopoulos, S. and Armenakis, A. (1999) Media and nationalism: the Macedonian question, *The Harvard International Journal of Press Politics*, 4(3): 26–50.

Eriksen, T. (1995) *Small Places, Large Issues.* London: Pluto Press.

Fakiolas, R. (2003) Regularising the undocumented migrants in Greece: procedures and effects, *Journal of Ethnic and Migration Studies*, 29(3): 535–61.

Featherstone, K. (1996) Introduction, in Featherstone, K. and Ifantis, K (eds) *Greece in a Changing Europe.* Manchester: Manchester University Press, 3–16.

Girard, R. (1972) *La Violence et le Sacre.* Paris: Grasset.

Greenfeld, L. (1992) *Nationalism: Five Roads to Modernity.* Cambridge: Harvard University Press.

Hall, S. (1996) Who needs identity? in Hall, S. and Du Gay, P. (eds) *Questions of Cultural Identity.* London: Sage, 1-17

Hroch, M. (1996) From national movement to the fully-formed nation: the nation-building process in Europe, in Balakrishnan, G. (ed.) *Mapping the Nation.* London: Verso, 78–97.

Kitromilides, P (1990a) *Enlightenment, Nationalism, Orthodoxy.* Great Yarmouth: Galliard.

—— (1990b) Imagined communities and the origins of the national question in the Balkans, in Blinkhorn, M. and Veremis, T. (eds) *Modern Greece: Nationalism and Nationality.* Athens: Eliamep, 23–66.

Kohn, H. (1945) *The Idea of Nationalism.* New York: Macmillan.

Mai, N. (2003) The cultural construction of Italy in Albania and vice versa: migration dynamics, strategies of resistance and politics of mutual self-definition across colonialism and post-colonialism, *Modern Italy*, 9(1), 77–94.

McLuhan, M. (1987) *Understanding Media: The Extensions of Man.* London: Ark Paperbacks.
Moerman, M. (1965) Ethnic identification in a complex civilization: who are the Lue?, *American Anthropologist*, 67(5): 1215–29.
Pantazopoulos, A. (2001) *For the People and the Nation: The Time of Andreas Papandreou 1965–1989.* Athens: Polis (in Greek).
Pettifer, J. (1996) Greek political culture and foreign policy, in Featherstone, M. and Ifantis, K. (eds) *Greece in a Changing Europe.* Manchester: Manchester University Press, 17–23.
Plamenatz, J. (1976) Two types of nationalism, in Kamenka, E. (ed.) *Nationalism: The Nature and Evolution of an Idea.* New York: St. Martin's Press, 22–36.
Rozakis, C. (1996) The international protection of minorities in Greece, in Featherstone, K. and Ifantis, K. (eds) *Greece in a Changing Europe.* Manchester: Manchester University Press, 95–116.
Said, E. (1978) *Orientalism.* London: Routledge & Kegan Paul.
Sofos, S. and Tsagarousianou, R. (1994) The politics of identity: nationalism in contemporary Greece, in *The Resurgence of Nationalist Movements in Europe.* Bradford: University of Bradford, School of European Studies, Occasional Paper 12.
Sugar, P. (1969) External and domestic roots of Eastern European nationalism, in Sugar, P. and Lederer, I. (eds) *Nationalism in Eastern Europe.* Seattle: University of Washington Press, 3–54.
Taguieff, P. (1987) *La Force du Préjuge – Essais sur le Racisme et ses Doubles.* Paris: La Découverte.
—— (1997) *Le Racisme.* Paris: Flammarion.
Teodorova, M. (1997) *Imagining the Balkans.* Oxford: Oxford University Press.
Triandafyllidou, A. (2002) Greece, in ter Val, J. (ed.) *Racism and Cultural Diversity in the Mass Media.* Vienna: EUMC, 149–70.
Triandafyllidou, A. and Mikrakis, (1995) A ghost wanders through the capital, in Baumgartl, B. and Favell, A. (eds) *New Xenophobia in Europe.* The Hague: Kluwer, 164–79.
Triandafyllidou, A. and Veikou, M. (2002) The hierarchy of Greekness, *Ethnicities*, 2(2): 189–208.
Tsoukalis, L. (1996) Is Greece an awkward partner? in Keatherstone, K. and Ifantis, K. (eds) *Greece in a Changing Europe.* Manchester: Manchester University Press, 24–30.
Veremis, T. (1995) *Greece's Balkan Entanglement.* Athens: Eliamep.
Wieviorka, M. (1998) *Le Racisme.* Paris: La Découverte.
Willis, P. (1990) *Common Culture.* Buckingham: Open University Press.

8

Better than Muslims, not as good as Greeks

Emigration as experienced and imagined by the Albanian Christians of Lunxhëri

GILLES DE RAPPER

My first encounter with Albanian emigration happened in 1995–6, when I was doing fieldwork in the border district of Devoll, in south-eastern Albania. I was staying in an Albanian-speaking Christian village, up in the mountains and close to the Greek border. Villagers told me about people from the closest Muslim village, down in the valley: 'Look at them, down there. At the time of the cooperative, they used to insult us by calling us "damned Greeks", "bloody Greeks". But today they all work in Greece and have Greek names, while we did not go to Greece. Who is Greek then?' As a matter of fact, people from the Christian villages – who insist on their Albanian national identity and refuse to be called Greek – have been moving to the town and even more to the United States, where they retain links dating back to the time of the pre-World War II migration known as *kurbet*. Meanwhile, their Muslim neighbours started in the early 1990s to migrate to Greece, where most of them changed their names and some converted to Orthodoxy.

Emigration appeared to be a matter of negotiation of identity not only for those who were living in the host society, but also for the ones living at home, giving new forms to boundaries inside local society. In this chapter, I look at the impact of migration on the construction of collective identity in a more complex local society. If the district of Devoll is clearly divided between a Muslim majority and a few Christian villages higher up in the mountains, the district of Gjirokastër, on which this paper focuses, is divided into several intermingled groups, based on religion, territory, language and national identity. Each of these groups seems to have its specific migration strategy, using different networks. I focus here on the sense of belonging and identity of the people involved in the migration, i.e. the migrants and their families, either in Albania or in Greece.

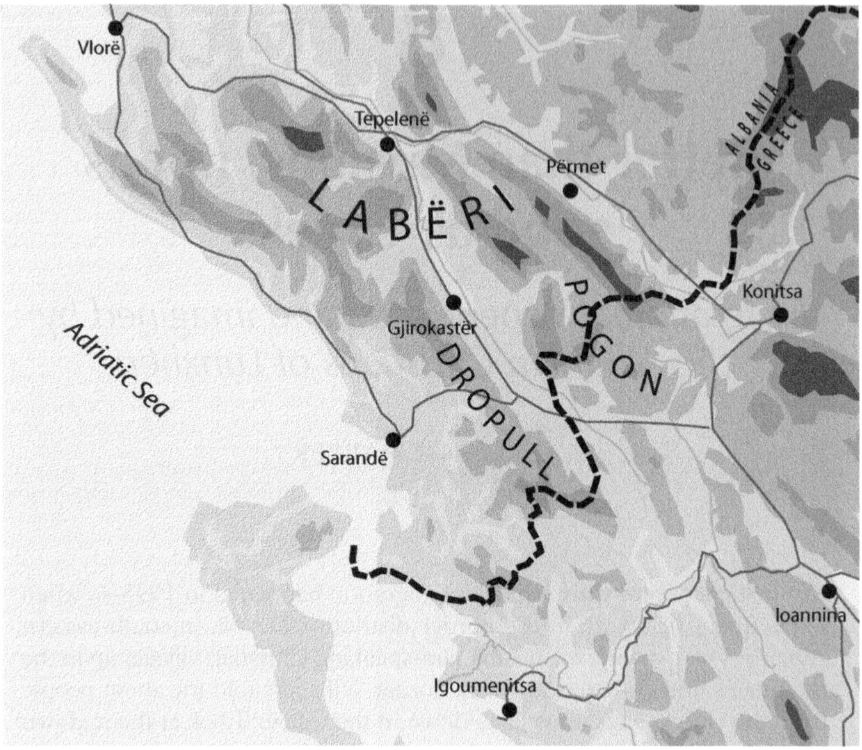

Figure 8.1 Southern Albania

My main fieldwork location is the group of around a dozen villages named Lunxhëri, on the slopes of the mountain range facing the town of Gjirokastër.[1] See figures 8.1 and 8.2 for location maps, first of Southern Albania, and second of the area of Lunxhëri. Until the 1960s, Lunxhëri was mainly inhabited by Albanian-speaking Orthodox Christians called the Lunxhots. By then, and starting during and just after the Second World War, many of them had left their villages to settle in Gjirokastër and in the towns of central Albania, where living conditions and employment opportunities were considered better. They were replaced, from the end of the 1950s on, by Vlachs, forced by the regime to settle in agricultural cooperatives. Some Muslim families from Kurvelesh, in the mountainous area of Labëria, also came to Lunxhëri at the same time – in fact, many of them were employed as shepherds in the villages of Lunxhëri even before the

Second World War. While Lunxhëri practiced (as did many other regions) a high level of (territorial) endogamy, marriage alliances started to occur between Christian Lunxhots and members of the Greek minority of the districts of Gjirokastër (Dropull, Pogon) and Sarandë. Such alliances were both encouraged by the regime and used by people to facilitate internal mobility and obtain a better status and life-chances.

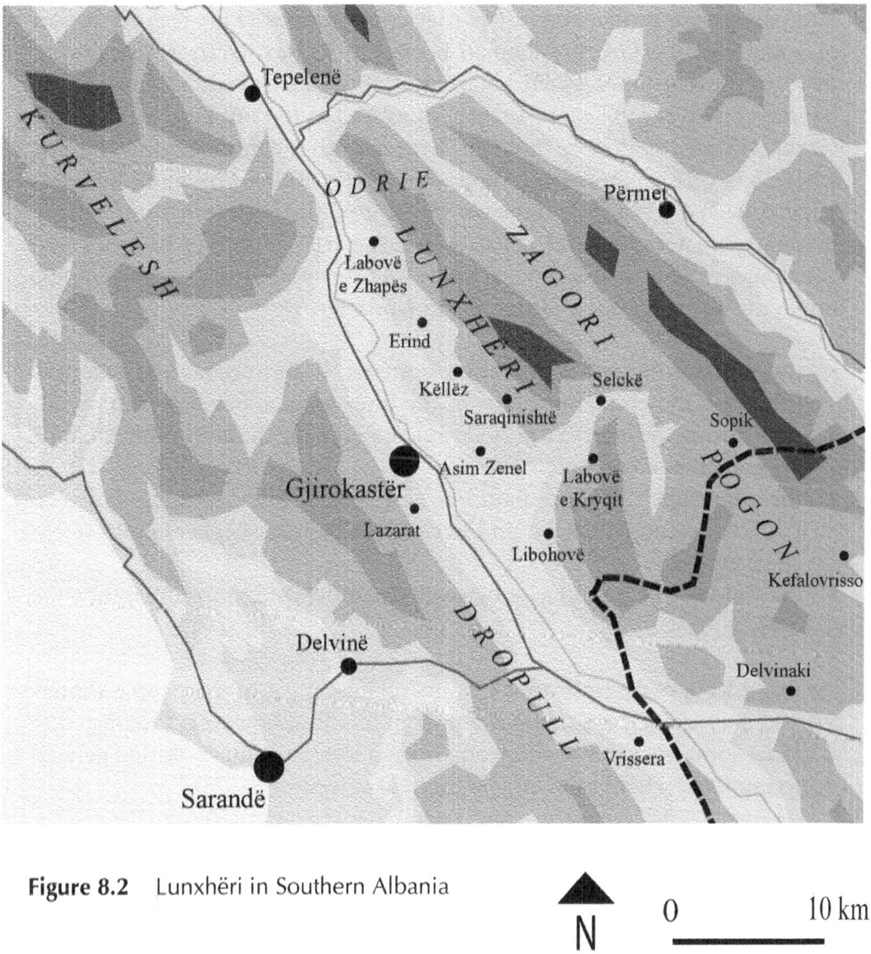

Figure 8.2 Lunxhëri in Southern Albania

Today, the population of Lunxhëri is perceived as composed of three main groups:

- the Lunxhots, who call themselves 'ethnic Lunxhots' or '*autoktonë*', and are called 'villagers' (*fshatarë*) by the others;
- the Vlachs,[2] who call themselves '*çoban*' or 'Greek-Vlachs' and are still referred to by the Lunxhots as 'newcomers' (*të ardhur*);

- and finally the Muslims, whether they trace their origin in Labëri or claim to be autochthonous (as is the case for instance in the village of Erind). They refer to themselves as Muslims or Turks (*myslyman, turk*).

The various terms used in this categorisation will be discussed further below.

Its complex ethnic composition and social history make Lunxhëri an interesting case in the study of border communities. This chapter is part of a study of the Greek–Albanian border in Epirus, from its creation in 1913 to present time, which I started in 2001. I made short stays (up to ten days) in every village of Lunxhëri, as well as in Gjirokastër and in the Greek villages of Pogon (both in Greece and Albania), and in Tirana, where lots of Lunxhots have migrated. The material presented here has been collected through interviews with Lunxhotes living in Lunxhëri, in Tirana or in Greece, and consists in large part of family histories and genealogies. This enables me to focus on three main topics regarding the impact of the international border on Lunxhëri:

- the transformation of migration patterns, both internal and external, following the changing status of the international border (from openness during the interwar period to closure during the communist regime and openness again after 1991);
- the marriage alliance patterns, especially intermarriage between Christians and Muslims, and between Albanian-speakers and Greek-speakers;
- the fluid ethnic boundaries between the different groups inhabiting the area.

As usual for a male anthropologist in Albania, most of the people I interviewed are men. By spending my time in families, however, I managed to conduct some interviews with women, or at least to witness, during general conversations, where men and women disagreed.

The impact of migration on the construction of identity

It is common-sense to say that the politics of immigration and the reception of migrants by the host society have an impact on the migrants' individual strategies – such as in the case of changing one's personal name. It is also acknowledged that emigration has an impact on the economy of the country of origin, mainly through remittances. This chapter aims to illustrate that the impact of migration goes beyond remittances and personal strategies, and affects also the construction of collective (and individual) identity in the society of origin: that is to say that the people who do not leave, or who do not directly benefit from remittances, are also affected by migration in the way they perceive themselves.

In that sense, emigration to Greece has rendered more visible some distinctions and lines of division of local Albanian society: for instance between *minoritarë*, or members of the Greek minority in Albania, and Albanians; or between Orthodox Christians and Muslims. New categories have also emerged – such as 'Northern Epirotes'[3] – which have become central in the way migrants themselves perceive their migratory experience, and which influence some of their decisions. In other words, every migrant, before leaving Albania, is confronted by these oppositions and categories, when he or she has to think about the means of departure: legally, if documents can be easily obtained; or illegally, if the individual believes on the contrary that his/her religious affiliation, first name, or place of origin, will make it difficult to obtain the documents. Those categories and lines of division were certainly not unknown in the original society, but some of them had been denied by the communist regime (the case of religious affiliation – although it was still relevant in social relations) or were not openly mentioned (as in the case of national or linguistic minorities).

The notion of *kurbet*, already mentioned above, and described in a little more detail in Chapter 1, is a good example of how past and present migration to a foreign land, both as facts and as representations, shape the social relations inside local society.[4] It is striking for instance how, of the three groups under consideration here, only the Lunxhots claim – and to a certain extent are acknowledged to have – an exclusive connection with the *kurbet*. Lots of aspects of social life are said to have been inherited from the *kurbet*. For instance, the Lunxhot female traditional costume, which acts as a marker of Lunxhot identity *vis-à-vis* the Vlachs, Greeks and Muslims, is said to reflect the prosperity of Lunxhot migrants in Istanbul and to be influenced by models originating from the capital city of the empire.[5] The ritual of hospitality, particular pieces of furniture, and varieties of trees cultivated in the courtyards and gardens are also said to have been brought in by Lunxhot *kurbetllinj* (returnees). Altogether, and most important, the Lunxhots claim a higher level of 'culture' than all other areas of Southern Albania, because of their old practice of *kurbet*. The time of the *kurbet* is thus generally presented as a golden age for Lunxhëri, a time when the villages enjoyed prosperity, development, and when the Lunxhots formed a kind of *aristokraci* in the whole area. Needless to say, this idealised memory of the *kurbet* stands in sharp opposition to the actual migration to Greece that Lunxhëri has experienced from 1991 on. As we shall see, present migration to Greece is said to bring no good at all to Lunxhëri, and to mean on the contrary the end of everything (people are leaving, shops are closed, fields and gardens abandoned, etc.).

It is also necessary to note that the idealisation of the era of *kurbet* – which opposes *kurbet* to present migration as if communism had no impact at all on the villages – is mainly a characteristic of men's discourse on local society. During one evening conversation with a couple of neighbours in the village of Këllëz, one of the men started to tell me about the *kurbet* which 'opened us to the world, brought us culture'. He was immediately interrupted by one the women who told him: 'What are you saying? When we went for the first time to Greece [after 1991], we did not even know how to flush the toilet, nor to use knives and forks!' Thus the glorification of the *kurbet* on the part of men whose sons are now working in Greece should not be taken as a general feature of Lunxhot identity, although it plays a role in the way the Lunxhots define themselves and in the way they consider today's migration to Greece.

The opening of the border to Greece and new opportunities of migration have not had the same impact on the different categories of population. The Vlachs seem to have been the first to depart on a large scale from the villages and go to Greece. This is a result of their bad condition in Lunxhëri, where they were still considered foreigners and had suffered more than the others from persecution during communism. Their migration also drew on their connections with kin living in Greece, as all of them trace their origin to the village of Kefalovrisso (the old Mexhide), in Greek Epirus (Sintès 2003). As they were the first ones to leave, they were also the first ones to come back, starting in 1993–4. Some of them came back to the 'home' village, where they opened a small shop – most of the times the only one existing in the village – and/or bought a minibus to transport goods and travellers between the village and the town of Gjirokastër. In several villages, such as Saraqinishtë, this economic power, added to their demographic weight, allowed them to gain some political power by being elected as village heads (*kryetar i fshatit*). Others continued to work as masons or carpenters, as they did in Greece, working either in the villages or in Gjirokastër. Some of them actually left the village to settle in Gjirokastër where the labour market offers more opportunities. More recently, they were also the first ones to use the lands they possess to grow grapes and vegetables on a commercial scale rather than for domestic use only, as is usual among other villagers. Altogether, they became prominent in the villages; their success is a source of envy and jealousy for the other villagers.

The two other groups, the Lunxhots and the Muslims, soon followed the example of the Vlachs. In their accounts of their first experience in Greece, they often refer to the Vlachs as guides and well-connected people from whom they could expect assistance in Greece. Actually, there is evidence that Vlachs – as well as Lab shepherds from Lazarat – already played that role before the opening of the border, when they were supposed to know hidden tracks across the border that even the border guards were not aware of. A young male informant from Këllëz thus used the 'Vlach network' through Sopik (Albanian Pogon) and Kefalovrisso/Mexhide (Greek Pogon) to go to Veria in 1991, before moving on to Athens three months later to look for a distant cousin. Just as the Vlachs present themselves as 'Greek-Vlachs', most of the Lunxhots and, although with less ease, the Muslims who migrate to Greece pretend to be Greeks, or of Greek origin, or at least Christians. It is interesting to note however that, due to the very limited number of intermarriages with Vlachs and to the generally bad reputation the Vlachs have in the area, the Lunxhots do not claim a Greek identity through an invented Vlach identity, but rather directly, through intermarriage with the Greek minority members in Dropull, Pogon and Sarandë.

Local society and its lines of division

Southern Albania forms a particularly complex society as far as collective identity is concerned. At first sight, it can be described as a juxtaposition of small units identified by specific ethnonyms and/or toponyms. Although they are usually not administrative units, most of them are known and recognised by the whole population and even by the State, for instance through official ethnography. Lunxhëri is thus an 'ethnographic region' (*krahinë etnografike*) surrounded by others, namely Zagori, Pogon, Dropull and Kurvelesh, and a part of the larger ethno-linguistic unit called Labëri (Zojzi 1962).[6] These units are also characterised by a high level of endogamy, which is a good illustration of their relevance for local populations. It is usual for its inhabitants to define Lunxhëri as an endogamous unit. As often happens, endogamy is more ideal than real, as people are actually marrying in and out. Even so, things are seen as following a specific pattern: girls from Lunxhëri should not be married out, except if they have a physical handicap or a low morality. Men are marrying in, in contradiction to the patri-virilocal rule of residence, but this is explained – at least in local discourse – by the situation of Lunxheri in the context of the *kurbet*: men being abroad for long periods of time, it was not easy to find a husband inside Lunxhëri, and men from outside were looking for these unions, as it allowed them to enter the prosperous and prestigious villages of Lunxhëri.

A closer examination reveals, however, a much more complex and dynamic situation: most of these small units have porous and changing borders (as can be expected in the case of ethnically-based groups), and the meaning they have for their members, as well as for outsiders, is also changing according to time and circumstances. The question of the boundaries of Lunxhëri is thus a matter of discussion among educated Lunxhots as well as among ethnographers. First comes a group of seven villages whose inclusion into Lunxhëri cannot be disputed: Nokovë, Mingull, Këllëz, Dhoksat, Qestorat, Saraqinishtë and Stegopull form the 'heart' of Lunxhëri and are considered the most ancient and aristocratic villages. Two other villages, Erind to the north and Selckë to the south, are usually added to this core. Then comes a group of villages which are generally lower in altitude and share the fact of having been parts of *çiflik* or land estates owned by Muslims before World War Two, whereas Lunxhëri is proud of its history of 'independence' and exclusive Orthodox Christian character. Those villages are called by others 'below' (*poshtë*) and their inhabitants are *poshtarak*, 'lowlanders', with a rather strong derogatory meaning: they live lower down, closer to the river, and are also seen as of low morality and culture, partly because of their mixed origin (people working on the *çiflik* lands came from different parts of the country), partly because they did not experience the *kurbet*.[7] Finally, one is told about 'geographic Lunxhëri' (as opposed to 'ethnographic Lunxhëri'), a kind of larger Lunxhëri that includes also the area known as Odrie to the north and the village of Labovë e Kryqit to the south. People from Odrie, for instance, issued tapes of traditional music under the name of 'Grupi i Lunxhërisë'. On the part of 'ethnographic Lunxhëri', the extension beyond the 'ethnic border' has the advantage of bringing into Lunxhëri the historically and architecturally valuable villages of Labovë e Kryqit (with its twelfth-century Byzantine church) and Labovë e Zhapës (home of the successful nineteenth-century *kurbetlli* Vangjel Zhapa and of several patriots from the Meksi family). As can be seen from the presentation of the different geographic meanings of Lunxhëri, there are both a stress on local identity (and this is not specific to Lunxhëri) and a wide spectrum of ways to understand the content and meaning of this local identity.

Two main lines of division seem significant in the case of Lunxhëri and determine most of the process of construction of ethnic boundaries. The first one is religion, the second ethno-national belonging. As in other parts of Albania (de Rapper 2002), and notwithstanding official ideology on the lack of relevance of religious affiliation, local society is strongly organised in terms of religious communities, or *fe*: Lunxhot identity, as it is expressed today, relies on the belonging to Orthodox Christianity. The Lunxhots are proud of being Christians, proud of the numerous and sometimes historically and architecturally valuable churches and monasteries that are spread all over Lunxhëri. Religious festivals such as Shën Sotir, celebrated on 6 August at Drenovë monastery in Mingull, are supposed to gather most of the population,[8] and Christian holidays structure the whole year. This is important as more and more migrants follow the rhythm of the Greek Orthodox year, with breaks for Christmas, Easter and mid-August, instead of the two-season cycle that first characterised Albanian emigration to Greece, when migrants left their homes from April to October. As a matter of fact, the revival of Christian holidays in Lunxhëri may be seen, at least partially, as a consequence of migration to Greece, after several decades of proscribed religious practice. The ban on religious personal names during communism did not affect them too much (Lunxhots appear to have been on the right side at that time, many of them becoming army officers, high-ranked officials, etc.) and they almost all bear Christian names. Those who did not, got baptised in the 1990s, either in Albania or in Greece, and others got religiously married many years after their civil marriage.

By insisting on their religious affiliation, and especially in front of a French and allegedly Christian anthropologist, the Lunxhots are opposing themselves to the other main religious community in the area, the Muslims.[9] This opposition is expressed at different levels. It is first directed against the Muslim Lunxhots, most of whom are considered as foreigners (*të ardhur*), as they moved from Labëri (Kurvelesh) to Lunxhëri before and after the Second World War. The sense of otherness is not only due to their origin outside Lunxhëri, but mainly to the fact that they are Muslims (Christians moved from other places to Lunxhëri at the same time, but their origin is generally forgotten today, or not considered relevant). The Muslims from Erind – the only village in Lunxhëri to be Muslim in majority – are not perceived as the descendants of migrants from other Muslim areas, but they are nonetheless definitely different, and the relations between Erind and the neighbouring villages are marked by the same stereotypes as the relations between Muslims and Christians usually are: people from Erind are said to be violent and dirty, to have no culture, and to be responsible for anything bad happening in the area.

At another level, the Christian Lunxhots oppose themselves to the neighbouring area of Kurvelesh, in Labëri. This opposition is expressed in two ways: by telling stories relating to events dating back to a vague 'before' (*më përpara*), and by presenting more recent events, especially those of 1997, as the repetition of earlier ones. In the stories the Lunxhots tell about the *kurbet*, the Labs were often portrayed as bandits who robbed the rich *kurbetlli* on their return from Istanbul, kidnapped villagers to ransom their families, and organised expeditions to steal sheep from the Christians. Again in stories of the Second World War, the Labs (and Muslims in general, including inhabitants of Libohovë and Lazarat) are always connected to the Ballists (the bad side, from the Lunxhots' point of view) whose main purpose in fighting was to attack the Christian Lunxhots as Christians rather than as Partisans. At the same time, and probably under the influence of official ideology, the Labs are recognised as brave and heroic patriots (*atdhetar*), whose violent character has been devoted to the affirmation and defence of the nation. But this construction seems to be limited to the times of war and of communism. After this parenthesis, the image of the Labs is again what it used to be in earlier times. The events of 1997 (and to a lesser extent, those of 1990–2) are interpreted in terms of a never-ending conflict between the Christian Lunxhots and the Muslim Labs: as before, Labs came to Lunxhëri (using the knowledge of the area and its inhabitants they got by working there as shepherds and woodcutters), robbed the travellers and – most significantly – stole the bells from the churches.[10]

At a third level, finally, all Albanian Muslims in general are seen as responsible for all the troubles and destruction that happened in Albania, and as a majority group oppressing the Christian minority; they are considered as Others against whom the Lunxhots as Christians must fight and resist. This idea is not expressed by all the Lunxhots. Actually, if the official ideology did not prove strong enough to erase the traditional Muslim-Christian opposition at the local level, it seems to have had an effect on the way local people perceive the nation: as a place where Muslims and Christians are all alike and where difference does not matter. In that respect, religious difference is relevant only at the local level, in everyday social relationships. On the other hand, the people who 'came out' in the 1990s as opponents to communism, frequently parallel communism and Islam – both attempted to eradicate the Christian religion, both took the land from Christian landowners, both are related to fanatism and intolerance. It is they who state that, as a Christian minority, the Lunxhots must be aware of the Muslim threat to their existence. The issue of a couple of new villages created during communism illustrates this case. The village of Asim Zenel, named after a partisan from Kurvelesh who was killed in July 1943, was created as the centre of an agricultural cooperative in 1947 on the road leading from Lunxhëri to Dropull. The people who were settled in the new village were mainly shepherds from Kurvelesh, and were Muslims. The same thing happened for the village of Arshi Llongo, while other Muslims from Kurvelesh settled in the villages of lower Lunxhëri (Karjan, Shën Todër, Valare) and in Suhë. As a result, it is not exceptional to hear today from the Lunxhots, such as one of my informants, a retired engineer living in Tirana, that 'in 1945 a Muslim buffer-zone was created between Dropull and Lunxhëri to stop the Hellenisation of Lunxhëri. Muslims were thought to be more determined against Greeks. At that time, the danger of Hellenisation was real in Lunxhëri'. In the village of Këllëz people also regret that 'Lunxhëri has been surrounded by a Muslim buffer-zone by Enver Hoxha, who was himself a Muslim'.

The relevance of religious communities (*fe*) in local and collective identity is also obvious in the fact that the Vlachs are often said by the Lunxhots to be of another *fe*, although they are both Orthodox Christians and go to the same churches. The feeling of otherness that characterises so strongly the relation between Vlachs and Lunxhots is thus expressed in term of religious communities; at the same time, the definition of Vlachs as another *fe* justifies the reluctance for intermarriage with them as well as a lack of trust and sympathy.

Apart from religion, ethno-national affiliation appears to be of great relevance today. It is clear that, in this border area, it has always been important to identify oneself with one or other of the national groups. It is also well-known that, in this part of the Balkans, and back into the Ottoman times, the ethnonyms 'Greek' and 'Orthodox Christian' were largely synonymous, so that it was difficult to be Orthodox *and* to claim not to be Greek. Lunxhëri is an illustration of that ambiguity or contradiction. By the beginning of the nineteenth century and later on, the British, French and

Austrian travellers who visited Lunxhëri, most of them arriving from Ioannina, described the Lunxhots as Albanian-speaking Orthodox Christians, and had the feeling that, starting north of Delvinaki, they were entering another country, although the political border did not exist at the time. Greek was not spoken as it was further south; there was a change in the way of life and manners of the peasants. As one traveller reported (Hobhouse 1813: 93, 99–100):

> Every appearance announced to us that we were now in a more populous country. (. . .) the plain was every where cultivated, and not only on the side of Argyro-castro [Gjirokastër] . . . but also on the hills which we were traversing, many villages were to be seen. The dress of the peasants was now changed from the loose woollen brogues of the Greeks, to the cotton kamisa, or kilt of the Albanian, and in saluting Vasilly they no longer spoke Greek. Indeed you should be informed, that a notion prevails amongst the people of the country, that Albania, properly so called, or at least, the native country of the Albanians, begins from the town of Delvinaki; but never being able, as I have before hinted, to learn where the line of boundary is to be traced, I shall content myself with noticing the distinction in the above cursory manner.
>
> In this place [Qestorat, in Lunxhëri] everything was on a very different footing from what it had been in the Greek villages. We experienced a great deal of kindness and attention from our host; but saw nothing in his face (though he was a Christian) of the cringing, downcast, timid look of the Greek peasant. His cottage was neatly plastered, and white-washed, and contained a stable and small ware-room below, and two floored chambers above, quite in a different style from what we had seen in Lower Albania. It might certainly be called comfortable; and in it we passed a better night than any since our departure from Ioannina.

By the end of the nineteenth century, however, during the period of the *kurbet*, the Lunxhots were moving between two extreme positions regarding ethnic and national affiliation. On the one hand, there were those who joined the Albanian national movement, especially in Istanbul, and made attempts to spread a feeling of Albanian belonging in Lunxhëri. The well-known Koto Hoxhi (1825–95) and Pandeli Sotiri (1843–91), who participated in the opening of the first Albanian school in Korçë in 1887, were both from Lunxhëri (from the villages of Qestorat and Selckë). On the other hand were those who insisted on the Greekness of the Lunxhots and were opposed to the development of an Albanian national identity among the Christians. We recall here the names of the famous Christodoulos (1820–98) and Jorgos (1863–1920) Zografos – the latter having been the head of the Governement of Autonomous Northern Epirus in Gjirokastër during the First World War – and of Vangelis Zappas (or Vangjel Zhapa, 1800–65), all of them from Lunxhëri (Qestorat and Labovë e Zhapës). Between those two extreme positions were the majority of the people, and it is almost impossible today to say how they perceived themselves. What is sure is that, in the context of the *kurbet*, most of them declared themselves as Greeks: memories of the *kurbet* show that in Istanbul the Lunxhots were living together with other Orthodox Christians from Greece and going to the same churches, and were part of the Greek minority there. In America as well, it seemed easier, or more meaningful, to declare themselves as Greek rather than as Albanians.[11]

At the same time, it seems certain that most of the women spoke only Albanian, and no Greek, just as, in the first decades of twentieth century, Pogoni women spoke Greek and no Albanian (Winnifrith 2002). Greek was, however, used in church services all over Lunxhëri, and an old woman from the village of Këllëz recalled that 'we, the women, did not understand what the priest was saying'. It is also suggested, in the memories of the *kurbet*, that young men leaving Lunxhëri for Istanbul spoke only Albanian and would learn Greek and Turkish in Istanbul.

These fluid identities were to be crystallised at the time of the creation of the Albanian state (1913) and during the process of Albanisation that followed. Lunxhëri was actually included in the definition of Northern Epirus as a land of Hellenism that should have been given to the Greek state in 1913, and many families left the area, and Albania, during and after the First World War, to avoid becoming citizens of the new Albanian state. These people are called in Albanian propaganda *filogrek* and seem to have been powerful enough at some times to force pro-Albanian families to leave Lunxhëri. It the interwar period for instance, the village of Selckë is said to have been 'full of *filogrek*' and an informant told me the story of her husband's father, who secretly left the village one night with his wife, after a cousin told him that his pro-Albanian commitment did not please a powerful pro-Greek family. They left for America, while the pro-Greek family eventually left for Greece. Their house is now occupied by a Vlach family. It must be noted that the development of those national feelings did not automatically follow the linguistic border between Greek and Albanian. The stress on language as a criterion of national identification was probably stronger in the minds of nationalist activists and members of the international commission for the drawing of the border than among the local population. As T. J. Winnifrith reports from the notes of a British archaeologist in 1924:

> On 24 January Clarke left [Hllomo, in Albanian Pogon] for Labovë. He noted that then as now he was crossing a linguistic border from an area where Greek is spoken to one where it was merely understood. But he also said that there was little difference between the architecture of Labovë and of the villages he had previously visited, and that both in Labovë and farther north at Saraganishtë [*sic* for Saraqinishtë] there was a certain amount of pro-Greek feeling. (Winnifrith 2002)

Due to the departures of the *filogrek* and to the policy of Albanisation undertaken by the Albanian state since its creation, the sense of national belonging in Lunxhëri was, until recently, quite clear: not only are the Lunxhots ethnically and nationally Albanian, as opposed to the Greeks and Vlachs, they are even supposed to be the only true Albanians of the area, as opposed to the Muslims of Labëria who are seen as having abandoned their religion to become 'Turks' and, in so doing, have betrayed. The slightest variation from this discourse was suspected of being *filogrek*.

It must be noted that when people leave the question of national identity aside, for instance to tell their family histories, things become much less clear: shifts from one national identity to another are not rare, and they do not seem to be a problem as far as the individual or familial level is concerned. Several families thus acknowledge a Greek origin a few generations ago, others recognise branches that 'became' Greek just by crossing the border, and so on. This is for instance the case of an informant from Qestorat, who, although being definitely Albanian as far as national identity is concerned, and very critical *vis-à-vis* the Greeks, tells the story of his father, arrived from Athens in 1942 and who 'learned Albanian here, by himself'.

In fact, if 'exclusive Albanianness' is still dominant as a discourse, emigration and the loosening of state control have brought radical changes in the sense of belonging. To claim a Greek origin or Greek familial connections is not a problem anymore as regards the state, and it is even considered a positive feature as far as emigration to Greece is concerned. Most of the Lunxhots in Greece present themselves as Northern Epirotes, and any evidence of Greek nationality, *kombësi greke*, is looked for as a positive feature in the context of migration.

The impact of migration in Lunxhëri

As can be seen, the construction of collective identity in Lunxhëri cannot be separated from the vicinity of the Greek border and from the previous migration phase, *kurbet*. In fact, both the changing status of the border and whether mobility is permitted or not, have contributed to shape the local discourse on what it is to be a Lunxhot. This is illustrated by the way local people talk about themselves today in relation to emigration, and on how they perceive the changes to their identity brought by emigration.

According to the people living in Lunxhëri, the first characteristic of the new period of migration since 1990 is its demographic aspect: people have left massively (*kanë ikur shumë*), the villages have turned into deserted places (*shkretëtirë*), and only older people have remained (*vetëm pleqtë kanë mbetur*). As a matter of fact, a walk through the villages reveals – as in other parts of Albania – lots of closed or abandoned houses, and the land is obviously not cultivated everywhere. In the village of Selckë for instance, from 65 families (*familje*, i. e. married couple and children; two couples living in the same house count as two families) in 1990, only 22 have remained, with 53 individuals. The ones who left have gone mainly to Greece (33 families), and some also to Gjirokastër (5) and to other places in Albania (5). This desertification is opposed both to the period of communism, when most of the villages had their own school, several shops and small workshops, a museum and sometimes a clinic or a hospital (*ambulancë*); and to the period of the *kurbet*, which is paradoxically remembered as a time of dense social relationships. In fact, when the consequences of the *kurbet* are considered, it is mainly in positive terms, that is in terms of wealth and culture (*kulturë*) as well as in terms of demographic expansion. The *kurbet* is sometimes explained as resulting from the inability of the land to bear such a large population.

By contrast, the new emigration brings only negative consequences: the migrants do not return as the *kurbetlli* used to, and do not send money back to support the development of the village. In other words, they stop being members of the village, turning it into a desert. Although there is evidence of migrants sending money to restore the church or buy new icons, this is considered very little in comparison to the complete churches, schools, roads and bridges that the *kurbetlli* are said to have funded. In Qestorat for instance, people regret that when each migrant family was asked to contribute 20,000 drachmas (approximately 70 euros) for the restoration of the small church of Saint Mary, only some actually sent money.

For younger generations, who did not live at the time of the *kurbet*, the present-day situation is opposed to the one that prevailed during communism, 'at the time of the cooperative' (*në kohën e koperativës*). Those times of dense social relationships are recreated only during religious feasts, when the migrants come back to the village for a few days.

Together with the demographic aspect, there is a sense of cultural loss. As many Lunxhots say, 'with emigration, everything goes away': houses, with their traditional architecture and furniture, fall in ruins, customs and rituals vanish, the sense and pride of belonging disappear, schools and shops are closed.

Moreover, the demographic aspect has an ethnic dimension which is frequently mentioned by the Lunxhots: the first ones to have left the village, with no plan to return, were the Vlachs. Forming a large part of the population in almost every village by the end of communism, they are said to be responsible for the death of the villages. If we introduce this ethnic dimension into the figures for migration concerning the village of Selckë, we do indeed find that Vlach families are more likely to be in Greece.

It is true that in several villages (Selckë, Nokovë, Mingull, Stegopul), the Vlachs outnumbered the 'villagers' (*fshatarë* – this is how the Lunxhots call themselves and are called by the Vlachs) by 1990 and that they were the first ones to leave, in consequence of both their feeling of fear and actual experience of persecution dating back to communist time, and the connections they had kept (or easily reactivated) on the other side of the border.

It is, however, difficult to make a clear distinction between the Vlachs and the others in terms of relationship to the village (table 8.1); and the image of the former as being responsible for the death of the villages is something of a stereotype. As a matter of fact, if the Lunxhots have remained more numerous, it is often because they have fewer possiblities to leave, and thus are forced to remain.

Table 8.1 Migration of families in the village of Selckë

	Vlach families	Lunxhot families	Total
Still in the village	9	13	22
In Greece	19	14	33
In Gjirokastër	2	3	5
Other places in Albania	3	2	5
Total	33	32	65

Although it is not expressed as such by people, it must be stressed here that emigration has also brought a change in the ethnic relations between Vlachs and villagers: the former moved from a position of substantial inferiority (their integration in Lunxhëri was never complete, as the lack of intermarriage clearly shows) to a position of economic success. This raises envy and jealousy among the villagers. The biggest and most luxurious houses belong to the Vlachs, who are also the most dynamic and successful entrepreneurs. In consequence, far from contributing to the vanishing of ethnic differentiation between the two groups, migration has given rise to a new formulation of the boundary: the Vlachs are now the victims of a form of segregation developed by people, the Lunxhots, who suffer from their new position of inferiority in front of people who were traditionally considered as inferior. If most of the Lunxhots still speak in bad terms of the Vlachs, as they did in communist times (although all discriminatory behaviour was officially forbidden), they publicly insist on their qualities. The Vlachs are not only considered as backward and illiterate shepherds; people also praise their (cunning) intelligence and their courage as well as the fact that they are the most hardworking and successful in the new economic system.

At the same time, it appears that the present behaviour of the Vlachs recalls the behaviour of the Lunxhots themselves in earlier times – the 1950s and 1960s – when they massively left their villages to move to Tirana and other Albanian cities. Just like the Vlachs, most of them had no will to return and they abandoned or sold their houses (which were then occupied by the Vlachs). However, the Lunxhots never present themselves as having abandoned their villages. The development of village nostalgia among urban migrants from Lunxhëri in the 1990s is indicative of the will of the Lunxhots to differentiate themselves from the Vlachs. Living either in Gjirokastër, Durrës or Tirana, the activists of the Society Lunxhëria, created in 1995, cultivate their Lunxhot origin by constructing an image of the past from which the Vlachs are excluded, and by actually excluding them from joining the Society ('they have their own Vlach society anyway').

Connected to this new formulation, or renegotiation of the ethnic boundary between Lunxhots and Vlachs, is the stress on a specific Lunxhot identity, exclusive of both the Muslims and the Vlachs and, as will be illustrated later, based on a rather ambiguous relationship to the Greeks. Basically, to be a Lunxhot is to be Christian (and not Muslim), Albanian (and not Greek), and 'autochthonous' (*autokton*) in opposition to foreigners (like the Vlachs). It is striking how most of the Lunxhots, living either in Lunxhëri or in Gjirokastër or elsewhere in Albania (or even in Greece), insist on the fact that they are *autokton*. These people who left what they consider their place of origin, or who plan to leave it, all claim to have a homeland or, as it is sometimes used in Albanian, 'roots' (*rrënjë*) in Lunxhëri.[12] On the whole, this is not surprising from migrants and second-generation migrants. The interesting point is that by using the word *autokton*, instead of the Albanian word *vendas*, they attempt to give the fact a kind of scientific reality: the use of *autokton* comes as the result or summary of a long historical argumentation that cannot be discussed further here. Their belonging to the place is not only a matter of fact, but has to do with historical truth. It gives them a specific and stable position on the ethno-historical map of Epirus, and a kind of historical and moral priority. 'Lunxhëri is an ancient land', says a retired ethnographer now living in Tirana, 'its inhabitants descend from the Chaones [an Illyrian tribe], they are pure Albanians (*puro shqiptar*). This is evidenced by Antigone [an archaeological site south-west of Saraqinishtë]: Lunxhëri was populated by the inhabitants of Antigone when the city was burned down'. This historical continuity is also stressed by the historian Zija Shkodra who writes: 'numerous archaeological findings in the villages Këllëz, Dhoksat, Erind, and especially in the ancient city of Antigonea to the south-west of Saraqinishtë evidence that Lunxhëri has been populated since the dawn of History'(Shkodra 2002: 16).

In the same way, when they want to mark the boundary with the Muslims and the Vlachs, the Lunxhots call themselves 'ethnic Lunxhots' (*lunxhotë etnikë*). The word 'ethnic' refers here to blood and descent, but also to a closure of social relationships, expressed by the stress on endogamy: ethnic Lunxhots marry 'inside' (*brenda për brenda*) and are proud to do it, as a marker of their aristocratic character. The concept of 'ethnic Lunxhot' (as well as the Lunxhot category itself) is used to maintain or recreate the links between the migrants who have left Lunxhëri to go to other parts of Albania, Greece, or elsewhere, as is clearly shown by the creation of the 'cultural and patriotic association Lunxhëria' (*shoqata kulturore atdhetare Lunxhëria*) in 1995. One of the aims of the association, according to its first president, is to revitalise the links between the descendants of the *kurbetlli* who stayed abroad, and the Lunxhots who live in Albania. The association intends also to preserve the culture and history of the area, by collecting songs and proverbs, editing books and videos on traditional life in Lunxhëri. It is mainly through the work of the association that the new Lunxhot identity is being created, and its main activists are of course urban and educated people in search of an idealised rural origin. Quite significantly, all inhabitants of Lunxhëri are *de facto* members of the association, except Vlachs and Muslims, who have to justify fifty years of presence in Lunxhëri to join the association.

Finally, and perhaps most importantly, migration and the opening of the border brought radical changes in the way the Lunxhots perceive their relation with Greece and the Greeks. During communism, when Greece was an enemy and the Greeks of Albania suspected of sympathy with the enemy, the Lunxhots seem to have stressed their Albanianness in order to keep away from their Greek neighbours of Pogon and Dropull. This was facilitated when the main common characteristic that might be seen as uniting Greeks and Lunxhots, religion, was abolished in 1967. Many of them having joined the partisans during the Second World War, and subsequently welcomed the communist regime, they have been very receptive to nationalist propaganda. In this context, Greece was the enemy of the Albanian nation and tried to destroy it by using religion and violence. It is thus extremely difficult to find people in Lunxhëri who support the Greek claims on Northern Epirus and who talk in positive terms of the politics of Greece at the time the state border was established (1912–20); most of the Greek supporters went away at the end of the First World War, others in 1944. At the same time, intermarriage between Greeks (from the minority) and Lunxhots occurred more and more often, probably as a result of the exclusion of the Muslims and Vlachs from matrimonial strategies, when lots of Lunxhot families had left to go and settle in Central Albania.[13] Such marriages could also be a way for Greeks to get a better life-chance – as it is acknowledged that during communism some members of the Greek minority declared themselves Albanian in order to get better living conditions.

The nineteenth-century figures of Kristaq and Jorgo Zografi, already mentioned, are a good illustration of the ambiguous, fluid and evolving position of Lunxhots *vis-à-vis* Greece and the Greeks. Until 1990, Kristaq (Christodoulos) and his son Jorgo (Iorgos) Zografi (Zographos) were stigmatised in Albanian historiography as *shovinistë* and *borgjezë* (chauvinist, bourgeois) who had worked to destroy the Albanian nation by pretending that all Orthodox Christians were Greek or should be Greek, and by supporting the opening of Greek schools in Lunxhëri and elsewhere. In consequence of this negative propaganda, the last people who still hold the family name Zografi in their village of origin, Qestorat, were persecuted during communism. It is worth mentioning that, notwithstanding the common family name, the actual link between those people and their alleged ancestors Kristaq and Jorgo is not at all clear, and it was probably safer in earlier times not to insist on that link. Today however, the last Zografi openly claim to be direct descendants of Kristaq and Jorgo, as they are now becoming positive characters – especially Kristaq. At a time when *kurbet* is presented as a golden age, Kristaq Zografi appears as a hero, a glorious son of Lunxhëri who became a rich and influential man in the capital city, Istanbul. Even more, he used his wealth and influence to help his village: the school he opened and supported in Qestorat between 1874 and 1891 (Kitsou 1985) is now presented as one of the best examples of the high cultural level of Lunxhëri, and its re-opening as a museum of Lunxhëri has been overseen by the association Lunxhëria. Several bridges, churches and roads around Qestorat are connected to the name of Kristaq Zografi, who is said to have paid for them. However, the statue that was erected in front of the school building in 1989 is not that of Kristaq, but of Koto Hoxhi, the Albanian nationalist from Qestorat who fought against Kristaq and his Greek school (and whose granddaughter married Kristaq's grandson). Today nevertheless, even among communists, people go as far as to talk of Kristaq as a 'patriot' (*atdhetar*).

All this is only one example of how the construction of a new Lunxhot identity uses parts of the Greek past of the area and overlooks the previous polarisation between being Greek or Albanian. Stories about the Second World War are another example of how the Lunxhots emphasise their good relations with the Greeks and their ability to communicate with them: Greek soldiers and officers seem to have been welcome in the Lunxhots' houses during the counter-offensive against the Italian invasion army in 1940–1, and people recall today how well the Greek officers were treated by the Greek-speaking and aristocratic Lunxhots who had lived in Istanbul or in the United States. A villager from Këllëz thus recalls how Iorgos (George) Papadopoulos (who was to lead the 1974 *coup*) stayed six months in his house from June to December 1940 (*sic*). 'Italian soldiers did not know how to fight. The Greeks were cleverer. Greeks were welcomed here, even though they pretended it was their own country'.[14]

The relations with Greece in the new context of migration are even more complicated. On the one hand, there is a feeling of gratitude (even more if the experience of migration has been successful) and of cultural proximity: many Lunxhot migrants (or their parents) had had contact with the Greek side of the border before the war, and memories of that time are being revitalised, mainly in a quest for potential support in migration (see Sintès 2003). Religion is also a ground on which proximity with the Greeks is openly claimed: as has been said before, the Lunxhots insist today on their Christian identity, and Christianity offers in a way a large community that unites Albanian Christians and Greeks beyond national antagonism. People usually talk about their re-discovery and re-appropriation of religion in Greece, which took the form of baptism, wedding and participation in the main Orthodox Christian holidays.

At the same time, whatever the Lunxhots say about their level of development, or the cultural advance and prosperity brought either from the *kurbet* or from communism, they recognise – although not all the time openly – that Lunxhëri, as a part of post-communist Albania, is much less developed than Greece, and that the Lunxhots feel, and are usually treated, as all other Albanians feel and are treated in Greece: as coming from a backward country, and still not on a par with the standards of living of modern European society.

On the other hand, there is a feeling of exclusion and anger when people talk about the difficulties they encounter when they want to go to Greece. They complain (as do many other Albanian migrants) about the cost and scarcity of visas, about violence and racism in Greek society and about the extremely uneasy situation of most Albanian migrants in Greece. They envy members of the Greek minority who not only can easily migrate to Greece but also, if they decide to stay in Albania, are able to cross the border wherever they like to go shopping in Ioannina. They also envy the 'pension of the Greek' (*pensioni i grekut*) that Greece offers to retired people of the Greek minority in Albania.

Conclusion: new transnationalism?

What is striking in the discussion on the rise of new collective identities at local level, in the context of new migration, is that more or less the same elements are used by everyone to assess their own specificity and excellence. For instance, when the Lunxhots talk about their Christian identity, their high level of culture and the experience of *kurbet* from which it originates, they do not seem to be aware that their neighbours in Zagori, Pogon and Dropull do more or less the same. It seems that the conjunction of the border context, national enculturation processes (Karakasidou 1997) and migratory experience offers a rather limited number of traits that can be used in the formulation of local identities. The situation on the Greek–Albanian border is not that far from the one described by Michael Kearney on the US–Mexico border (Kearney 1998):

> Denied permanent residence in their homeland by economic necessity and denied naturalisation by the United States, Mixtec 'alien' migrants construct a new identity out of the bricolage of their transnational existence. What form does this transnational identity take? It coalesces as ethnicity, as an ethnic consciousness, which is the supremely appropriate form for collective identity to take in the age of transnationalism. In my research I have observed how Mixtec ethnicity arises as an alternative to nationalist consciousness and as a medium to circumscribe not space, but collective identity precisely in those border areas where nationalist boundaries of territory and identity are most contested and ambiguous.

In this context, it seems that Albanian national identity is only a part of the new Lunxhot ethnic identity: you have to be Albanian in order to be a Lunxhot, as you have to be Christian, but that is not enough. Everything is as if ethnicity was built on this contradiction, of being Albanian and Greek at the same time, or rather of being potential Greeks that chose to be Albanians. It is striking how the Lunxhots emphasise their knowledge of the border area, of the other side of the border, and the familiarity they used to have with the Greek side before the border was closed. It is also striking that people who most openly claim an Albanian identity and loyalty to the Albanian nation are at the same time making attempts to get forged certificates of Greek nationality!

Emigration and the opening of the border have brought a change in the local conception of identity: the Albanian-Greek opposition has given way to a more complex 'bricolage' based on memory of the *kurbet* and on a cultural and geographic proximity, and this can be seen as the marker of a new situation of transnationalism between Greece and Albania. This is the way the Lunxhots respond to the challenge of getting access to the Greek labour market.

National categories are still relevant at certain levels between Greece and Albania, and transnationalism in the border area does not mean the disappearance of national identification. However, in order to understand how things are working at lower levels, and especially in relation to migrants' strategies and behaviour, it is necessary to take into account other more ambiguous and changing categories.

As far as Lunxhëri is concerned, the idea of a national space closed by the state border has turned into the image of a transnational space occupied by several ethnic groups competing for job opportunities in Greece. These ethnic groups are not equal and their boundaries are, as ethnic boundaries usually are, mobile and negotiated. It is not easy, however, to assess to what extent this ethnicisation is due to the creation, by the migration process, of a transnational space where social antagonism is expressed in terms of ethnicity, or is a reaction to the end of the nationalist propaganda of the communist time.

Notes

1 The chapter is based on fieldwork conducted in Lunxhëri and other locations in southern Albania in 2001 and 2002, sometimes in collaboration with Pierre Sintès of the *Ecole Française* in Athens. My research has been mainly funded by the French CNRS, through the project *La question d'Epire: intégration et développement de la region frontalière gréco-albanaise.* Thanks to Pierre Sintès for the maps.

2 On the Vlachs in southern Albania, see Kahl (1999), especially Map 6.

3 This is a new category, as it could not be used during the communist period.

4 Deriving from the Turkish *gurbet*, meaning 'exile in a distant land', *kurbet* was the term habitually used to denote early migration from Albania (see Papailias

2003). Like many inhabitants of Epirus and Macedonia, male Lunxhotes used to migrate to Istanbul, Izmir and, later on, to Greece and the United States.

5 Another hypothesis maintains that the costume is of direct Illyrian origin, deriving from the original inhabitants of Albania.

6 Its population, however, is said to be 'non-Lab', the Labs inhabiting the area 'between the three bridges of Drashovicë, Tepelenë and Kalase' (Zojzi 1962).

7 For sure, this sharp opposition between low and high villages vanishes when one looks at the family histories: individuals and families have always been moving from one side to the other, through marriage or work opportunities.

8 However, in 2002 no more than 50 people attended the celebration, as a result of mass outmigration in the previous decade.

9 It should be noted that here, as in other parts of Albania, the distinction is generally not made by the Orthodox Christians between Sunni and Bektashi Muslims, both of them being classified just as Muslims.

10 It is hardly necessary to point out what this image (and the relationship it expresses) has in common with the image of the (Muslim) Albanian migrant in Greece: both the Lab and the migrant are culturally constructed as Muslim, poor, living in or connected to wilderness (through shepherding, forest work or the need to hide away); both are ungrateful guests who betray their hosts, and so on.

11 This is illustrated by the story of third-generation migrants from Lunxhëri living today in Mexico and who, while doing research on their family history, discovered that their origin was in Albania, and not in Greece like their grandfather had always told them. When asked, the grandfather explained that at that time no one in Mexico knew about Albania, while they had heard about Greece, and that is why he kept saying they were from Greece. This story was collected in Saraqinishtë, from the grandfather's brother.

12 On 'roots' as a metaphor in the Balkans, see Schwartz (1997).

13 From what can be seen from genealogies, the Lunxhots who moved from Lunxhëri married other urban Lunxhots rather than marrying back in Lunxhëri.

14 On the Greek occupation of Southern Albania, see Fischer (1999: 79–81).

References

de Rapper, G. (2002) Espace et religion : chrétiens et musulmans en Albanie du Sud, *Etudes Balkaniques. Cahiers Pierre Belon*, 9: 17–39.

Fischer, B. J. (1999) *Albania at War 1939–1945*. London: Hurst.

Hobhouse, J. C. (1813) *A Journey through Albania and other Provinces of Turkey in Europe and Asia, to Constantinople, during the years 1809 and 1810*. London: James Cawthorn.

Kahl, T. (1999) Ethnizität und räumliche Verteilung der Aromunen in Südosteuropa, *Münstersche Geographische Arbeiten*, 43.

Karakasidou, A. N. (1997) Women of the family, women of the nation: national enculturation among Slav-speakers in north-west Greece, in Mackridge, P. and Yannakakis, E. (eds) *Ourselves and Others. The Development of a Greek Macedonian Cultural Identity Since 1912*. Oxford: Berg, 91–109.

Kearney, M. (1998) Transnationalism in California and Mexico at the end of empire, in Wilson, T. M. and Donnan, H. (eds) *Border Identities, Nation and*

States at International Frontiers. Cambridge: Cambridge University Press, 117–41.

Kitsou, K. (1985) *Ta Zografeia Didaskaleia (Kestorati Argyrokastrou: 1874–1891)*. Ioannina: Idryma Boreioipeirotikon Ereynon.

Papailias, P. (2003) 'Money of *kurbet* is money of blood': the making of a 'hero' of migration at the Greek–Albanian border, *Journal of Ethnic and Migration Studies*, 29(6): 1059–78.

Schwartz, J. (1997) 'Roots' and 'Mosaic' in a Balkan border village. Locating cultural production, in Fog Olwig, K. and Hastrup, K. (eds) *Siting Culture. The Shifting Anthropological Object*. London and New York: Routledge, 255–67.

Shkodra, Z. (2002) Lunxhëria pellazge. *Rilindja Demokratike*, 31 March 2002.

Sintès, P. (2003) Les Albanais en Grèce. Le rôle des réseaux préexistants, *Balkanologie* 7(1): 111–33.

Winnifrith, T. J. (2002) *Badlands–Borderlands. A History of Northern Epirus/Southern Albania*. London: Duckworth.

Zojzi, R. (1962) Ndamja krahinore e popullit shqiptar, *Etnografia shqiptare* 1: 16–94.

9

The uses of origin

Migration, power-struggle and memory in southern Albania

GEORGIA KRETSI

Public and policy debates on migration generally focus on the receiving countries. In particular, only limited social research has been carried out on the issue of emigration from Eastern and South-Eastern Europe after the Cold War concerning the impact on demographic, social or ideological patterns *within* the countries of this region.

Public debates in reception countries are usually based on the assumption that immigration is related to 'problems' rather than to already-existing social phenomena. Accordingly, the discussions related to Albanian migration to Greece (e.g. Marvakis *et al.* 2001) commonly refer to the country of immigration, wherein migrants are the vehicles of an unprecedented 'cultural diversity' within a country of a supposedly high level of 'ethnic homogeneity'. Moreover, they are considered to be a 'problem' that appeared in the Greek society as a result of external factors – globalisation, poverty in the country of origin, insufficient control at the borders etc. (Lykovardi and Petroula 2003: 4–5). Additionally immigrants are considered potentially as both a part of the problem they presumably themselves provoke, namely xenophobia, and a part of the problem they are required to solve, namely the need for an inexpensive workforce. This complex of stereotypes and mistaken assumptions culminates in a chain reaction of migrants being forced into a condition of 'illegality', and thus potentially 'criminal', and legitimises their social exclusion and exploitation (on the genesis of the Albanian criminal stereotype in Greece see Karydis 1996; Kretsi 1997). On the other hand, it has to be acknowledged that the problems of Albanian migrants in Greece during the first migration period (1990–7) have decreased since the legalisations of 1998 and subsequent years.

Additionally for the Greek state the Albanian migration contains issues of repatriation/immigration of a kin minority. The present chapter deals with certain aspects of this issue. My study does not attempt to draw conclusions on the general issue of Albanian migration to Greece, but focuses on the case of population groups who are connected to kin minority policies. Till the final decade of the twentieth century the members of the Greek minority in Albania were considered to live and 'suffer' under the 'Albanian regime'; Greece as a 'mother-country' was alleged to be responsible for their protection (despite the fact that Greece was unwilling to nullify the 'law of war' with Albania dating from 1940 and to reconsider diplomatic relations). In the Greek national ideology the so-called Northern Epirots (*Vorioepirotes*) were incorporated as brothers and sisters, *homogeneis,* in an emotional patriotic and irredentist discourse.[1]

When these Albanian citizens of 'Greek origin' came to migrate and settle in Greece after 1990, this perception started to change; the presence of the *Vorioepirotes* in Albania was considered of vital importance for Greece's foreign policy in the Balkans.[2] However, after the collapse of the Albanian socialist system, the minority decided out of socio-economic necessity to migrate to Greece, as thousands of other Albanian citizens did. Thus their 'value' for national politics and ideology seemed to vanish after their massive emigration to Greece, as Konidaris also notes in his discussion of this issue in Chapter 3 of this book.

Although in terms of everyday life in Greece they experienced almost similar conditions to the Albanian migrants (occupying similarly disadvantageous positions in the labour market etc.), the status of *homogeneis* gave without doubt an advantage over the latter group in acquiring entry and work permits in Greece as well as welfare benefits.

Under these circumstances (Greek foreign policy/national ideology and migrants' needs), the certificate of Greek minority membership or a certificate of 'Greek origin' came to acquire a tremendous social and economic value in Albania. Different identity cards were provided first by elites of the Greek kin minority, or by certain associations of *homogeneis* and North Epirots, to Albanian citizens of supposedly 'Greek origin' (see Christopoulos 2002; Kretsi 2003). The associations, however, then widened their clientele to include mostly Christians (e.g. Vlachs) claiming Greek minority identity for migration reasons, or even Muslims who became 'Christians' by falsifying their papers. By means of migration allowances, social benefits, scholarships and educational institutions, this clientele network, based on 'ethnic affiliation', could be extended beyond the 'real' minority. This happened on the one hand because of the numerical decline of the Greek minority in Albania, and was obviously in accordance with Greek 'national concerns' that the minority's demographic political power *within* Albania was fading away (see Pavlou 2002 and 2003). On the other hand the business of certificates of 'Greekness' became a lucrative enterprise in Albania that involved both the Greek consulate and Albanian and Greek agents, who were profiting from the desperation of thousands of Albanian citizens who wanted to migrate to Greece.

In recent years a certain amount of research has been carried out regarding these crucial issues of Albanian migration to Greece. However, very few studies have focused on transformations relating to migration *within* the countries of emigration themselves (for exceptions see the various chapters in Kaser *et al.* 2002; also Kretsi 2003; Pichler 2002). The heretofore slim insights into migration dynamics in the emigration countries prevent an understanding of the migration phenomenon as a whole, especially as regards social inequalities and relations of dependence reflected in the processes of migration as part of ideological, global and international hierarchies (cf. Balibar and Wallerstein 1990).

On the basis of this desideratum of research, this chapter will explore issues of social change in the southern Albanian border region as prompted through emigration and connected to 'kin policies' of the Greek state. It will focus on three villages, and particularly on the (traditionally) Christian-Orthodox village of Mursi in the district of Sarandë. My analysis will elucidate the ways in which the migration to Greece, beyond providing the material basis of livelihood, brought to the surface old and new political disputes over national identity, myths of origin and past affiliations at the local Albanian level. I will also discuss the ways in which such contestations, as well as the new conflicts resulting from these, are situated within the wider political framework of Albanian migration to Greece, Greek migrant policies and Greek–Albanian political relations. The chapter is based on data from the author's doctoral thesis (Kretsi 2004) which involved participant observation, life-course interviews and group discussions in the villages of Konispol, Mursi and Xarrë during 1999–2001.

Views on local demographic changes within Albania in the post-socialist era

Let us start by setting out some local data about migration movements in southern Albania. The selected data on population mobility come from three neighbouring villages that feature different religious legacies (Christian, Muslim and mixed), and will be used to check the argument that there is an indicative correlation between local population developments in Albania and Greek identity policies towards Albanian migrants.

The first village, Xarrë, contains a mixed population in regard to confession and language.[3] The village is about 15 km from the Albanian-Greek border crossing point (for pedestrians) of Qafë Bota and around 30 km from the district capital, Sarandë. The second community, Mursi, consists of a rather homogenous population in terms of religious affiliation and language (Christian and Albanian-speaking) and is located just 1 km away from Xarrë. The third village, Konispol, around 10 km distant from these villages, is a traditionally Muslim, Albanian-speaking settlement and is situated close to the 'green line' with Greece.

Table 9.1 An indicative measure of the scale of migration in three villages in Sarandë district, southern Albania, 2001

	Konispol	Mursi	Xarrë
Vital registration data			
Total population	2406	2178	2228
Number of families	586	450	499
Census data			
Total population	2015	537	894
Number of families	469	159	255
Decrease (%)			
Total population	17	76	60
Number of families	20	65	49

Table 9.1 compares the vital registration data for the three villages for 30 April 2001 with the data from the 2001 population census, taken in the same month. The comparison generates an approximation of the scale of outmigration from the settlements – an extremely high 76 per cent in the case of Mursi, followed by 60 per cent from Xarrë and a much lower 17 per cent from Konispol. I assume that the depopulation rates recorded are overwhelmingly due to migration to Greece. Local checking and field enquiries reveal this to be a realistic assumption: there is no evidence of differential mortality amongst the villages or of migration to other countries. Migration within Albania, i.e. to urban centres such as Tirana, is also to be considered as a minor factor in the demographics of these border settlements.

This wide variation of the percentages could be explained by the fact that different migration policies towards the three communities have been followed by the Greek state or its agencies. This means that the possibility of acquiring a visa – at least in the 1990s – was not same for every Albanian citizen, but rather was linked to assumed ethnic/religious affiliations (cf. Christopoulos 2002; Kretsi 2003; Pavlou 2002), which have prevented or facilitated migration in the three villages. This argument was also put forward by most villagers when asked about the quantitative differences in migration rates. I now explore the realistic likelihood of this assumption.

Beyond the Greek policy, it was observable that other – probably minor – factors (we may call them 'internal factors') also contributed to these quantitative differences, such as the distance to the border crossing and livelihood structures. For example, the village of Konispol is very close to the border, so its inhabitants have had the possibility to cross over to Greece for work and return to their homes, as indeed happened since the early 1990s. The so-called 'refugee economy' (i.e. economic activities of the border-crossers who enter Greece clandestinely) was flourishing in the village in the first decade of the transformation period, as well as the livestock trade with Greek cattle-breeders at the borders. By these livelihood strategies, Konispol's inhabitants could circumvent the necessity for family migration, so the village's population remained more stable demographically.

At first glance one could suppose that the striking mobility differences between Konispol (17 per cent) and Mursi (76 per cent) arose from these internal aspects of border location and consequent opportunity structures, and not necessarily from visa politics. Since these border opportunities were available for Konispol inhabitants, but restricted for Mursi's, the latter, according to this assumption, had to migrate to Greece with their families. In order to validate this assumption the community of Xarrë was also studied.

In the case of Xarrë one can observe that, despite the same location as Mursi, the mobility percentages differ somewhat from the latter (60 versus 76 per cent). Therefore, the border location proves to have had only a partial importance for the scale of migration from the village. This argument becomes more cogent if we consider that the village of Xarrë has similar material bases to Konispol. Especially its Vlach population, traditionally livestock breeders, took up this profession again in the post-socialist area, making business-related exchanges with dairy dealers in the Greek border zone. Accordingly, despite the common starting point with Konispol relating to economic activities, we observe that the demographic developments between Konispol and Xarrë are quite different. The argument that this disparity was affected only little by internal factors, and was rather due to the substantial impact of external factors, namely foreign policies regarding migration from Albania, hence becomes more likely.

These selective examples give evidence about the *potential* effect of the Greek policies of privileged treatment of the 'Christians', people of 'Greek origin' in Albania. This effect can be exemplified in areas of religious and ethnic mixture, such as the village of Mursi, to which we now turn.

Re-invention of the 'Greek past'

Very often during my fieldwork in the area I came to hear furious complaints about Christians being privileged by Greek policy, and particularly the village of Mursi having been granted a special treatment. Neighbouring non-Christian villages would accuse Mursi people of a monopolisation of access to Greek visas. This was always commented upon as discrimination against Muslims or 'non-Greeks' by the Greek state. Some activists of Mursi were branded for having followed a 'hellenisation strategy' in order to gain social and economic advantages from Greece. Indeed, privileges for entry and working permit allocation were granted by Greek immigration policy for those having 'Greek origin'.[4]

Thus it is not surprising that a history of 'rival origins', pertaining to the 'Albanian' or 'Greek belonging' of the community, were being negotiated daily in the Mursi public space.[5] It was obvious from my first visit to the village that there was a tense relation between the proponents of the 'Greek' and of the 'Albanian' version of the local history. These disputes corresponded to a great extent with the attempts of some local activists to let Mursi be recognised by the Greek Consulate as a Greek minority village.[6] Almost all interlocutors put this development down to the activities of a woman who moved to Mursi upon marriage and who was a member of the Greek minority. She was said to have achieved control over the visa-policies in the border region, which implied in the Albanian context a great amount of political power. According to information from my field research, the diaspora Mursiots in Greece contributed a great deal to this effort as well.[7]

These village politics of Mursi were denied with anger and fury as 'hellenisation policy' by neighbouring villagers, and also by those Mursi inhabitants professing the community's 'Albanian origin'. Consequently, such disputes were not just based on pragmatic socio-economically informed migration strategies. They also reveal their own specific historicity, differences in individual migration experience and future expectations as well as on-going collective processes of questioning old values and redefining cognitive patterns.

Narrating 'authentic customs'

I now move to the statements of the aforementioned Mursi woman who was actively engaged in local politics. The interlocutor would not dispute that an application had been made to the Greek Ministry of Foreign Affairs to register the village as Greek. She claimed that the application was made at the request of the 'North Epirote association' of the Mursiots in Athens.[8] On the grounds of this request the Greek Consul came to Mursi, in order to diagnose the 'Greek identity' of the community.[9] Which criteria came in useful for that? The grecophile activist claimed as follows:

> Mursi is a village of Greek nationality, this has been proved by its own history . . . confirmed through its religion and history, whose recognition we demanded at the relevant offices, in the Albanian Parliament, in the Greek Ministry of Foreign Affairs and in the Greek Consulate. We made an application to be recognised as [part of the] minority, like the other villages. And I cannot do this for Konispol, I cannot, only its inhabitants can . . . They should demand their own rights themselves. Even the village of Mursi, for example, was acknowledged till four years ago as Albanian, so it was not

given any preference. In 1998 . . . the new consul came here. With our traditions, our customs, even our accent in our language, when we speak Albanian, it sounds similar to Greek. Also the students are very good in Greek here, because we have a group that learns Greek, with all the bits and pieces, with the dances, with customs, we are who we are! And our dances are Epirotic.
GK: Is this not a Greek and an Albanian culture simultaneously?
[No] we talk about our culture, that's what we have, the Greek one. When I make the weddings, the mass, funerals, I do it in my [Greek] culture. These are our customs.

From the activist's narrative, Mursi's (Greek) history became a matter of power at the present time (cf. Rappaport 1990: 15); this became obvious in the claim for institutionalisation of exclusive ethnic/national history by the 'competent offices'. Furthermore, the activist pleaded for Konispol to convert to Christian Orthodoxy, and by doing this to restore its own history, to reverse the events, as if the time of Islam existed only outside the 'correct flow of history' (Giordano and Kostova 2002: 78). The visit of the consul further attested an authoritative acknowledgement of the local 'customs and traditions' as 'authentic Greek'. Herewith, the attempt to *reverse* the historical narratives that used to perceive Mursi as an Albanian village was legitimised and sealed by an authority and its powerful discourse of origin.

Last but not least, these 'expert comments' yielded unambiguous benefits for the whole community. The same activist continues:

[In] 1998 the first one-year visas were handed over to Mursi inhabitants. In 1999, 2000, 2001 this went on. And the Mursiots were going with the 'small passport' [a form of ethnic-Greek identity card] and took their visa . . . And this doesn't happen because they [the Greeks] make discriminations because of [us] being Christians. But because the village demanded it. We asked to be what we are. Nobody can deprive us from our origin, the village demanded it. And we proved it. We made an outline of the history of the village, six pages, it was sent to the Greek Ministry of Foreign Affairs, to the Albanian Parliament . . . We sent it to the Greek Consulate in Gjirokastër. The Greek Consul wanted to come to inspect every single thing close up with his own eyes. He came and he verified that here more than the half of the population speaks Greek. The songs, the dances, the food, these all were [Greek].

The intertwining of historical discourses of legitimisation, state identity politics and local interests towards maximising chances in the migration scenario becomes starkly evident in the above interview extract. The interlocutor considers the right of 'origin' and the exclusive national collective identity to be an issue of public, even state concern – apparently, in accordance with the above-mentioned dominant national discourses. The very pragmatic interaction of this ethnic/national discourse with the politics of visa acquisition is stated very self-confidently by her. Even more, the claim for favourable treatment in getting entry and working permits in Greece is postulated as an inherited, historical and cultural right of the we-group.[10]

Narrating the 'right language'

Nonetheless, not all Mursi inhabitants approved this one-dimensional, ethnic interpretation of local history. The disagreements related to this triggered a contradictory revitalisation of memories of the local past within the realm of daily negotiations in the village. In doing so, the past was reflected and reformulated, especially regarding the historicity of language. Language was seen as the anchor of collective identification, that potentially affiliates the community with the Albanian nation or, alternatively, ties it to the Greek domain.

The dynamic interplay of Albanian and Greek in-between culture, both geographically and metaphorically, is reflected in the narrations of the inhabitants. Apparently, bilingualism rather than a clear-cut language structure had emerged within the borderland community in the past. Elder inhabitants of Mursi claimed that their parents, besides Albanian, used to speak Greek and attended Greek schools. Some of the interviewees claimed further that everybody spoke Albanian at home, while others would argue that a long time ago people were Greek-speakers and this was to be confirmed by the high rate of intermarriages with inhabitants of Greek-speaking villages at the Greek border zone.

The pervasiveness and perplexity of memories of the local past are closely related to the traditional cross-border relations, which did not provide the village with a single option of 'national identity'. Even at present some inhabitants use the self-ascription *arbanitas*[11] or *minoritarë* in order to designate Mursi residents and their intrinsic bonds to Greece. This indicates the specific historicity of the group formation processes in this borderland community.

In fact the identity 'dilemma' of the community reflects a long history, which is worth mentioning at this point. In 1917 the teacher Vasil Raptopulli transformed by his own initiative the Greek school of Mursi into an Albanian one. This basically meant that he began teaching the Albanian instead of the Greek language at school and started a pro-Albanian campaign in the region. In the socialist historiography this teacher has been portrayed as a progressive scholar who did 'glorious patriotic work' in the region: 'Vasil fulfilled a glorious mission, he albanianised the names of the people and assigned them new names of Albanian origin'. In this way, according to this depiction, Mursi preserved its language from the hellenisation policies of the Orthodox Church. According to the same source 'Mursi not only avoided assimilation by aliens, but maintained its pure ethnic and local characteristics'.[12]

In this mainstream socialist narrative of the local past, rejection of Greek identity policies was central.

In the eyes of those people who honour him for his commitment to the national cause, the teacher – never forcefully, always via mental vigour – convinced the residents to change their names, since the new ones would 'sound beautiful' and 'be good for the nation'. Traces of these name conversions are to be found today in the village (Kretsi 2003). An elderly informant mentioned that he used to have the family name 'Rroshomani' until it was changed by the teacher to 'Duro'. As well as family names Raptopulli would also change first names, e.g. Chrysaugi ('golden dawn' in Greek) into Agimtare (the same in Albanian). However, the interviewee disliked this tactic, since he believed that they had 'a tradition of beautiful Greek names', which the teacher 'destroyed'.

A café owner, for example, named his shop 'Papajorgji' in memory of the family name of his ancestors, since Raptopulli had changed it. The explanation he gave for this past change was that the name 'Papajorgji' suggested a Greek origin and Raptopulli as an Albanian national proponent was eager to replace such practices. In contrast to the previous interviewee, he approved this sort of 'restoration' of the community's history:

> Raptopulli was one of the most progressive teachers of the nation, not only in Mursi but also in Konispol. He didn't want any foreigners. He was an Albanian. Because, earlier there was a Greek school in Mursi, and he transformed it into an Albanian one. And I totally agree with the views of this man, who did a lot at this time . . . because we are on Albanian territory, and it is proper for us to learn Albanian and be good Albanians.

The character of Raptopulli has often been a focus for differing and conflictive articulations, where struggles over the production of historical meanings occur in the context of asymmetrical relations between Albania and Greece. Both the aforementioned Greek activist and the Orthodox priest of the community favoured the Greek version of the community's history, and voiced their aversion to the activities of Raptopulli. Both of them depicted his actions as a forceful manipulation of local culture. For them the deeds of the teacher were a prime example of 'forced albanisation'. According to this historical recollection it was the socialistic historiography that imposed on the basis of his deeds an Albanian collective ascription of the village and attempted to eliminate the 'actual Greek' past and origin.

Contested rights, emotions and political legacies

Memories of the community's past emerged in the discursive field of negotiating national belonging and through it challenging (transnational) structures of power and rights. In this context the chapter of Albania's interwar history is particularly important for understanding past discourses (as shown above with the example of the interwar albanophile teacher in Mursi), for processes of we-group formation along national lines took place mainly in this period. Moreover this period proved conducive to the mobilisation of the past in the post-socialist era. The projection by current discourses of the socialist historical period as a phenomenon of discontinuity in national history links immediately the national present with what was 'before', namely the pre-socialist period, seen as 'correct' (cf. Giordano and Kostova 2002: 77). In this respect the interwar period has a proliferating value in signalling other 'correct' collective identities, transmitting symbolic messages and claiming rights. The aforementioned 'grecophile' activist said further:

> Here there were people Islamised in the years of Zogu. The Agas came down here, as we know, and everybody who would serve the interests of a party, he would be given services in return. So anybody representing the interests of Zogu would be given what? Land . . . The Konispol inhabitants had lots of lands. The Mursi inhabitants had none. Can you explain, how this came to happen, namely that Konispolats had land in Mursi, but the Mursiots didn't have any in Mursi? Zogu gave it to them, definitely, he made them Agas.

This statement is not from the usual anachronistic denouncement for national and/or religious disloyalty and opportunism directed against Muslims.[13] This moralising impetus attempts to de-legitimise their claims for rights, such as landed property. This invokes evidently a certain kind of 'telescoping' of time, since neither did the Konispolats convert to Islam during Zogu's time (but rather in the eighteenth and nineteenth century), nor did King Zog award the residents with *Aga*-titles (they dated back to the Ottoman period). Notwithstanding, also the priest of the village remembered through similar 'telescoping' of past events the property issue in our interview:

> Mursi kept its honour . . . [whereas] the Konispolats have their pockets full. They sold their soul, they changed both their religion and their identity [for] gaining land, our part, do you understand? They did their own thing . . . Because Zogu came and he was a Moslem. These lands, these pastures, belonged at all times to Mursiots . . . And [nowadays] I feel that history is being falsified.

The Zogu era has an outstanding importance for both of the grecophile interviewees who associate this historic period with 'Islamisation'. It is most likely that this inaccuracy derives from the fact that at that time Zogu secularised part of the monasteries' estates (cf. Fishta 2000–1: 419; Schmidt-Neke 1987: 222–6). This also affected ecclesiastical properties in Mursi, which the Orthodox Church was at the time of my research trying to claim back (unsuccessfully) from the state. In the post-socialist period widespread confusion emerged *vis-à-vis* property titles. This consequently prompted discourses of historic legitimisation, wherein the period of appropriation of 'Christian' property was designated as the era of 'Islamisation'. Discourses of origin and morals of religious belonging thus became materially relevant for the present and as well for the future.

The issue of the village's (and the individual's) ethnic and religious origins has become increasingly passionately disputed. For some, such as the grecophile activist and the priest, the land issue with Konispol was crucial; for others this problem was non-existent, since at the time of my fieldwork the issue of land privatisation had been settled and relations between the two villages were good. Moreover, the social use of the debate over 'origin' was seen in different ways by different actors: some claimed the exclusiveness of one, 'authentic', option; others believed in multiple options, or were prepared to shift interpretations, memories and identity processes according to changing socio-economic opportunity structures, especially as these related to resources emanating from Greece (cf. Elwert 1997).

In the present context, the fact that representatives of the Greek state introduced an 'identity option' in relation to migration opportunities had a lasting influence on the discourses of belonging in the village. If the village could manage to be recognised as 'Greek', the chances of obtaining an entry and working permit for Greece increased. The members of the younger generation had already profited from this and had migrated to Greece in large numbers. Advantages of this politically-motivated identity-switching were also achievable for the elderly inhabitants of Mursi, since they could be granted pensions from Greece.[14] These benefits from Greek agents gave rise to envy from other villages, as well as to conflict within Mursi.

Here follow some excerpts from a heated debate in the village café that demonstrate the ambiguity of positions of different local actors. The dialogue illustrates how the past conditions the present, and how the present modifies or determines perceptions of the past.

While an elder discussant pleaded that he was bound to Greece by 'religion, blood and origin' and was not about to 'throw the blood away', the younger discussant (aged 40, the proprietor of the café, and a former migrant in Greece) challenged him to say *how else* he was bound to Greece. Thereupon the older man began talking about the pension he was receiving from Greece, which he designated as a 'social benefit for old people' (*ndihmë shoqerore*). When asked by me whether the pension depended on the question of origin, he gave a remarkable answer:

> No, also Muslims were given something.
> *GK*: Was this benefit organised by *Omonia* [the Greek minority's political organisation]?
> No, this was a help that probably came from the Council of Europe, from the World, to help Albania.
> *GK*: Who brings the pension here?
> No, I go by myself and get it in Greece. Not from *Omonia*. It is a help from the Greek state for its own people, which have the Christian

religion. This is the political trend. That . . . they help their own folk, because, those here [means Greek minority] have the Greek nationality [*kombësi greke*]! Due to them [the Greek minority] we are also included [in the minority's regulation], as the community of Mursi!

GK: As Greeks?

No, not as Greeks. Because I am Mursiot, I am an Albanian. I'm not gonna lose my nationality now. Because I am Albanian! And I will die as an Albanian! But for my present interests, if for example they give me the pension, I will cry 'long live' . . . So they included us in this regulation, only to help us! But they were obliged to help us! I told you already, because we've been for 1200 years in prison and have been interned, because we made propaganda for the Greeks. But this was not true. Neither Konispolats nor Mursiots made propaganda! This was the fashion of Enver Hoxha!

The interviewee did not question the fact of his being Albanian; he negotiated his way through an awkward situation by trying to justify the preferential treatment, or the 'positive discrimination', of the Christian against the Muslim population as a 'geographical accident' (Mursi was located close to the Greek minority villages). His complex and shifting accounts pointed to this ambivalent embarrassment: the Muslims would take benefits, while Greeks at the same time would prefer only 'their own folk'; Mursi was treated as a Greek minority village, whereas in fact it was not; and in the end, Greeks owed them social allowances, since they were sentenced for many years detention due to accusations of being 'grecophile' by Hoxha's regime, despite the fact that they were not making propaganda for the Greeks.

To this 'performed ambiguity' of the elderly man, another informant reacted giving following clarification: 'Mursiots are Albanians, but *graecoman* Albanians!' Indeed, during the socialist era Mursi was designated as a 'grecophile' community, situated not only within the restricted border zone (*zona kufitare*), but also within the more restricted security zone (*brez kufitar*), a 500-metre strip edging the border. Under the conditions of authoritarian control of a regime that outlawed not only migration, but also any contacts with abroad for decades (cf. King *et al.* 1998), the historic cross-border relations with the 'enemy' burdened, on the one hand, the community with political allegations of national treason.[15] On the other, Greece became for the inhabitants of the border zone who were persecuted something like a 'big friend' and political 'homeland'. This seemed to have been the case of the main interviewee cited above, as it was for many of the other older interviewees in Mursi, who were found in my subsequent discussions with them to have been detained for several years (between 7 and 12) for their alleged 'grecophilia'. It is noteworthy that the discussants referred to the individual fate of imprisonment as a group experience, expressed in the aggregated account of the years-in-prison ('1200 years for Mursi').

This collectivisation of the years-in-detention indicates in a striking way the nature of the persecution experienced. It is perceived as a result of collective stigmatisation of the community due to ethnic affiliations to Greece. Otherwise it also goes along with today's discourses of identity that favour a collective self-portrayal of a politically victimised community. Since the 'ethnic' allegations against Mursi were effective for the regime as well as traumatic for the residents in the socialist period, the latter interpret the pensions from Greece in their own vein, as a moral compensation for their predicament. This discursive transformation of the previous negative bias ('national betrayal') into a prospective outlook ('sacrifice for Greece') coincides for a number of villagers today with the claim for reparation (e.g. social welfare payments) from Greece, due to the fact that the Albanian state is unable to provide this to them.

Considering that the Greek actors and agents never brought the argument of 'political loyalty' fairly into play, but rather insisted on 'racial/ethnic bonds', this link between persecution and compensation is a highly constructed one. Apart from that, this line of argument does not convince all the members of the community. In particular, it could be observed that opinions and views floated increasingly around generational lines. The older generations were more flexible over the question of ethnic/national belonging than the younger ones. This may reflect several factors. First, most of the elders remember personally another epoch, before the socialist isolation of the country, when cross-border relations were practiced; and they subsequently experienced stigmatisation by the regime due to this. Secondly this flexibility towards ethnic/national identifications is related to their marginal situation and economic dependence within a national state that does not provide them any social security (cf. Sampson 1995).

This flexible attitude towards the 'protective patron', Greece, was very often disavowed by younger inhabitants, who hold them accountable for a 'compromised, chameleonic behaviour, left-over from the communist time'. The café proprietor, for instance, challenged the older man quoted above, who did not directly declare his Albanian belonging, in the following words:

> Who are you? Tell this lady coming from Germany, who you are! When she goes back to Germany she will say to her friends: I was in Albania, where there are no Albanians!

The old man, who previously declared his gratitude to Greece for his pension, said in a manner that revealed he was somehow unsure of himself, that he was 'both Albanian and Greek. Why not to be able to be both'. In rebuffing his mutability, the café proprietor contradicted him vehemently: 'Old man, when you die, what will be written on your grave? It will be written that here is buried a nobody!'.

Here, in this stark and painful exchange, the 'spiritual' bondage between national and personal sense of belonging was put simply to the test. Such discursive struggles make it apparent that identities and memories are less descriptive than highly selective and, moreover, emotionally inscribed.

Aftermath

The café proprietor had been working for several years in Greece; he was a barman on a Greek tourist island. After a period of hard work and learning in the café-business he eventually decided to return – in his own words – to his homeland, where he would have full rights, be respected and where he could employ his skills for his own economic advance. In contrast to the nation-transcending narrations of the elders, the café proprietor contradicted flexibility in order to reject any dependence on the neighbouring country; and for the sake of his own dignity, which he had to define and vice-versa defend during migration through a painful struggle against albanophobic prejudices and the pervasive national stereotypes about Albanians held in Greece. The acquisition of a positive, exclusive national self-portrayal therefore corresponds to a social pattern of self-defining and challenging of international (i.e. Greek) dominance in Albania.

The elders insisted, till the end of our discussion, upon multidimensional self-perceptions, expressed profoundly in the phrase: 'It is better that you say neither Albanian nor Greek, but *Epirote*! . . . Epirus and Pyrrhus the Great! Pyrrhus the Great, that is [what we are]!' In this fashion they tried to exhaust the transnational potential of Epirus (the borderland territory shared by Albania and Greece) and of its mythic hero, Pyrrhus, and to perform a compatible way out of the 'national dilemma' they have been subjected to via migration and identity politics in the post-socialist area. For the elders, the flexibility between 'being Greek/Albanian' signalled a switching, grounded in their marginality within the realm of a national economy that is fully dependent on migration for its survival. By participating in the biased pensions scheme or visa politics, they appropriated the protective kin policies of Greece, transformed them via their own historical notions and designated them as political rights, which the community was entitled to claim.

It becomes obvious, then, that at the local level the main attribute of the 'uses of origin' discourse is ambivalence. This becomes even more evident when one considers the arguments of the 'grecophile' actors in contrast to the 'albanophiles'. Nonetheless, the various contradictory positions have as a common denominator the activities of actors whose agency mediated the Greek influence in the village. Be they the local actors interviewed or Mursiot villagers in the diaspora in Greece, they encouraged Greek kin policies in the village with obvious protective character.

The subordination of social opportunities and the legal frame of immigration to the distinction of how close or far prospective migrants are to the norm of the Greek national ideal leads to discrimination between citizens. The conflict-potential of this within the immigration country has been described elsewhere (Christopoulos 2002; Pavlou 2002). Here I would also observe how it triggered further conflicts between Christian and non-Christian villages and how this pervaded the demographic, social and ideological realm within Albania as well. The claim for the institutionalisation of a 'new history', that would exclude Muslim rights, and testify to the 'Greek origin', is not to be disregarded in its ideological and discursive power. The social inequalities intertwined and reproduced with this discourse of the past should not be ignored. Beyond the fact that key actors might gain control over visas and social welfare payments, and thus exercise crucial power over Albanian citizens, they also work as mechanisms of clientelistic intermediation between citizens, prospective migrants and both the home and the reception country. The absence of an Albanian welfare state provides the terrain for the Greek state to intervene and to promote foreign policy issues by widening such nepotistic networks through 'ethnic brokers', such as church agents or 'kin' members etc. The underlying rhetoric for such strategies are 'history' and 'origin' in terms of 'blood and/or beliefs' as criteria for defining a 'Greek consciousness'.

Hence, for the people involved, at stake are social goods in respect of human and civil rights (mobility, social security etc.), but for the (Greek) protective state there are notions of internal 'homogeneity' and relative 'national interests' abroad, for the purpose of which it engages the discourse of 'origin'. In a global perspective, the outcome of this discrepancy is likely to be a continuation of the subaltern ideological and social position of a great number of Albanian citizens and prospective migrants. To the degree that they are awarded social benefits and prospects by the way of clientelistic mechanisms, they are not by any means assured of their true civil rights.

On the one hand, the connection between the narratives of origin and the wider political framework of Albanian migration to Greece reveals strategies of power. Local actors appropriate an interpretation of the past favoured by the immigration state (Greece), for the purpose of surviving within (or out of) a home state (Albania), beset by economic, political and social distress. On the other hand, it discloses the ideological mechanisms of subordination, which are subject to global dependence structures between states, becoming particularly evident in the context of migration. For residents of Albania and the migrants, disputes over memory also reveal a position of powerlessness in view of their subaltern position in defining their 'origin'.

Notes

1 *Homogeneis* are 'aliens of Greek descent'. The opposite notion of this term is the *allogeneis* (Greek citizens of non-Greek descent), which emerged in the

national legal order with the aim of ruling out the existence of national minorities (Christopoulos and Tsitselikis 2003). The concept of *homogeneia* (cf. *genos*, race) both implies a racial criterion of the definition of the 'nation' and supplements the belief-system of the Greek national consciousness. As Pavlou (2002) notes about the principles underlying the legal status of *homogeneis*, 'the interesting thing about this pair of "blood and beliefs" criteria – which seems to be rather incompatible rather than complementary – is that it is selectively used by the administration in an alternative manner for different kin minorities coming from different countries'.

2 For this reason ethnic-Greek Albanians were not granted citizenship in Greece: they occupied a position 'somewhere in between the status of citizen and that of the alien or non-native' (Christopoulos and Tsitselikis 2003: 5).

3 This mixed composition refers to socio-occupational, ethnic, linguistic and religious legacies which, however, played a minor role during the socialist era, when all the population groups were integrated as co-nationals, i.e. as Albanians in the People's Republic of Albania. In Xarrë the relevant groups were Albanian-speaking Christians, Çam people (or Chams – the Albanian-speaking Muslim minority settled in northern Greece/Epirus in the 1920s and 1940s), Vlachs (cattle-breeders, speaking a Latin-based language), Roma, and some members of the Greek minority.

4 On the racialisation of Greek immigration procedures see Christopoulos (2002); and on the clientelistic operation of the visa trade see Baltsiotis (2003), Pavlou (2002), Tsitselikis and Christopoulos (2003).

5 Discussions cited here took place mainly in the village's central café, which is considered as a public forum where opinions are exchanged, and in other public spaces. Albanian was the main language spoken. The interview with the priest and the 'grecophile' activist took place respectively in the churchyard and in the yard of the activist's house, both in the presence of other people.

6 Mursi was located just outside what was called in the socialist era the *zona minoritare*, the recognised ethnic-Greek minority zone. This location, close to but not in the minority region, meant that Mursi was officially an Albanian village, part of the majority population. Whilst during socialism religious legacies were rather irrelevant, during the interwar years religion had been of striking importance for community life. Then, Mursi used to have close social, economic and intermarriage relations with Greek-speaking Orthodox communities on the Greek side of the border. These ties were closer than those with neighbouring villages within the Albanian state. Consequently, an almost bilingual culture emerged in the village. Most of the population, though, probably had Albanian as their mother-tongue.

7 I was not able to verify this since fieldwork in Greece lay beyond the range of this research project.

8 Such associations are numerous in Greece and are described by Christopoulos (2002) as special vehicles for clientelistic mediation between the various communities and the Greek state.

9 In this paper I make no judgements on the activist's power over the visa distribution process, nor about the influence of the Greek officials on their visits. For the purposes of my analysis, what is important is the *perceived* importance of both for the local population.

10 The issue of 'ethnic kinship' as a priority criterion in the context of migration concerns has other examples too, such as the case of ethnic Germans from Eastern Europe, permitted full migration and citizenship rights in Germany.

11 Like the Albanian-speaking Christian groups living within Greek territory who are known as *arvanitë* (in Greek *Arvanites*).

12 The quotes in this paragraph are from the local (Sarandë) newspaper *Fitorja*, 28 February 1979.

13 For a review of the 'negative incorporation' of Islam in Albanian historiography, and an account of the associated myths which have accompanied the *problematique* of Albanians' 'European identity', see Lakshman-Lepain (2002).

14 The pension issue is almost completely overlooked in the literature of the Greek politics of '*homogeneis*', although some attention has been given to the granting of scholarships, grants and social welfare benefits (Baltsiotis 2003; Schwandner-Sievers 1998).

15 The xenophobia of Hoxha's regime has yet to be fully investigated; it is beyond the scope of this chapter to do this. Certainly the obsessive phobia against enemies of the communist regime can hardly be exaggerated, but this was not the only case; on the Greek side of the border a policy of strict military control was imposed and fears against the 'communist enemy' were widespread. Both are to be understood within the geo-strategic logic of the Cold War. One difference is significant, however: in communist Albania mobility and contacts abroad were criminalised; not so in the Greek case. See Kretsi (2004).

References

Balibar, E. and Wallerstein, I. (1990). *Rasse-Klasse-Nation. Ambivalente Identitäten.* Hamburg: Argument.

Baltsiotis, L. (2003) The Greek minority of Albania: an attempt to approach a society in transformation, in Tsitselikis, K. and Christopoulos, D. (eds) *The Greek Minority of Albania.* Athens: Kritiki, Studies of the Research Centre for Minority Studies (KEMO), 45–125 (in Greek).

Christopoulos, D. (2002) Greece of the homogeneia: from mother-homeland to capitalistic metropol, *O Politis*, 109: 9–20 (in Greek).

Christopoulos, D. and Tsitselikis, K. (2003) Treatment of minorities and *homogeneis* in Greece: relics and challenges, in *Legal Aspects of Religious and Linguistic Otherness in Greece.* http://www.kemo.gr/archive/papers/ChristTsitsel.htm [12 November 2003].

Elwert, G. (1997) Switching of we-group identities: the Alevis as a case among many others, in Kehl-Bodrogi, C. (ed.) *Syncretistic Religious Communities in the Near East.* Leiden: Brill, 65–85.

Fishta, I. (2000–1) Agrarproblem und Agrarreform im Albanien der Zwischenkriegszeit, *Südost-Forschungen, Internationale Zeitschrift für Geschichte, Kultur und Landeskunde Südosteuropas*, 59/60: 387–422.

Giordano, C. and Kostova, D. (2002) The social production of mistrust, in Hann, C. M. (ed.) *Postsocialism: Ideals, Ideologies and Practices in Eurasia.* London and New York: Routledge, 74–91.

Kaser, K., Pichler, R. and Schwandner-Sievers, S. (eds) (2002) *Die weite Welt und das Dorf. Albanische Emigration am Ende des 20. Jhs.* Vienna-Cologne-Weimar: Böhlau.

King, R., Iosifides, T. and Myrivili, L. (1998) A migrant's story: from Albania to Athens, *Journal of Ethnic and Migration Studies*, 24(1): 159–75.

Kretsi, G. (2003). Actual and historical dimensions of anthroponymic behaviour in Albanian society, *Mnimon*, 25: 111–45. (in Greek).

—— (2004) Politische Verfolgung und Gedächtnis im (post)sozialistischen Albanien am Beispiel der südlichen Grenzregion, Freie University Berlin, Department for Political and Social Sciences, Institute for Social Anthropology, Berlin, unpublished doctoral thesis.

Lakshman-Lepain, R. (2002) Albanian Islam – development and disruptions, in Kressing, F. and Kaser, K. (eds.) *Albania – a Country in Transition. Aspects of Changing Identities in a South-East-European Country*. Baden-Baden: Nomos, 39–64.

Lykovardi, K. and Petroula, E. (2003) Greece. Hellenic League for Human Rights, in Niessen, J., Schible, Y. and Magoni, R. (eds) *EU and US Approaches to the Management of Immigration*. Brussels and Athens: Migration Policy Group, 1–27.

Marvakis, A., Parsanolgou, D. and Pavlou, M. (eds) (2001) *Migrants in Greece*. Athens: Ellinika grammata (in Greek).

Pavlou, M. (2002) Greek state policy from 'irredentism' to 'home-coming'/'immigration': the case of two repatriated kin minority groups, in *The Protection of National Minorities by their Kin-State*, Strasbourg: Council of Europe Publications, Science and Technique of Democracy Series, No. 32, 197–207.

—— (2003) The Greeks of Albania in Greece, in Tsitselikis, K. and Christopoulos, D. (eds) *The Greek Minority of Albania*. Athens: Kritiki, Studies of the Research Centre for Minority Studies (KEMO), 265–308 (in Greek).

Pichler, R. (2002) Strategies of migrant workers in the highland villages of Southern Albania in the 19th and 20th centuries, in Kressing, F. and Kaser, K. (eds) *Albania – a Country in Transition. Aspects of Changing Identities in a South-East-European Country*. Baden-Baden: Nomos, 125–45.

Rappaport, J. (1990) *The Politics of Memory: Native Historical Interpretations in the Columbian Andes*. Cambridge: Cambridge University Press.

Sampson, S. (1995) All is possible, nothing is certain: the horizons of transition in a Romanian village, in Kideckel, D. A. (ed.) *East European Communities. The Struggle for Balance in Turbulent Times*. Boulder and Oxford: Westview Press, 159–78.

Schmidt-Neke, M. (1987) *Entstehung und Ausbau der Königsdiktatur in Albanien (1912–1939). Regierungsbildungen, Herrschaftsweise und Machteliten in einem jungen Balkanstaat*. München: den Oldenbourg (Südosteuropäische Arbeiten 84).

Schwandner-Sievers, S. (1998) Ethnicity in transition: the Albanian Aromanians' identity politics, *Ethnologia Balkanica*, 2: 167–84.

Tsitselikis, K. and Christopoulos, D. (2003) The Greek minority of Albania: uncertain moments of national truths, in Tsitselikis, K. and Christopoulos, D. (eds) *The Greek minority of Albania*. Athens: Kritiki, Studies of the Research Centre for Minority Studies (KEMO), 17–44 (in Greek).

Contributors

Kosta Barjaba, Professor of Sociology at the University of Tirana and former Director of the Department of Migration in the Albanian Ministry of Labour and Social Affairs, is at present doing a Mid-Career Master in Public Administration at the JF Kennedy School of Government, Harvard University.

Panos Hatziprokopiou is Research Fellow in Social Policy in the School of Health and Social Sciences at Middlesex University.

Gazmend Kapllani is a Ph.D student at Panteion University, Athens; he also works as a journalist.

Ellen Kelly is the International Programme Manager for the Liberal Democrats in London.

Russell King is Professor of Geography at the University of Sussex, where he also co-directs the Sussex Centre for Migration Research.

Gerasimos Konidaris is Lecturer in International Politics in the Department of Politics, University of Sheffield.

Georgia Kretsi is Lecturer in the Institute of Social Anthropology at the Freie University of Berlin.

Lois Labrianidis is Professor of Economic Geography in the Department of Economic Sciences, University of Macedonia, Thessaloniki.

Nicola Mai is Morris Ginsberg Fellow in Sociology at the London School of Economics.

Aida Orgocka has recently completed her Ph.D in Human Development and Family Studies at the University of Illinois at Urbana-Champaign.

Flavia Piperno is Researcher on International Migration and Development at the Centro Studi di Politica Internazionale (CeSPI) in Rome.

Gilles de Rapper is Chargé de Recherche in Social Anthropology at the Institut d'Ethnologie Méditerranéenne et Comparative, Maison Méditerranéenne des Sciences de l'Homme, Aix-en-Provence.

Stephanie Schwandner-Sievers is formerly Nash Fellow and Lecturer in Albanian Studies at the School of Slavonic and East European Studies, University College London.

Index

Printed and bound by CPI Group (UK) Ltd, Croydon, CR0 4YY

13/09/2026

14961101-0003